Tkinter GUI Application Development H⊕TSHOT

Develop exciting and engaging GUI applications in Python and Tkinter by working on 10 real-world applications

Bhaskar Chaudhary

BIRMINGHAM - MUMBAI

Tkinter GUI Application Development HOTSHOT

First published: October 2013

Production Reference: 1211013

Published by Packt Publishing Ltd.
Livery Place
35 Livery Street
Birmingham B3 2PB, UK.

ISBN 978-1-84969-794-1

www.packtpub.com

Cover Image by Manu Gangadhar (manug30@gmail.com)

Credits

Author
Bhaskar Chaudhary

Reviewers
Ankur Aggarwal
Mike Driscoll
Anshuman Pandey
Alejandro Rodas de Paz

Acquisition Editor
Pramila Balan

Lead Technical Editor
Chalini Snega Victor

Technical Editors
Jalasha D'costa
Dipika Gaonkar
Kapil Hemnani
Akashdeep Kundu
Mrunmayee Patil

Project Coordinator
Angel Jathanna

Proofreaders
Simran Bhogal
Maria Gould

Indexer
Rekha Nair

Graphics
Abhinash Sahu

Production Coordinators
Alwin Roy
Nitesh Thakur

Cover Work
Nitesh Thakur

About the Author

Bhaskar Chaudhary is a professional programmer and information architect. He has almost 9 years of consulting, contracting, and educating experience in the field of software development. He has worked with a large set of programming languages on various platforms over the years.

He is an electronics hobbyist and musician in his free time.

I would like to thank my parents for everything that they have done for me. Thanks to my wife Sangita who provided valuable support at every stage of writing of this book. Thanks to my friend Souvik, sisters Priyanki and Shambhavi, and nephew Praneet and niece Aakansha for being around. Anurag you are always remembered and a source of inspiration.

I would like to thank Angel Jathanna, the Project Coordinator, for her timely input and feedback during the course of writing. I'd also like to thank Pramila Balan, the Acquisition Editor, and Chalini Snega Victor, the Lead Technical Editor, for making several helpful suggestions with regard to the book's structure, technical accuracy, and quality control. Thanks to Reshma Raman, the Author Relations Executive for getting me involved in the project.

I would also like to thank my reviewers Alejandro Rodas for providing countless suggestions to improve the code, Michael Driscoll for pointing out otherwise unnoticeable errors, Anshuman for testing out programs and pointing errors, and Ankur Aggarwal for providing suggestions for making the book more reader friendly.

Finally thanks to the Python community for being such a supportive group and to entire team at Packt Publishing, for publishing great books in the open source domain.

About the Reviewers

Ankur Aggarwal is currently working in the Education and Research department of Infosys Limited. He loves to play with Unix and Linux tools. He has created various automation tools using Python, PHP, and is learning Linux Kernel Development. He is also an author of various international magazines and portals such as Open Source For You (previously Linux For You), Ubuntumanual.org, and Richnusgeek. He runs a Linux based blog too on www.flossstuff.wordpress.com. He loves coding and listening to metal music. He is a die hard fan of Iron Maiden and loves playing the guitar in his free time.

Mike Driscoll has been programming in Python since Spring 2006. He enjoys writing about Python on his blog: http://www.blog.pythonlibrary.org/. He also occasionally writes for the Python Software Foundation, i-Programmer, and Developer Zone. He enjoys photography and reading a good book. Mike has also been a technical reviewer for *Python 3 Object Oriented Programming, Python 2.6 Graphics Cookbook*, and the *Python Web Development Beginner's Guide* among others.

I would like to thank my wonderful wife, Evangeline, for always supporting me. I would also like to thank friends and family for all that they do to help me. And I would like to thank Jesus Christ for saving me.

Anshuman Pandey holds a Bachelor's Degree in Technology in Computer Science and Engineering. Being a software developer, he is always eager to learn and build upon new technologies. He is also an avid blogger, endurance runner, and tennis enthusiast. Currently employed as an Analyst at a software consulting firm, Anshuman has extensive hands on experience with data analysis and programming. He picked up Python by himself as an undergraduate, and has since worked on a variety of Python projects as well as reviewed books on the subject.

Being enthusiastic about sharing ideas and collaborating with like-minded individuals, Anshuman is an up-and-coming blogger. He manages his own website "Twisted Thoughts", where he shares his thoughts on everything from cool new technologies and nifty software tricks to tennis and life lessons. His blog has proved to be a good portal to network with young professionals with similar interests.

I would like to thank my parents for being supportive in my first venture as a book reviewer, my band of friends for encouraging me, and Packt Publishing for giving me the wonderful opportunity to review this book.

Alejandro Rodas de Paz is a Computer Engineer from the University of Seville (Spain). He started programming in Python for artificial intelligence and data mining projects, and discovered Tkinter as an easy and effective way to develop GUI applications. He worked at research institutions such as the Web Engineering and Early Testing group, and the MediaLAB Amsterdam.

I would like to thank my grandmother Crescencia for her unconditional support, trust, and love during all my life.

www.PacktPub.com

Support files, eBooks, discount offers, and more

You might want to visit www.PacktPub.com for support files and downloads related to your book.

Did you know that Packt offers eBook versions of every book published, with PDF and ePub files available? You can upgrade to the eBook version at www.PacktPub.com and as a print book customer, you are entitled to a discount on the eBook copy. Get in touch with us at service@packtpub.com for more details.

At www.PacktPub.com, you can also read a collection of free technical articles, sign up for a range of free newsletters, and receive exclusive discounts and offers on Packt books and eBooks.

http://PacktLib.PacktPub.com

Do you need instant solutions to your IT questions? PacktLib is Packt's online digital book library. Here, you can access, read and search across Packt's entire library of books.

Why Subscribe?

- ▸ Fully searchable across every book published by Packt
- ▸ Copy and paste, print and bookmark content
- ▸ On demand and accessible via web browser

Free Access for Packt account holders

If you have an account with Packt at www.PacktPub.com, you can use this to access PacktLib today and view nine entirely free books. Simply use your login credentials for immediate access.

Table of Contents

Preface

Tkinter GUI Application Development Hotshot is a step-by-step guide that will walk you through the process of developing real-world graphical applications using Python and Tkinter; the built-in GUI module of Python.

This book attempts to highlight features and capabilities of Tkinter, while demonstrating a few of the myriad ways you can use Tkinter to develop exciting, fun, and useful pieces of GUI applications with Tkinter and Python.

We hope to take you on a fun journey through more than 10 projects from different problem domains. As we develop new applications in each project, the book also builds up a catalogue of some commonly used strategies for developing real-world applications.

What this book covers

Project 1, *Meet Tkinter*, begins from scratch, providing an overview of Tkinter covering details on how to create root windows, how to add widgets to a root window, how to handle layout with geometry managers, and how to work with events.

Project 2, *Make a Text Editor like Notepad*, develops a text editor in procedural style of programming. It gives the reader their first taste of several features of Tkinter and what it is like to develop a real application.

Project 3, *Programmable Drum Machine*, uses object-oriented programming to develop a drum machine capable of playing user composed rhythms. The application can also save those compositions and later edit or replay them. Here, you also learn to write multithreaded GUI applications.

Project 4, Game of Chess, develops a game of chess, introducing key aspects of structuring a GUI application as a model-view program. It also teaches the art of taking a real-world object (chess), and modeling it in notations that your program can manipulate. It also introduces the reader to the power of Tkinter Canvas widget.

Project 5, Audio Player, takes up the task of building an audio player. This project introduces the concepts of working with external libraries while showing you how to work with many different Tkinter widgets.

Project 6, Drawing an Application, develops a drawing and graphic editor. This project also shows how to develop and work with a GUI framework, thereby creating reusable code for all of your future programs.

Project 7, Some Fun Project Ideas, works through a series of small but functional projects, demonstrating problems from different domains such as network programming, database programming, graphing, basic animation, and multithreaded programming.

Appendix A, Miscellaneous Tips, discusses some vital aspects of GUI programming not covered in previous projects, but form a common theme in many GUI programs.

Appendix B, Quick Reference Sheets, lists down a handy reference sheet of all Tkinter and ttk options and methods along with a brief description on their input, usage, and output.

What you need for this book

The programs discussed in this book have been developed on Windows platform. However given the multi-platform abilities of Tkinter, you can easily work along on other platforms such as Linux distributions or Mac OS.

The following software is required for this book:

▸ Python 2.7 version with Tkinter 8.5 included in the distribution

The link to download and install other project specific modules and software are mentioned in the respective projects.

Who this book is for

This book assumes that you are familiar with Python programming language, at a beginner level. However, a motivated Python newbie with a background in writing programs can fill in gaps in knowledge with a little outside research.

Conventions

In this book, you will find a number of styles of text that distinguish between different kinds of information. Here are some examples of these styles, and an explanation of their meaning.

Code words in text are shown as follows: "We can include other contexts through the use of the include directive."

A block of code is set as follows:

```
from Tkinter import *
class MyFirstGUI():
  def __init__(self):
    self.root = Tk()
    self.root.mainloop()
if __name__ == '__main__':
app = MyFirstGUI()
```

When we wish to draw your attention to a particular part of a code block, the relevant lines or items are set in bold:

```
from Tkinter import *
class MyFirstGUI():
  def __init__(self):
    self.root = Tk()
    self.root.mainloop()
if __name__ == '__main__':
app = MyFirstGUI()
```

Any input on Python interactive shell is written as follows:

```
>>> import Tkinter
>>> help(Tkinter.Label)
```

New terms and **important** words are shown in bold. Words that you see on the screen, in menus or dialog boxes for example, appear in the text like this: "When a user specifies a new number and clicks on the **Update Record** button it calls a method."

Warnings or important notes appear in a box like this.

Tips and tricks appear like this.

Reader feedback

Feedback from our readers is always welcome. Let us know what you think about this book—what you liked or may have disliked. Reader feedback is important for us to develop titles that you really get the most out of.

To send us general feedback, simply send an e-mail to feedback@packtpub.com, and mention the book title via the subject of your message.

If there is a topic that you have expertise in and you are interested in either writing or contributing to a book, see our author guide on www.packtpub.com/authors.

Customer support

Now that you are the proud owner of a Packt book, we have a number of things to help you to get the most from your purchase.

Downloading the example code

You can download the example code files for all Packt books you have purchased from your account at http://www.packtpub.com. If you purchased this book elsewhere, you can visit http://www.packtpub.com/support and register to have the files e-mailed directly to you.

Errata

Although we have taken every care to ensure the accuracy of our content, mistakes do happen. If you find a mistake in one of our books—maybe a mistake in the text or the code—we would be grateful if you would report this to us. By doing so, you can save other readers from frustration and help us improve subsequent versions of this book. If you find any errata, please report them by visiting http://www.packtpub.com/submit-errata, selecting your book, clicking on the **errata submission form** link, and entering the details of your errata. Once your errata are verified, your submission will be accepted and the errata will be uploaded on our website, or added to any list of existing errata, under the Errata section of that title. Any existing errata can be viewed by selecting your title from http://www.packtpub.com/support.

Piracy

Piracy of copyright material on the Internet is an ongoing problem across all media. At Packt, we take the protection of our copyright and licenses very seriously. If you come across any illegal copies of our works, in any form, on the Internet, please provide us with the location address or website name immediately so that we can pursue a remedy.

Please contact us at copyright@packtpub.com with a link to the suspected pirated material.

We appreciate your help in protecting our authors, and our ability to bring you valuable content.

Questions

You can contact us at questions@packtpub.com if you are having a problem with any aspect of the book, and we will do our best to address it.

Project 1
Meet Tkinter

Welcome to the exciting world of GUI programming with Tkinter. This project aims at getting you acquainted with Tkinter, the built-in **graphical user interface (GUI)** interface for all standard Python distributions.

Tkinter (pronounced tea-kay-inter) is the Python interface to Tk, the GUI toolkit for Tcl/Tk.

Tcl (pronounced "tickle" and is an acronym for **Tool Command Language**) is a popular scripting language in the domains of embedded applications, testing, prototyping, and GUI development. Tk on the other hand is an open source, multiplatform widget toolkit that is used by many different languages for building GUI programs.

The Tkinter interface is implemented as a Python module, `Tkinter.py`, which is just a wrapper around a C-extension that uses Tcl/Tk libraries.

Tkinter is suited for application to a wide variety of areas ranging from small desktop applications, to use in scientific modeling and research endeavors across various disciplines.

We believe that the concepts you will develop here will enable you to apply and develop GUI applications in your area of interest. Let's get started!

Mission Briefing

The purpose of this project is to make you comfortable with Tkinter. It aims at introducing you to various components of GUI programming with Tkinter.

By the end of this project, you will have developed several partly functional dummy applications such as the one shown as follows:

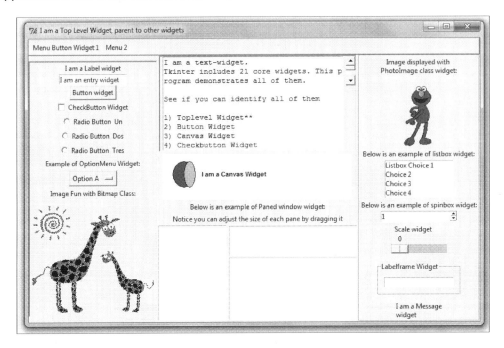

The applications developed in this project are "dummy applications" because they are not fully functional. In fact, the purpose of each small dummy application is to introduce you to some specific aspects of programming with Tkinter. This will set up the context for developing some fun and fully functional project ideas from *Project 2, Making a Text Editor*, onwards.

Why Is It Awesome?

The ability to program a GUI application (as opposed to a simple console application) opens a whole world of possibilities for a programmer. It shifts the focus of the program from the programmer to the end user, enabling the programmer to reach out to a wider audience.

When a person learning Python needs to graduate to GUI programming, Tkinter seems to be the easiest and fastest way to get the work done. Tkinter is a great tool for programming GUI applications in Python.

The features that make Tkinter a great choice for GUI programming include:

▸ It is simple to learn (simpler than any other GUI package for Python)
▸ Relatively little code can produce powerful GUI applications

- ▸ Layered design ensures that it is easy to grasp
- ▸ It is portable across all operating systems
- ▸ It is easily accessible as it comes pre-installed with standard Python distribution

None of the other GUI toolkits has all of these features at the same time.

Your Hotshot Objectives

The key concepts that we want you to take from this project include:

- ▸ Understanding the concept of root window and main loop
- ▸ Understanding widgets—the building blocks for your programs
- ▸ Acquainting yourself with a list of available widgets
- ▸ Developing layouts using three geometry managers: pack, grid, and place
- ▸ Learning to apply events and callbacks to make your program functional
- ▸ Styling your widgets with styling options and configuring the root widget

Mission Checklist

An elementary knowledge of data structures, syntax, and semantics of Python is assumed. To work along with this project, you must have a working copy of Python 2.7.3 installed on your computer.

The Python download package and instructions for downloading for different platforms are available at `http://www.Python.org/getit/releases/2.7.3/`.

We will develop our application on the Windows 7 platform. However, since Tkinter is truly cross-platform, you can follow along on Mac or Linux distributions without any modifications to our code.

After the installation, open the IDLE window and type:

```
>>>from Tkinter import *
```

If you have installed Python 2.7, this shell command should execute without any errors.

If there are no error messages the Tkinter module is installed in your Python distribution. When working with examples from this book, we do not support any other Python version except for Python 2.7, which comes bundled with Tkinter Tcl/Tk Version 8.5.

To test if you have the correct Tkinter version on your Python installation, type the following commands in your IDLE or interactive shell:

```
>>> import Tkinter
>>>Tkinter._test()
```

This should pop up a window where the first line in the window reads **This is Tcl/Tk version 8.5**. Make sure it is not 8.4 or any earlier version, as Version 8.5 is a vast improvement over its previous versions.

You are ready to code your Tkinter GUI applications if your version test confirms it as Tcl/Tk version 8.5. Let's get started!

The root window – your drawing board

GUI programming is an art, and like all art, you need a drawing board to capture your ideas. The drawing board you will use is called the **root window**. Our first goal is to get the root window ready.

Engage Thrusters

The following screenshot depicts the root window we are going to create:

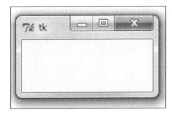

Drawing the root window is easy. You just need the following three lines of code:

```
from Tkinter import *
root = Tk()
root.mainloop()
```

Save this with the .py file extension or check out the code 1.01.py. Open it in the IDLE window and run the program from the **Run** menu (*F5* in IDLE). Running this program should generate a blank root window as shown in the preceding screenshot. This window is furnished with functional minimize, maximize, and close buttons, and a blank frame.

The description of the code is as follows:

- The first line imports all (*) classes, attributes, and methods of Tkinter into the current workspace.

- The second line creates an instance of the class Tkinter.Tk. This creates what is called the "root" window that you see in the screenshot provided. By convention, the root window in Tkinter is usually called "root", but you are free to call it by any other name.

- The third line executes the mainloop (that is, the event loop) method of the root object. The mainloop method is what keeps the root window visible. If you remove the third line, the window created in line 2 will disappear immediately as the script stops running. This will happen so fast that you will not even see the window appearing on your screen. Keeping the mainloop running also lets you keep the program running until you press the close button, which exits the main loop.

Objective Complete – Mini Debriefing

Congratulations! You have completed your first objective, which was to draw the root window. You have now prepared your drawing canvas (root window). Now get ready to paint it with your imagination!

Commit the three lines of code (shown in *code 1.01.py*) to memory. These three lines generate your root window, which will accommodate all other graphical components. These lines constitute the skeleton of any GUI application that you will develop in Tkinter. All code that will make your GUI application functional will go between line 2 (new object creation) and line 3 (mainloop) of this code.

Classified Intel

This section describes the different styles of importing Tkinter modules.

In the preceding example, we imported Tkinter using the following command:

```
from Tkinter import *
```

This method of import eases the handling of methods defined in the module. That is to say, you can simply access the methods directly. Generally, it is considered a bad practice to import all (*) methods of a module like we did here. This is because if you import all methods from some other module with a common method name, it would lead to the overwriting of methods.

There are several ways to import Tkinter in which this overlapping can be avoided, a common one being:

```
import Tkinter
```

This style of importing does not pollute the namespace with a list of all methods defined within Tkinter. However, every method within Tkinter will now have to be called using the format `Tkinter.methodA` instead of directly calling the method.

Another commonly used import style is as follows:

```
import Tkinter as Tk
```

Here too, you do not pollute the current namespace with all Tkinter methods and now you can access methods such as `Tk.methodA`. "Tk" is a convenient, easy-to-type alias commonly used by many developers for importing Tkinter.

The big picture

As a GUI programmer, you will generally be responsible for deciding three aspects of your program:

- ► **What components should appear on screen?**: This involves choosing the components that make the user interface. Typical components include things such as buttons, entry fields, checkboxes, radio buttons, scroll bars, and the like. In Tkinter, the components that you add to your GUI are called widgets.

- ► **Where should the components go?**: This involves deciding the positioning or placement of each component in the overall design structure. This includes decisions to be made on issues of positioning and the structural layout of various components. In Tkinter, this is referred to as **geometry management**.

▶ **How do components interact and behave?**: This involves adding functionality to each component. Each component or widget does some work. For example, a button, when clicked on, does something in response; a scrollbar handles scrolling; and checkboxes and radio buttons enable the user to make some choices. In Tkinter, the functionality of various widgets is managed by command binding or event binding using **callback functions**.

Let us delve deeper into each of these three components in the context of Tkinter.

Widgets – building blocks for your GUI program

Now that we have our Toplevel window ready, it is time to think over the question, what components should appear in the window? In Tkinter jargon, these components are called **widgets**.

Engage Thrusters

The syntax for adding a widget is as follows:

```
mywidget = Widget-name (its container window,**configuration options)
```

In the following example (refer to the code 01.02.py), we add two widgets, a label and a button, to the root frame. Notice how all widgets are added in between the skeleton code we defined in the first example.

```
from Tkinter import *
root = Tk()
mylabel = Label(root,text="I am a label widget")
mybutton = Button(root,text="I am a button")
mylabel.pack()
mybutton.pack()
root.mainloop()
```

The description of the code is listed as follows:

- ▶ This code adds a new instance, `mylabel`, for the **Label** widget. The first parameter defines `root` as its parent or container. The second parameter configures its text option as `"I am a label widget"`.

- ▶ We similarly define an instance of a **Button** widget. This is also bound to the root window as its parent.

- ▶ We use the `pack()` method, which is essentially required to position the label and button widgets within the window. We will discuss the `pack()` method and several other related concepts under the Geometry management task. However, you must note that some sort of geometry specification is essential for the widgets to display within the Toplevel window.

- ▶ Running this code will generate a window as shown in the following screenshot. It will have a custom label and a custom button:

Objective Complete – Mini Debriefing

In this iteration, we have learned the following:

- ▶ What widgets are.

- ▶ How widgets are instantiated and displayed within a container window frame.

- ▶ How to set options for the widgets at the time of instantiation.

- ▶ The importance of specifying a geometry option such as `pack()` to display a widget. We will discuss more about this in a subsequent task.

Classified Intel

- ▶ All widgets are actually objects derived from their respective **widget class**. So, a statement such as `mybutton = Button(myContainer)`, actually creates the button instance from the `Button` class.

▸ Each widget has a set of options that decides its behavior and appearance. This includes attributes such as text labels, colors, font size, and many more. For example, the Button widget has attributes to manage its label, control its size, change its foreground and background colors, change the size of the border, and so on.

▸ To set these attributes, you can set the values directly at the time of creation of the widget as we have done in the preceding example. Alternatively, you can later set or change the options of the widget by using the .config() or .configure() method. Note that the .config() or .configure() method are interchangeable and provide the same functionality.

You can also add the pack() method on the same line in which you create a new instance of the widget. For example, consider the following code:

```
mylabel = Label(root,text="I am a label widget")
mylabel.pack()
```

If you are instantiating the widget directly, you can write both the lines together as follows:

```
Label(root,text="I am a label widget").pack()
```

You may keep a reference to the widget created (as in the first example, mylabel) or you can create a widget without keeping any reference to it (as in the second example).

You should ideally keep the reference if the widget content is likely to be modified by some action at a later stage in the program. If the widget state is to remain static after its creation, you need not keep a reference for the widget.

Also, note that calls to pack() (or other geometry managers) always returns None. So, consider you create a widget keeping a reference to it and add the geometry manager (say pack()) on the same line as shown:

```
mylabel = Label(...).pack()
```

In this case, you are actually not creating a reference to the widget but instead creating a None type object for the variable mylabel.

So, when you later try to modify the widget through the reference, you get an error as you are actually trying to work on a None type object.

This is one of the most common errors committed by beginners.

Getting to know core Tkinter widgets

In this iteration, we will get to know all core Tkinter widgets. We have already seen two of them in the previous example—the Label and Button widgets. Let's now see all other core Tkinter widgets.

Prepare for Lift Off

Tkinter includes 21 core widgets. These are as follows:

Toplevel widget	Label widget	Button widget
Canvas widget	Checkbutton widget	Entry widget
Frame widget	LabelFrame widget	Listbox widget
Menu widget	Menubutton widget	Message widget
OptionMenu widget	PanedWindow widget	Radiobutton widget
Scale widget	Scrollbar widget	Spinbox widget
Text widget	Bitmap Class widget	Image Class widget

Let's write a program to include these widgets on our root window.

Engage Thrusters

The format for adding widgets is the same as we discussed in the previous task. To give you a flavor, here's some sample code for adding some common widgets:

```
Label(parent, text=" Enter your Password:")
Button(parent, text="Search")
Checkbutton(parent, text='RememberMe', variable=v, value=True)
Entry(parent, width=30)
Radiobutton(parent, text=Male, variable=v, value=1)
Radiobutton(parent, text=Female, variable=v, value=2)
OptionMenu(parent, var, "Select Country", "USA", "UK", "India", Others")
Scrollbar(parent, orient=VERTICAL, command=mytext.yview)
```

Can you spot the pattern common to each widget? Can you spot the differences?

As a reminder, the syntax for adding a widget is:

```
Widget-name (its container window, *configuration options)
```

The method for creating all the previously mentioned widgets is the same. Most of the configuration options will also be similar. However, a few configuration options vary from widget to widget.

For example, the Button and Label widgets will have an option to configure their text, but scrollbars do not have a text-configuration option.

Using the same pattern, let's now add all the 21 core Tkinter widgets into a dummy application (code `01.03.py`).

Do not be intimidated by the size of the program. Instead look for a common pattern that is used to initialize and display all the widgets. To reiterate, the syntax for adding a widget is:

```
mywidget = Widget-name (container, all widget-options)
```

Notice how the configuration options for each widget differ slightly from each other depending on the type of widget being initialized.

Refer to the code `1.03.py` for a demo of all Tkinter widgets. A summarized code description for `1.03.py` is as follows:

▶ We create a Toplevel window and create a main loop as seen in the earlier examples.

▶ We add a Frame widget that we named `menubar`. Note that Frame widgets are just holder widgets that hold other widgets. Frame widgets are great for grouping widgets together. The syntax for adding a frame is the same as that of all other widgets:

```
myframe = Frame(root)
myframe.pack()
```

▶ Keeping the `menubar` frame as the container, we add two widgets to it, the Menubutton and Menu widgets.

▶ We create another frame and name it `myframe1`. Keeping `myframe1` as the container/parent widget, we add seven widgets to it:

  ❏ The Label, Entry, Button, Checkbutton, Radiobutton, OptionMenu, and Bitmap Class widgets.

▶ We then proceed to create `myframe2`, another Frame widget. We add six more widgets to it:

  ❏ The Image Class, Listbox, Spinbox, Scale, LabelFrame, and Message widgets.

- ▶ We then create `myframe3`, another Frame widget. We add two more widgets to it, the Text and Scrollbar widgets.

- ▶ Finally we create the last frame, `myframe4`, another Frame widget. We add two more widgets to it, the Canvas and PanedWindow widgets.

All these widgets constitute the 21 core widgets of Tkinter.

Read through the code explanation, and find the corresponding piece of code in the example code `01.03.py`. Look at how each widget is created. Try to identify each widget's class name as used in Tkinter. Look what remains the same in all widgets, and what changes between one widget and another?

A few minutes spent reading and understanding the code in `1.03.py` will really help you appreciate the simplicity and overall structure of a Tkinter program.

Finally, note that we have used `.pack()` on each widget to display it inside its container frame. We discuss `.pack()` in the next task. However, for now just note that we have used something called `pack()`, without which the widgets would not have displayed at all.

Objective Complete – Mini Debriefing

You have reached a major milestone in your GUI programming effort.

You now know all the 21 core widgets of Tkinter. You can identify them by their class names, and you can create them on a root frame or on a subframe within the root. You now know how to configure options of widgets.

With this you have now seen the first and the most important building block of a Tkinter program. You have mastered Tkinter widgets.

Classified Intel

Widget options can be set at instantiation time as we have done in the examples so far. Alternatively, the options can be configured after instantiation using the following syntax:

```
widget.configure(**options)
```

This is a very handy tool that lets you change widget options dynamically after the widget has been created. We will be using this very often in all our projects.

For common widget configuration options, refer to the *Options common to widgets* section in *Appendix B, Quick Reference Sheets*.

Geometry management

Having seen all the core Tkinter widgets, let us now turn our attention to the second component of GUI programming—the question of where to place those widgets.

This is taken care of by the geometry manager options of Tkinter. This component of GUI programming involves deciding the position of the widget, overall layout, and relative placement of various widgets on the screen.

Prepare for Lift Off

Recall that we used the `pack()` method for adding widgets to the dummy application we developed in the previous section. `pack()` is an example of geometry management in Tkinter.

`pack()` is not the only way you can manage the geometry in your interface. In fact, there are three geometry managers in Tkinter that let you specify the position of widgets inside a Toplevel or parent window.

The geometry managers are as follows:

- ▸ `pack`: This is the one we have used so far. Simple to use for simpler layouts but may get very complex for slightly complex layouts.

- ▸ `grid`: This is the most commonly used geometry manager that provides a table-like layout of management features for easy layout management.

- ▸ `place`: This is least popular, but provides the best control for absolute positioning of widgets.

Engage Thrusters

Let us now see examples of all three geometry managers in action.

The pack geometry manager

The `pack` geometry derives its name from the fact that it literally packs widgets on a first-come-first-serve basis in the space available in the master frame in which widgets are pushed.

The `pack` geometry manager fits "slave widgets" into "parent spaces". When packing the slave widgets, the `pack` manager distinguishes between three kinds of spaces:

- ▸ The unclaimed space
- ▸ The claimed but unused space
- ▸ The claimed and used space

The most commonly used options in `pack()` include:

- ▸ `side`: LEFT, TOP, RIGHT, and BOTTOM (these decide the alignment of the widget)
- ▸ `fill`: X, Y, BOTH, and NONE (these decide whether the widget can grow in size)
- ▸ `expand` :1/0 or Yes/No (corresponding to values respectively)
- ▸ `anchor`: NW, N, NE, E, SE, S, SW, W, and CENTER (corresponding to the cardinal directions)
- ▸ Internal padding (`ipadx` and `ipady`) and external padding (`padx` and `pady`), which all defaulted to a value of zero

Let's take a look at some demo code that illustrates some of the `pack` features. Here's the code snippet (code `1.04.py`) that generates a GUI like the following screenshot:

```
from Tkinter import *
root = Tk()
Button(root, text="A").pack(side=LEFT, expand=YES, fill=Y)
Button(root, text="B").pack(side=TOP, expand=YES, fill=BOTH)
Button(root, text="C").pack(side=RIGHT, expand=YES, fill=NONE, anchor=NE)
Button(root, text="D").pack(side=LEFT, expand=NO, fill=Y)
Button(root, text="E").pack(side=TOP, expand=NO, fill=BOTH)
Button(root, text="F").pack(side=RIGHT, expand=NO, fill=NONE)
Button(root, text="G").pack(side=BOTTOM, expand=YES, fill=Y)
Button(root, text="H").pack(side=TOP, expand=NO, fill=BOTH)
Button(root, text="I").pack(side=RIGHT, expand=NO)
Button(root, text="J").pack(anchor=SE)
root.mainloop()
```

The description of the code is listed as follows:

- ▸ When you insert button **A** in the `root` frame, it captures the left-most area of the frame, it expands, and fills the *Y* dimension. Because expand and fill options are specified in affirmative, it claims all the area it wants and fills the *Y* dimension. If you increase the size of the root window pulling it down, you will notice that the button **A** expands in the downward direction (along the *Y* coordinate) but a side-wise increase in the window does not result in a horizontal increase in the size of button **A**.

- ▸ When you insert the next button, **B**, into the root window, it picks up space from the remaining area but aligns itself to `TOP`, expand-fills the available area, and fills both *X* and *Y* coordinates of the available space.

- ▸ The third button, **C**, adjusts to the right-hand side of the remaining space. But because fill is specified as `NONE`, it takes up only that much space as is required to accommodate the text inside the button. If you expand the root window, the button **C** will not change its size.

- ▸ The `anchor` attribute used in some lines provides a means to position a widget relative to a reference point. If the `anchor` attribute is not specified, the `pack` manager places the widget in the center of the available space or the **packing box**. Other allowed options include the four cardinal directions (`N`, `S`, `E`, and `W`) and a combination of any two directions. Therefore, valid values for the `anchor` attribute are: `CENTER` (default), `N`, `S`, `E`, `W`, `NW`, `NE`, `SW`, and `SE`.

The description for the rest of the lines is left as an exercise for you to explore. The best way to study this piece of code would be to comment out all lines of code and introduce each successive button one after another. At each step, try to resize the window to see the effect it has on various buttons.

We will use the `pack` geometry manager in some of our projects, so it would be a worthwhile exercise to get acquainted with `pack` and its options.

Note that the value for most of the Tkinter geometry manager attributes can either be specified in capital letters without quotes (like `side=TOP`, `anchor=SE`) or in small letters but within quotes (like `side='top'`, `anchor='se'`).

For a complete `pack` manager reference refer to the *The pack manager* section in *Appendix B, Quick Reference Sheets*.

Where should you use the pack() geometry manager?

Using the `pack` manager is somewhat complicated compared to the `grid` method that we will discuss next, but it is a great choice in situations such as:

▶ Having a widget fill the complete container frame

▶ Placing several widgets on top of each other or in a side by side position (as in the previous screenshot). See code `1.05.py`.

While you can create complicated layouts by nesting widgets in multiple frames, you can find the `grid` geometry manager more suitable for most of the complex layouts.

The grid geometry manager

The `grid` geometry manager is most easy to understand and, perhaps, the most useful geometry manager in Tkinter. The central idea of the `grid` geometry manager is to divide the container frame into a two-dimensional table divided into a number of rows and columns. Each cell in the table can then be targeted to hold a widget. In this context, a **cell** is an intersection of imaginary rows and columns. Note that in the `grid` method, each cell can hold only one widget. However, widgets can be made to span multiple cells.

Within each cell you can further align the position of the widget using the `STICKY` option. The `sticky` option decides how the widget is expanded, if its container cell is larger than the size of the widget it contains. The `sticky` option can be specified using one or more of the N, S, E, and W, or NW, NE, SW, and SE options.

Not specifying stickiness defaults to stickiness to the center of the widget in the cell.

Let us now see a demo code that illustrates some of the features of the `grid` geometry manager. The code in `1.06.py` generates a GUI-like figure as shown:

```
from Tkinter import *
root = Tk()
Label(root, text="Username").grid(row=0, sticky=W)
Label(root, text="Password").grid(row=1, sticky=W)
Entry(root).grid(row=0, column=1, sticky=E)
Entry(root).grid(row=1, column=1, sticky=E)
Button(root, text="Login").grid(row=2, column=1, sticky=E)
root.mainloop()
```

The description of the code is listed as follows:

- ▸ Take a look at the grid position defined in terms of rows and column positions for an imaginary grid table spanning the entire frame. See how the use of `sticky=W` on both labels makes them stick to the west or left-hand side, resulting in a clean layout.

- ▸ The width of each column (or height of each row) is automatically decided by the height or width of the widgets contained in the cell. Therefore, you need not worry about specifying the row or column width as equal. You may specify the width for widgets, if you need that extra bit of control.

- ▸ You can use the argument `sticky=N+S+E+W` to make the widget expandable to fill the entire cell of the grid.

In a more complex scenario, your widgets may span across multiple cells in the grid. To enable a grid to span multiple cells, the `grid` method offers very handy options such as `rowspan` and `columnspan`.

Furthermore, you may often need to provide some padding between cells in the grid. The `grid` manager provides `padx` and `pady` options to provide padding to place around the widget in a cell.

Similarly, there are `ipadx` and `ipady` options for internal padding. The default value of external and internal padding is `0`.

Let us see an example of the `grid` manager, where we use most of the common arguments to the `grid` method such as `row`, `column`, `padx`, `pady`, `rowspan`, and `columnspan` in action.

The code `1.08.py` is a demonstration of `grid()` geometry manager options:

```
from Tkinter import *
top = Tk()
top.title('Find & Replace')
```

```
Label(top,text="Find:").grid(row=0, column=0, sticky='e')
Entry(top).grid(row=0,column=1,padx=2,pady=2,sticky='we',columnspan=9)

Label(top, text="Replace:").grid(row=1, column=0, sticky='e')
Entry(top).grid(row=1,column=1,padx=2,pady=2,sticky='we',columnspan=9)

Button(top, text="Find").grid(row=0, column=10, sticky='ew', padx=2,
pady=2)
Button(top, text="Find All").grid(row=1, column=10, sticky='ew', padx=2)
Button(top, text="Replace").grid(row=2, column=10, sticky='ew', padx=2)
Button(top, text="Replace All").grid(row=3, column=10, sticky='ew',
padx=2)

Checkbutton(top, text='Match whole word only').grid(row =2, column=1,
columnspan=4, sticky='w')
Checkbutton(top, text='Match Case').grid(row =3, column=1, columnspan=4,
sticky='w')
Checkbutton(top, text='Wrap around').grid(row =4, column=1, columnspan=4,
sticky='w')

Label(top, text="Direction:").grid(row=2, column=6, sticky='w')
Radiobutton(top, text='Up', value=1).grid(row=3, column=6, columnspan=6,
sticky='w')
Radiobutton(top, text='Down', value=2).grid(row=3, column=7,
columnspan=2, sticky='e')

top.mainloop()
```

Notice how just 14 lines of core `grid` manager code generates a complex layout such as the one shown in the following screenshot. In contrast, developing this with the `pack` manager would have been much more tedious:

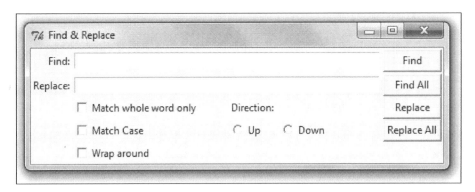

Another `grid` option that you can sometimes use is the `widget.grid_forget()` method. This method can be used to hide the widget from the screen. When you use this option, the widget exists in its place but becomes invisible. The hidden widget may be made visible again but any `grid` options that you had originally assigned to the widget will be lost.

Similarly, there is a `widget.grid_remove()` method that removes the widget, except that in this case when you make the widget visible again, all its `grid` options will be restored.

For a complete `grid()` reference, refer to the the *The grid manager* section in *Appendix B, Quick Reference Sheets*.

Where should you use the grid() geometry manager?

The `grid` manager is a great tool for developing complex layouts. Complex structures can be easily achieved by breaking the container widget into grids of rows and columns and then placing the widgets in grids where they are wanted.

It is also commonly used in developing different kinds of dialog boxes.

Now we will delve into configuring grid column and row sizes.

Different widgets have different heights and widths. So when you specify the position of a widget in terms of rows and columns, the cell automatically expands to accommodate the widget.

Normally the height of all grid rows is automatically adjusted to be the height of its tallest cell. Similarly, the width of all grid columns is adjusted to be equal to the width of the widest widget cell.

If you then want a smaller widget to fill a larger cell or to stay at any one side of the cell, you use the `sticky` attribute on the widget to control that.

You can, however, override this automatic sizing of columns and rows using the following code:

```
w.columnconfigure(n, option=value, ...)   AND
w.rowconfigure(N, option=value, ...)
```

Use these to configure the options for a given widget, `w`, in the column, `n`, specifying values for the options, `minsize`, `pad`, and `weight`.

The options available here are as mentioned in the following table:

Options	Description
minsize	The minimum size of column or row in pixels. If there is no widget in the given column or row, the cell does not appear despite this minsize specification.
pad	External padding in pixels that will be added to the specified column or row over the size of largest cell.
weight	This specifies the relative weight of the row or column, then distributes the extra space. This enables making the row or column stretchable.
	For example, the following code distributes two-fifths of the extra space to the first column and three-fifths to the second column:
	`w.columnconfigure(0, weight=2)` `w.columnconfigure(1, weight=3)`

The columnconfigure() and rowconfigure() methods are often used to implement dynamic resizing of widgets, especially on resizing the root window.

 You cannot use grid and pack methods together in the same container window. If you try doing that, your program will enter into an infinite negotiation loop.

The place geometry manager

The place geometry manager is the most rarely used geometry manager in Tkinter. Nevertheless, it has its uses in that it lets you precisely position widgets within its parent frame using the *X-Y* coordinate system.

The place manager can be assessed using the place() method on all standard widgets.

The important options for place geometry include:

  ▸ Absolute positioning (specified in terms of x=N or y=N)

  ▸ Relative positioning (key options include relx, rely, relwidth, and relheight)

Other options commonly used with place() include width and anchor (the default is NW). Refer to the code in 1.09.py for a demonstration of the common place option:

```
from Tkinter import *
root = Tk()
# Absolute positioning
```

```
Button(root,text="Absolute Placement").place(x=20, y=10)
# Relative positioning
Button(root, text="Relative").place(relx=0.8, rely=0.2, relwidth=0.5,
width=10, anchor = NE)
root.mainloop()
```

You may not see much of a difference between absolute and relative positions simply by looking at the code or the window frame. If, however, you try resizing the window, you will notice that the button placed absolutely does not change its coordinates, while the relative button changes its coordinates and size to fit the new size of the root window.

For a complete `place()` reference, check out the *The place manager* section in *Appendix B, Quick Reference Sheets.*

When should you use the place manager?

The `place` manager is useful in situations where you have to implement the custom geometry managers where the widget placement is decided by the end user.

While `pack()` and `grid()` managers cannot be used together in the same frame, the `place()` manager can be used with any other geometry manager within the same container frame.

The `place` manager is rarely used. This is because if you use it you have to worry about the exact coordinates. If say you make a minor change for one widget, it is very likely that you will have to change the *X-Y* values for other widgets as well, which can be very cumbersome.

We will not use the `place` manager in our projects. However, knowing that options for coordinate-based placement exist can be helpful in certain situations.

Objective Complete – Mini Debriefing

This concludes our discussion on geometry management in Tkinter.

In this section you implemented examples of `pack`, `grid`, and `place` geometry managers. You also understood the strength and weaknesses of each geometry manager.

You learned that `pack` is best for a simple side-wise or top-down widget placement. You also saw that the `grid` manager is best suited for handling complex layouts. You saw examples of the `place` geometry manager and the reasons why it is rarely used.

You should now be in a position to plan and execute different layouts for your programs using these geometry managers of Tkinter.

Events and callbacks – adding life to programs

Now that we have learned how to add widgets to our screen and how to position them where we want, let's turn our attention to the third component of GUI programming. This addresses the question of how to make the widgets functional.

Making the widgets functional involves making them responsive to events such as the pressing of buttons, the pressing keys on keyboards, mouse clicks, and the like. This requires associating callbacks to specific events.

Engage Thrusters

Callbacks are normally associated with specific widget events using the `command` binding the rules, which is elaborated on in the following section.

Command binding

The simplest way to add functionality to a button is called `command` binding, whereby the callback function is mentioned in the form of `command = some_callback` in the widget option.

Take a look at the following sample code:

```
def my_callback ():
    # do something
    Button(root,text="Click",command= my_callback)
```

Note that `my_callback` is called without parentheses `()` from within the widget `command` option. This is because when the callback functions are set, it is necessary to pass a reference to a function rather than actually calling it.

Passing arguments to the callback

If the callback does not take any argument, it can be handled with a simple function like the one we just used. However, if the callback needs to take some arguments, we can use the `lambda` function as shown in the following code snippet:

```
def my_callback (somearg):
   #do something with argument
   Button(root,text="Click",command=lambda: my_callback
   ('some argument'))
```

Python borrows syntax from a functional program called the `lambda` function. The `lambda` function lets you define a single-line, nameless function on the fly.

The format for using `lambda` is `lambda arg: #do something with arg in a single line`, for instance:

```
lambda x: return x^2
```

 Please note that the `command` option available with the Button widget is really an alternative function to ease programming the Button event. Many other widgets do not provide any equivalent `command` binding option.

The command button binds by default to the left mouse click and the Space bar. It does not bind to the Return key. Therefore, if you bind a button using the `command` function, it will react to the Space bar and not the Return key. This is counter-intuitive to many Windows users. What's worse is you cannot change this binding of the `command` function. The moral is that `command` binding, though a very handy tool, does not provide you the the independence to decide your own bindings.

Event binding

Fortunately, Tkinter provides an alternative form of event binding mechanism called `bind()` to let you deal with different events. The standard syntax for binding an event is as follows:

```
widget.bind(event, handler)
```

When an event corresponding to the event description occurs in the widget, it calls the associated handle passing an instance of the event object as the argument, with the event details.

Let us look at an example of the `bind()` method (refer to the code file `1.10.py`):

```
from Tkinter import *
root = Tk()
```

```
Label(root, text='Click at different\n locations in the frame below').
pack()
def mycallback(event):
  print dir(event)
  print "you clicked at", event.x, event.y
myframe = Frame(root, bg='khaki', width=130, height=80)
myframe.bind("<Button-1>", mycallback)
myframe.pack()
root.mainloop()
```

The description of the code is listed as follows:

- ▸ We bind the Frame widget to the event, `<Button-1>`, which corresponds to left-click of the mouse. On the occurrence of this event, it calls the function `mycallback`, passing along an object instance as its argument.

- ▸ We define the function `mycallback(event)`. Notice that it takes the event object generated by the event as the argument.

- ▸ We inspect the event object using `dir(event)`, which returns a sorted list of attribute names for the event object passed to it. This prints the list:

  - ❑ `['__doc__', '__module__', 'char', 'delta', 'height', 'keycode', 'keysym', 'keysym_num', 'num', 'send_event', 'serial', 'state', 'time', 'type', 'widget', 'width', 'x', 'x_root', 'y', 'y_root'].`

- ▸ Out of the attributes list generated by the object, we use two attributes, `event.x` and `event.y`, to print the coordinates of the point of click.

When you run this code, it produces a window like the one shown. When you left-click anywhere in the frame, it outputs messages to the console. A sample message passed to the console is as follows:

```
['__doc__', '__module__', 'char', 'delta', 'height', 'keycode', 'keysym',
'keysym_num', 'num', 'send_event', 'serial', 'state', 'time', 'type',
'widget', 'width', 'x', 'x_root', 'y', 'y_root']
You clicked at 63 36.
```

Event pattern

In the previous example, you saw how we used the event `<Button-1>` to denote the left-click of a mouse. This is a built-in pattern in Tkinter that maps it to the mouse's left-click event. Tkinter has an exhaustive mapping scheme that exactly identifies events such as this one.

Here are some examples to give you an idea of event patterns:

Event pattern	Associated Event
`<Button-1>`	Left-click of the mouse button
`<KeyPress-B>`	Keyboard press of the key *B*
`<Alt-Control-KeyPress- KP_Delete>`	Keyboard press of *Alt + Ctrl + Delete*

In general, the mapping pattern takes the following form:

```
<[event modifier-]...event type [-event detail]>
```

Typically an event pattern will comprise of:

- ▸ **An event type** (required): Some common event types include `Button`, `ButtonRelease`, `KeyRelease`, `Keypress`, `FocusIn`, `FocusOut`, `Leave` (mouse leaves the widget), and `MouseWheel`. For a complete list of event types, refer to the *The event types* section in *Appendix B, Quick Reference Sheets*.

- ▸ **An event modifier** (optional): Some common event modifiers include `Alt`, `Any` (used like in `<Any-KeyPress>`), `Control`, `Double` (used like in `<Double-Button-1>` to denote a double-click of the left mouse button), `Lock`, and `Shift`. For a complete list of event modifiers, refer to the *The event modifiers* section in *Appendix B, Quick Reference Sheets*.

- ▶ **The event detail** (optional): The mouse event detail is captured by number 1 for a left-click and number 2 for a right-click. Similarly, each keyboard keypress is either represented by the key letter itself (say *B* in `<KeyPress-B>`) or using a key symbol abbreviated as **keysym**. For example, the up arrow key on the keyboard is represented by the `keysym` value of `KP_Up`. For a complete `keysym` mapping, refer to the *The event details* section in *Appendix B, Quick Reference Sheets*.

Let's take a look at a practical example of the `event` binding on widgets. (See the code in `1.11.py` for the complete working example). The following is a modified snippet of code to give you a flavor of the commonly used the `event` bindings:

```
widget.bind("<Button-1>",callback)    #bind widget to left mouse click
widget.bind("<Button-2>", callback) # bind to right mouse click
widget.bind("<Return>", callback)# bind  to Return(Enter) Key
widget.bind("<FocusIn>", callback) #bind  to  Focus in Event
widget.bind("<KeyPress-A>", callback)# bind  to keypress A
widget.bind("<KeyPress-Caps_Lock>", callback)# bind to CapsLockkeysym
widget.bind("<KeyPress-F1>", callback)# bind widget to F1 keysym
widget.bind("<KeyPress-KP_5>", callback)# bind to keypad number 5
widget.bind('<Motion>', callback)  # bind to motion over widget
widget.bind("<Any-KeyPress>", callback) # bind to any keypress
```

Rather than binding an event to a particular widget, you can also bind it to the Toplevel window. The syntax remains the same except that now you call it on the root instance of the root window like `root.bind()`.

Levels of binding

In the previous section, you saw how to bind an event to an instance of a widget. This can be called **instance level binding**.

However, there might be times when you need to bind events to the entire application. At other times you may want to bind the event to a particular class of widget. Tkinter provides different levels of binding options for this:

> ► **An application-level binding**: Application-level bindings will let you use the same binding across all windows and widgets of the application, as long as any one window of the application is in focus.
>
> The syntax for application-level bindings is:
> ```
> w.bind_all(event, callback)
> ```
>
> The typical usage pattern is as follows:
> ```
> root.bind_all('<F1>', show_help)
> ```
>
> An application-level binding here means that no matter what widget is under the current focus, a press of the *F1* key will always trigger the show_help callback as long as the application is under active focus.

> ► **A class-level binding**: You can also bind events at a particular class level. This is normally used to set the same behavior of all instances of a particular widget class.
>
> This syntax for class level binding is as follows:
> ```
> w.bind_class(className, event, callback)
> ```
>
> The typical usage pattern is as follows:
> ```
> myentry.bind_class('Entry', '<Control-V>', paste)
> ```
>
> In the preceding example, all entry widgets will be bound to the <Control-V> event that would call a method called 'paste (event)'.

Event propagation

Most of the keyboard events and mouse events occur at the operating system level. It propagates from the source of the event, hierarchically up, until it finds a window that has a corresponding binding. The event propagation does not stop there. It propagates itself upwards looking for other bindings from other widgets until it reaches the root window. If it does reach the root window and no bindings are discovered by it, the event is disregarded.

Handling widget-specific variables

You need variables with a wide variety of widgets. You likely need a string variable to track what the user enters into the entry widget or text widget. You most probably need Boolean variables to track whether the user has checked the Checkbox widget. You need integer variables to track the value entered in a Spinbox or Slider widget.

In order to respond to changes in widget-specific variables, Tkinter offers its own variable class. The variable that you use to track widget-specific values must be subclassed from this Tkinter variable class. Tkinter offers some commonly used predefined variables. They are `StringVar`, `IntVar`, `BooleanVar`, and `DoubleVar`.

You can use these variables to capture and play with changes in the value of variables from within your callback functions. You can also define your own variable type, if required.

Creating a Tkinter variable is simple. You simply call the required constructor:

```
mystring = StringVar()
ticked_yes = BooleanVar()
option1 = IntVar()
volume = DoubleVar()
```

Once the variable is created, you can use it as a widget option, as follows:

```
Entry(root, textvariable = mystring)
Checkbutton(root, text="Remember Me", variable=ticked_yes)
Radiobutton(root, text="Option1", variable=option1, value="option1")
#radiobutton
Scale(root, label="Volume Control", variable=volume, from =0, to=10) #
slider
```

Additionally, Tkinter provides access to the value of variables using `set()` and `get()` methods:

```
myvar.set("Wassup Dude") # setting   value of variable
myvar.get() # Assessing the value of variable from say a callback
```

A demonstration of the Tkinter variable class is available in the code file `1.12.py`. The code generates a window like the following screenshot:

Objective Complete – Mini Debriefing

In this lesson, you learned:

▸ The `command` binding to bind simple widgets to certain functions

▸ Use of the `lambda` function, if you need to process arguments

▸ The `event` binding using the `widget.bind(event, callback)` method to bind keyboard and mouse events to your widgets and to invoke callbacks on the occurrence of some events

▸ How to pass extra arguments to a callback

▸ How to bind events to an entire application or to a particular class of widget using `bind_all()` and `bind_class()`

▸ How to use the Tkinter variable class to set and get values of widget specific variables

In short you now know how to make your GUI program functional!

Classified Intel

In addition to the `bind` method we previously saw, you might find these two event-related options useful in certain cases:

▸ `unbind`: Tkinter provides the `unbind` options to undo the effect of an earlier binding. The syntax is as follows:

```
widget.unbind(event)
```

The following are some examples of its usage:

```
entry.unbind('<Alt-Shift-5>')
root.unbind_all('<F1>')
root.unbind_class('Entry', '<KeyPress-Del>')
```

▶ **Virtual events**: Tkinter also lets you create your own events. You can give these virtual events any name you want.

For example, imagine you want to create a new event called `<<commit>>`, which is triggered by the *F9* key. To create this virtual event on a given widget, use the syntax:

```
widget.event_add('<<commit>>', '<F-9>')
```

You can then bind `<<commit>>` to any callback using a normal `bind()` method like:

```
widget.bind('<<commit>>', callback)
```

Other event-related methods are listed in the *Other event-related methods* section in *Appendix B, Quick Reference Sheets*.

Now that you are ready to dive into real application development with Tkinter, let's spend some time exploring a few custom styling options that Tkinter offers. We will also see some of the configuration options commonly used with the root window.

Doing it in style

So far, we have have relied on Tkinter to provide specific platform-based styling for our widgets. However, you can specify your own styling of widgets in terms of their color, font size, border width, and relief. A brief introduction of styling features available in Tkinter is covered in the following task.

Prepare for Lift Off

Recall that we could specify widget options at the time of its instantiation as shown:

```
mybutton = Button(parent, **configuration options)
```

Alternatively, you could specify widget options using `configure ()`:

```
mybutton.configure(**options)
```

Styling options are also specified as options to the widgets, either at the time of instantiation or later using the configure option.

Engage Thrusters

Under the purview of styling, we will cover how to apply different colors, fonts, border width, relief, cursor, and bitmap icons to our widgets. We will also look at some of the root configurations later in the section.

Let's first see how to specify color options for a widget. You can specify two types of color for most of the widgets:

- ▸ Background color
- ▸ Foreground color

You can specify the color using hexadecimal color codes using the proportion of red, green, and blue. Commonly used representations are #rgb (4 bits), #rrggbb (8 bits), and #rrrgggbbb (12 bits).

For example, #fff is white, #000000 is black, and #fff000000 is red.

Alternatively, Tkinter provides mapping for standard color names. For a list of predefined colors, open the program titled pynche in the Tools folder within your Python installation directory (in my case, C:\Python27\Tools\pynche). Within the program click on **View | Color list Window**.

Next, the easiest and the most common way to specify a font is to represent it as a tuple. The standard representation is as follows:

```
widget.configure( font= 'font family, fontsize, optional style
modifiers like bold, italic, underline and overstrike')
```

Here are some examples to illustrate the method for specifying fonts:

```
widget.configure (font='Times, 8')
widget.configure  (font = 'Helvetica 24 bold italic')
```

 If you set a Tkinter dimension in a plain integer, the measurements takes place in units of pixel. Alternatively, Tkinter accepts four other measurement units which are: m (millimeters), c (centimeters), i (inches), and p (printer's points, which is about 1/72").

The default border width for most Tkinter widgets is 2 pixels. You can change the border width of the widgets by specifying it explicitly, as shown in the following line:

```
button.configure (borderwidth=5)
```

The relief style of a widget refers to the difference between the highest and lowest elevations in a widget. Tkinter offers five possible relief styles: flat, raised, sunken, groove, and ridge.

```
button.configure (relief='raised')
```

Tkinter lets you change the style of mouse cursor when you hover over a particular widget. This is done using the option cursor as in the following example:

```
button.configure (cursor='cross')
```

For a complete list of available cursors, refer to the *List of available cursors* section in *Appendix B, Quick Reference Sheets*.

While you can specify styling options at each widget level, sometimes it may be cumbersome to do so individually for each widget. Widget-specific styling has several disadvantages:

  ▶ It mixes logic and presentation into one file making the code bulky and difficult to manage

  ▶ Any change in styling is to be applied to each widget individually

  ▶ It violates the **don't repeat yourself** (**DRY**) principle of effective coding as you keep specifying the same style for a large number of widgets

Fortunately, Tkinter now offers a way to separate presentation from the logic and to specify styles in what is called the external "option database". This is nothing but a text file where you can specify the common styling options.

A typical option database text file may look like the following:

```
*font: Arial 10
*Label*font: Times 12 bold
*background: AntiqueWhite1
*Text*background: #454545
*Button*foreground:gray55
*Button*relief: raised
*Button*width: 3
```

The asterisk (*) symbol here means that the particular style applies to all instances of the given widget.

These entries are placed in an external text (.txt) file. To apply this styling to a particular piece of code, you simply call it using the option_readfile() call early in your code, as shown here:

```
root.option_readfile('optionDB.txt')
```

Now that we are done discussing styling options, let us wrap up with a discussion on some commonly used options for the root window:

Method	Description
`root.title("title of my program")`	Specifying the title for the Title bar
`root.geometry('142x280+150+200')`	You can specify the size and location of a root window using a string of the form `width`x`height` + `xoffset` + `yoffset`

`self.root.wm_iconbitmap('mynewicon.ico')`
 	
or
 	
`self.root.iconbitmap('mynewicon.ico')`
	Changing the Title bar icon to something different from the default Tk icon

`root.overrideredirect(1)`	Removing the root border frame

Now let's take a look at an example where we apply all the styling options and root window options as discussed previously (see the code `01.13.py`):

```python
from Tkinter import *
root = Tk()

#demo of some important root methods
root.geometry('142x280+150+200') #specify root window size and
position
root.title("Style Demo") #specifying title of the program
self.root.wm_iconbitmap('brush1.ico')#changing the default icon
#root.overrideredirect(1) # remove the root border - uncomment #this
line to see the difference
root.configure(background='#4D4D4D')#top level styling

# connecting to the external styling optionDB.txt
root.option_readfile('optionDB.txt')

#widget specific styling
```

```
mytext = Text(root, background='#101010', foreground="#D6D6D6",
borderwidth=18, relief='sunken', width=16, height=5 )
mytext.insert(END, "Style is knowing \nwho you are, what \nyou want to
say, \nand not giving a \ndamn.")
mytext.grid(row=0, column=0, columnspan=6, padx=5, pady=5)

# all the below widgets derive their styling from optionDB.txt file
Button(root, text='*' ).grid(row=1, column=1)
Button(root, text='^' ).grid(row=1, column=2)
Button(root, text='#' ).grid(row=1, column=3)
Button(root, text='<' ).grid(row=2, column=1)
Button(root, text='OK', cursor='target').grid(row=2, column=2)
Button(root, text='>').grid(row=2, column=3)
Button(root, text='+' ).grid(row=3, column=1)
Button(root, text='v', font='Verdana 8').grid(row=3, column=2)
Button(root, text='-' ).grid(row=3, column=3)
fori in range(0,10,1):
  Button(root, text=str(i) ).grid( column=3 if i%3==0  else (1
  if i%3==1 else 2), row= 4 if i<=3  else (5 if i<=6 else 6))

#styling with built-in bitmap images
mybitmaps = ['info', 'error', 'hourglass', 'questhead', 'question',
'warning']
for i in mybitmaps:
  Button(root, bitmap=i,  width=20,
  height=20).grid(row=(mybitmaps.index(i)+1), column=4,
  sticky='nw')

root.mainloop()
```

The description of the preceding code is listed as follows:

▶ The first segment of code uses some important root methods to define the geometry, title of the program, icon for the program, and method to remove the border of the root window.

▶ The code then connects to an external styling file called `optionDB.txt` that defines common styling for the widgets.

▶ The next segment of code creates a Text widget and specifies styling on the widget level.

▶ The next segment of code has several buttons, all of which derive their styling from the centralized `optionDb.txt` file. One of the buttons also defines a custom cursor.

▶ The last segment of code styles some buttons using built-in bitmap images.

Running this program would produce a window like the following screenshot:

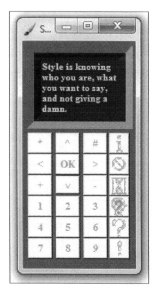

Objective Complete – Mini Debriefing

In this task, we explored how to use styling options to modify the default styling of Tkinter. We saw how to specify custom colors, fonts, reliefs, and cursors for our GUI programs. We also saw how to separate styling from the logic using the option database. Finally, we explored some of the common options for configuring our root window.

Mission Accomplished

This brings us to end of *Project 1*, *Meet Tkinter*. This project aimed to provide a high-level overview of Tkinter. We have worked our way through all the important concepts that drive a Tkinter program. We now know:

- ▸ What a root window is and how to set it up
- ▸ What the 21 core Tkinter widgets are and how to set them up
- ▸ How to layout our programs using `pack`, `grid`, and `place` geometry managers
- ▸ How to make our programs functional using events and callbacks
- ▸ How to apply custom styles to our GUI programs

To summarize, we can now start thinking of making interesting, functional, and stylish GUI programs with Tkinter!

A Hotshot Challenge

Time for your first Hotshot challenge! Your task is to build a simple calculator (or if you are ambitious, a scientific calculator). It should be fully functional and should have custom-styled buttons and a screen. Try to make it look as close to real physical calculators as you can.

When you are done, we invite you to search in your computer for complex GUI programs. These can range from your operating system programs such as the search bar, to some simple dialog-based widgets. Try to replicate any chosen GUIs using Tkinter.

Project 2
Making a Text Editor like Notepad

In the previous project, we got a fairly high-level overview of Tkinter. Now that we know some things about Tkinter's core widgets, geometry management, and bindings of command and events to callbacks, let us apply our skill to make a text editor in this project.

In the process, we will also take a closer look at individual widgets and learn how to tweak those widgets to our custom needs.

Mission Briefing

In this project, our goal is to build a fully-functional text editing pad with some cool nifty features. In its final form, the proposed editor should look as follows:

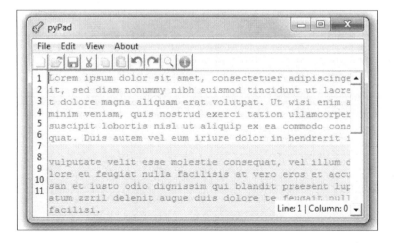

Some features we intend to include in the notepad are:

- Creating new documents, opening and editing existing documents, and saving documents

- Implementing common editing options such as cut, copy, paste, undo, and redo

- Searching within a file for a given search term

- Implementing line numbering and the ability to show/hide line numbers

- Implementing theme selection to let the user choose custom color themes

- Implementing about and help windows and more

Why Is It Awesome?

In this project you will build you first real and useful project. This project will provide you with further insights into the world of Tkinter. It will delve deeper into features of some commonly used widgets such as Menu, Menubutton, Text, Entry, Checkbutton, and Button widgets.

Particularly, we will go into the finer details of the Menu, Menubar, and Text widgets. We will also learn to easily handle custom dialogs windows such as the Open, Save, Error, Warning, and Info dialogs.

Your Hotshot Objectives

The project will be developed in seven consecutive iterations. The goals for each of these iterations are as follows:

- Set the user interface using the `pack` geometry using widgets such as Menu, Menubar, Text, Entry, Button, Checkbutton, and the like

- Implement some features using Tkinter's built-in widget options

- Implement dialogs using `ttk` dialogs and different types of Toplevel widgets

- Apply some Text widget features such as text index, tag, and mark to implement some custom features

- Apply some features using the Checkbutton and Radiobutton widgets

- Apply some custom event binding and protocol binding to make the application more user-friendly

- Add some miscellaneous features

Setting up the widgets

Our first goal is to implement the visual elements of the text editor. As programmers, we have all used notepad or some code editor to edit our code. We are mostly aware of the common GUI elements of a text editor. So, without much of an introduction, let's get started.

Prepare for Lift Off

The first phase implements the following six widgets:

- Menu
- Menubutton
- Label
- Button
- Text
- Scrollbar

Although we will cover all these in detail, you might find it helpful to look at the widget-specific options in the documentation of Tkinter maintained by its author Frederick Lundh at `http://effbot.org/tkinterbook/`.

You might also want to bookmark the official documentation page of Tck/Tk located at `http://www.tcl.tk/man/tcl8.5/TkCmd/contents.htm`.

The latter site includes the original Tcl/Tk reference. While it does not relate to Python, it provides a more detailed overview of each widget and is an equally useful reference. (Remember, Tkinter is just a wrapper around Tk)

You can also read the documentation provided with the original source code of Tkinter by typing these two lines in the interactive Python shell:

```
>>> import Tkinter
>>>help(Tkinter)
```

Engage Thrusters

In this iteration, we will complete the implementation of most of the visual elements of the program.

We will be using the pack () geometry manager to place all the widgets. We have chosen the pack manager because it is ideally suited for placing widgets side by side or in a top-down position. Fortunately in a text editor, we have all widgets placed either side-by-side or in top-down locations. Thus, it suits to use the pack manager. We could have done the same with the grid manager as well.

1. First, we will start by adding the Toplevel window, one that will contain all other widgets using the following code:

    ```
    from Tkinter import *
    root = Tk()
    # all our code is entered here
    root.mainloop()
    ```

2. In this step we add the top menu buttons to our code. See the code in 2.01.py. Menus offer a very compact way of presenting a large number of choices to the user without cluttering the interface. Tkinter offers two widgets to handle menus.

    ❑   The **Menubutton** widget – one that is part of the menu and appears on the top of application, which is always visible to the end user

    ❑   The **Menu** widget – one that show a list of choices when the user clicks on any menu button

    To add top-level menu buttons, you use the following command:

    ```
    mymenu = Menu(parent, **options)
    ```

    For example, to add a File menu, we use the following code:

    ```
    # Adding Menubar in the widget
    menubar = Menu(root)
    filemenu = Menu(menubar, tearoff=0 ) # File menu
    root.config(menu=menubar) # this line actually displays menu
    ```

Similarly, we add the Edit, View, and About menus at the top. Refer to step 2 of `2.01.py`.

Most of the Linux platforms support **tear-off menus**. When `tearoff` is set to `1` (enabled), the menu appears with a dotted line above the menu options. Clicking on the dotted line enables the user to literally tear off or separate the menu from the top. However, as this is not a cross-platform feature, we have decided to disable tear-off, marking it as `tearoff = 0`.

3. Now we will add menu items within each of the four menu buttons. As previously mentioned, all drop-down options are to be added within the menu instance. In our example, we add five drop-down menu choices in the File menu, namely New, Open, Save, Save As, and Exit menu items. See step 3 of `2.02.py`.

    Similarly, we add the following menu choices for other menus:

    - ❏ Under **Edit** we have **Undo**, **Redo**, **Cut**, **Copy**, **Paste**, **Find All**, and **Select All**
    - ❏ Under **View** we have **Show Line Number**, **Show Info Bar at Bottom**, **Highlight Current Line**, and **Themes**
    - ❏ Under **About** we have **About** and **Help**

    The format for adding menu items is as follows:

    ```
    mymenu.add_command(label="Mylabel", accelerator='KeyBoard
    Shortcut', compound=LEFT, image=myimage, underline=0,
    command=callback)
    ```

    For example, you would create the **Undo** menu item using the following syntax:

    ```
    mymenu.add_command(label="Undo", accelerator='Ctrl + Z',
    compound=LEFT, image=undoimage, command=undocallback)
    ```

4. Next we will add some labels. We will add the top label, which will later hold the shortcut buttons. We will also add a label to the left-hand side to display the line numbers:

The top label has been marked in a green background and the side label in a light cream background for illustration purposes.

When working with the `pack` geometry manager, it is important to add widgets in the order they will appear. This is because `pack()` uses the concept of available space to fit the widgets. If we do not maintain the order, the widgets will start occupying places in the order they are introduced. This is why we cannot introduce the text widget before the two label widgets as they appear higher up in the display.

Having reserved the space, we can later add shortcut icons or line numbers keeping the label as the parent widget. Adding labels is easy, we have done that in the past. See the code in `2.02.py` step 4. The code is as follows:

```
shortcutbar = Frame(root,  height=25, bg='light sea green')
shortcutbar.pack(expand=NO, fill=X)
lnlabel = Label(root,  width=2,  bg = 'antique white')
lnlabel.pack(side=LEFT, anchor='nw', fill=Y)
```

We have applied a colorful background to these two labels for now to differentiate it from the body of the Toplevel window.

5. Lastly, let's add the Text widget and Scrollbar widget to our code. Refer to step 5 of the code `2.02.py`.

```
textPad = Text(root)
textPad.pack(expand=YES, fill=BOTH)
scroll=Scrollbar(textPad)
textPad.configure(yscrollcommand=scroll.set)
scroll.config(command=textPad.yview)
scroll.pack(side=RIGHT, fill=Y)
```

The code is similar to all other code that we have used so far to instantiate widgets. Notice, however, that the scrollbar is configured to `yview` of the Text widget and the Text widget is configured to connect to the Scrollbar widget. This way, we cross connected both the widgets to each other.

Now when you go down the Text widget, the scrollbar reacts to it. Alternatively, when you pull the scrollbar, the Text widget reacts in return.

Some new menu-specific options introduced here are as follows:

- `accelerator`: This option is used to specify a string, typically the keyboard shortcut, which can be used to invoke the menu. The string specified as the accelerator appears next to the text of the menu item. Please note that this does not automatically create bindings for the keyboard shortcut. We will have to manually set them up, as we will see later.

- `compound`: Specifying a `compound` option to the menu item lets you add images beside the common text label of the menu. A specification such as `Compound=LEFT, label= 'mytext', image=myimage` means that the menu item has a compound label comprising of a text label and an image, where the image is to be placed on the left-hand side of the text. The images we use here are stored and referenced from a separate folder called `icons`.

- `underline`: The `underline` option lets you specify the index of a character in the menu text to be underlined. The indexing starts at 0, which means that specifying `underline=1` underlines the second character of the text. Besides underlining, Tkinter also uses it to define the default bindings for keyboard traversal of menus. This means that we can select the menu either with the mouse pointer, or with the *Alt* + `<character_at_the_underlined_index>` shortcut.

Therefore, to add the **New** menu item within the **File** menu, we use the following code:

```
filemenu.add_command(label="New", accelerator='Ctrl+N', compound=LEFT,
image=newicon, underline=0,  command=new_file)
```

Similarly, we add menu choices for the **Edit** menu.

Menu separators

Occasionally within your menu items, you will come across code such as `mymenu.add_separator()`. This widget displays a separator bar and is solely used to organize similar menu items in groups, separating groups by horizontal bars.

Other than the normal menu type that we implement for the **New** and **Edit** menus, Tkinter offers three more varieties of menu:

  ▶ **The Checkbutton menu**: This menu lets you make a yes/no choice by checking/ unchecking the menu

  ▶ **The Radiobutton menu**: This menu lets you choose one from among many different options

  ▶ **The Cascade menu**: This menu only opens up to show another list of choices

Our **View** menu demonstrates all these three types of menus as shown in the following screenshot:

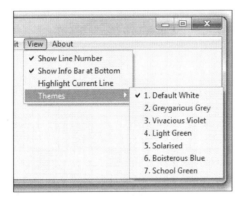

The first three choices under the **View** menu let the user select whether or not they want a certain thing to happen. The user can check/uncheck options against these menus and are examples of the Checkbutton menu.

The fourth menu choice under **View** menu reads as **Themes**. Hovering over this menu opens another list of choices. This is an example of a **Cascade** menu as it only serves the purpose of opening up another list of choices.

Within the **Cascade** menu, you are presented with a list of choices for your editor theme. You can, however, select only one of the themes. Selecting one theme unselects any previous selection. This is an example of the Radiobutton menu.

An example format for adding these three types of menu is as follows:

```
viewmenu.add_checkbutton(label="Show Line Number", variable=showln)
viewmenu.add_cascade(label="Themes", menu=themesmenu)
themesmenu.add_radiobutton(label="Default White", variable=theme)
```

Now that we need to track whether or not a selection has been made, we track it by adding a variable that can be `BooleanVar()`, `IntVar()`, or `Stringvar()` as we discussed in *Project 1, Meet Tkinter*.

For a complete list of configuration options for the Menubutton and Menu widgets, refer to the *The basic widget methods* section in *Appendix B, Quick Reference Sheets*.

Objective Complete – Mini Debriefing

This concludes our first iteration. In this iteration, we have completed laying down the majority of visual elements of our text editor.

Leveraging the power of built-in Text widget options

Tkinter's Text widget comes with some handy built-in functionality to handle common text-related functions. Let's leverage these functionalities to implement some common features in our text editor.

Engage Thrusters

1. Let's start by implementing the Cut, Copy, and Paste features. We now have our editor GUI ready. If you open the program and play with the Text widget, you will notice that you can perform basic functions such as cut, copy, and paste in the text area using the keyboard shortcuts *Ctrl + X*, *Ctrl + C*, and *Ctrl + V*. All these functions exist without us having to add a single line of code toward these functionalities.

    Clearly the text widget comes built in with these events. Rather than coding these functions ourselves, let's use the built-in functions to add these features to our text editor.

    The documentation of Tcl/Tk "universal widget methods" tells us that we can trigger events without any external stimulus using the following command:

    ```
    widget.event_generate(sequence, **kw)
    ```

    To trigger the cut event for our `textPad` widget, all we need is a line of code such as the following:

    ```
    textPad.event_generate("<<Cut>>")
    ```

Let's call that using a function cut, and associate it with our cut menu using the command callback. See the code `2.03.py` that bears the following code:

```
def cut():
    textPad.event_generate("<<Cut>>")
# then define a command callback from our existing cut menu like:
editmenu.add_command(label="Cut", compound=LEFT, image=cuticon,
accelerator='Ctrl+X', command=cut)
```

Similarly, we trigger the copy and paste functions from their respective menu items.

2. Next we will move on to implementing the undo and redo features. The Tcl/Tk text documentation tells us that the Text widget has an unlimited undo and redo mechanism, provided we set the -undo option as true. To leverage this option, let's first set the Text widget's undo option to true as shown in the following screenshot:

```
textPad = Text(root, undo=True)
```

Now if you open your text editor and try out the undo and redo features using *Ctrl + Z* and *Ctrl + Y*, you will see that they work fine. We now only have to associate the events to functions and callback the functions from our **Undo** and **Redo** menus respectively. This is similar to what we did for cut, copy, and paste. Refer to the code in `2.03.py`.

Objective Complete – Mini Briefing

Taking advantage of some built-in Text widget options, we have successfully implemented the functionality of cut, copy, paste, undo, and redo into our text editor with minimal coding.

Indexing and tagging

While we managed to leverage some built-in functionality to gain a quick advantage, we need a more precise control over the text area, so as to bend it to our will. This would require the ability to target each character or location of the text with precision.

Prepare for Lift Off

The Text widget offers us the ability to manipulate its content using **index**, **tags**, and **mark**, which lets us target a position or place within the text area for manipulation.

Index

Indexing helps you target a particular place within a text. For example, if you want to mark a particular word in bold style or in red or in a different font size, you can do so if you know the index of the starting point and the index of end point to be targeted.

The index must be specified in one of the following formats:

Index format	Description
x.y	The *y*th character on line *x*.
@x,y	The character that covers the x,y coordinate within the text's window.
end	The end of the text.
mark	The character after a named mark.
tag.first	The first character in the text that has been tagged with a given tag.
tag.last	The last character in the text that has been tagged with a given tag.
selection (SEL_FIRST, SEL_LAST)	This corresponds to the current selection. The constants SEL_FIRST and SEL_LAST refer to the start position and the end position in the selection. Tkinter raises a TclError exception if there is no selection.
windowname	The position of the embedded window whose name is windowname.
imagename	The position of the embedded image with the name imageName.
INSERT	The position of the insertion cursor.
CURRENT	The position of the character closest to the mouse pointer.

Indices can be further manipulated using modifiers and submodifiers. Some examples of modifiers and submodifers are as follows:

- ▶ end - 1 chars or end - 1 c refers to the index of one character before the end
- ▶ insert +5lines refers to the index of five lines ahead of the insertion cursor
- ▶ insertwordstart - 1 c refers to the character just before the first one in the word containing the insertion cursor
- ▶ end linestart refers to the index of the line start of the end line

Indexes are often used as arguments to functions. For example, refer to the following list:

- ▶ text.delete(1.0, END): This means you can delete from line 1, column 0 up till the end
- ▶ text.get(0.0, END): This gets the content from 0.0 up till the end
- ▶ text.delete(insert-1c, INSERT): This deletes one character at the insertion cursor

Tags

Tags are used to annotate text with an identification string that can then be used to manipulate the tagged text. Tkinter has a built-in tag called **SEL**, which is automatically applied to the selected text. In addition to SEL, you can define your own tags. A text range can be associated with multiple tags, and the same tag can be used for many different text ranges.

Some examples of tagging are as follows:

```
mytext.tag_add('sel', '1.0', 'end') # add SEL tag from start(1.0) to
end
mytext.tag_add("danger", "insert linestart", "insert lineend+1c")
mytext.tag_remove("danger", 1.0, "end")
mytext.tag_config('danger', background=red)
mytext.tag_config('outdated', overstrike=1)
```

 You can specify the visual style for a given tag with `tag_config` using options such as `background(color)`, `bgstipple (bitmap)`, `borderwidth (distance)`, `fgstipple (bitmap)`, `font (font)`, `foreground (color)`, `justify (constant)`, `lmargin1 (distance)`, `lmargin2 (distance)`, `offset (distance)`, `overstrike (flag)`, `relief (constant)`, `rmargin (distance)`, `spacing1 (distance)`, `tabs (string)`, `underline (flag)`, and `wrap (constant)`.

For a complete reference of text indexing and tagging, type the following command into your Python interactive shell:

```
>>> import Tkinter
>>> help(Tkinter.Text)
```

Engage Thrusters

Equipped with a basic understanding of indexing and tagging, let's implement some more features in our code editor.

1. The first feature that we will implement is the "Select All" feature. We know that Tkinter has a built-in SEL tag that applies a selection to a given text range. We want to apply this `sel` tag to the complete text contained in our widget.

    We simply define a function to handle this. Refer to the code in 2.04.py as shown in the following code snippet:

    ```
    def select_all():
        textPad.tag_add('sel', '1.0', 'end')
    ```

    After this we add a callback to our Select All menu item:

    ```
    editmenu.add_command(label="Select All", underline=7,
    accelerator='Ctrl+A', command=select_all)
    ```

Now, we are done adding the Select All functionality to our code editor. If you now add some text to the text widget and then click on the menu item **select all**, it should select the entire text in your editor. Note that we have not bound the *Ctrl + A* accelerator in the menu options. The keyboard shortcut will therefore not work. We will make the `accelerator` function in a separate step.

2. Next, let's complete the functioning of the **Find** menu item.

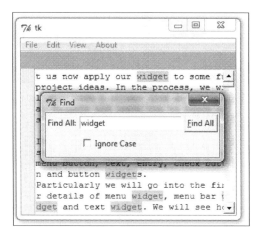

Here's a quick summary of the desired functionality. When a user clicks on the **Find** menu item, a new Toplevel window opens up. The user enters a search keyword, and specifies if the search is to be case-sensitive. When the user clicks on the **Find All** button, all matches are highlighted.

For searching through the document, we will rely on the `text.search()` method. The `search` method takes in the following arguments:

```
search(pattern, startindex, stopindex=None, forwards=None,
backwards=None, exact=None, regexp=None, nocase=None, count=None)
```

For our editor, we define a function called `on_find` and attach it as a callback to our **Find** menu item (refer to the code in `2.04.py`):

```
editmenu.add_command(label="Find", underline= 0,
accelerator='Ctrl+F', command=on_find)
```

We then define our function `on_find` as follows (refer to the code in `2.04.py`):

```
def on_find():
    t2 = Toplevel(root)
    t2.title('Find')
    t2.geometry('262x65+200+250')
```

```
    t2.transient(root)
    Label(t2, text="Find All:").grid(row=0, column=0, sticky='e')
        v=StringVar()
        e = Entry(t2, width=25, textvariable=v)
    e.grid(row=0, column=1, padx=2, pady=2, sticky='we')
    e.focus_set()
    c=IntVar()
    Checkbutton(t2, text='Ignore Case', variable=c).grid(row=1,
    column=1, sticky='e', padx=2, pady=2)
    Button(t2, text="Find All", underline=0,  command=lambda:
    search_for(v.get(), c.get(), textPad, t2, e)).grid(row=0,
    column=2, sticky='e'+'w', padx=2, pady=2)

def close_search():
  textPad.tag_remove('match', '1.0', END)
  t2.destroy()

t2.protocol('WM_DELETE_WINDOW', close_search)#override close
```

The description of the preceding code is as follows:

- When a user clicks on the **Find** menu item, it invokes a callback `on_find`.

- The first four lines of the `on_find()` function creates a new Toplevel window, adds a title `Find`, specifies it geometry (size, shape, and location), and sets it as a transient window. Setting it to transient means that it is always drawn on top of its parent or root window. If you uncomment this line and click on the root editor window, the **Find** window will go behind the root window.

- The next eight lines of code are pretty self-explanatory in that they set the widgets of the **Find** window. It adds the Label, Entry, Button, and Checkbutton widgets and provides for two variables, `e` and `c`, to track the value a user enters into the Entry widget, and whether or not the user has checked the check button. The widgets are arranged using the `grid` geometry manager to fit into the **Find** window.

- The **Find All** button has a `command` option that calls a function, `search_for()`, passing the search string as the first argument and whether or not the search is to be case-sensitive as its second argument. The third, fourth, and fifth arguments pass the Toplevel window, the Text widget, and the Entry widget as parameters.

❑ Prior to the `search_for()` method, we override the Close button of the Find window and redirect it to a callback named `close_search()`. The `close_search()` method is defined within the `on_find()` function. This function takes care of removing the tag `match` that was added during the search. If we do not override the Close button and remove these tags, our matched string will continue to be marked in red and yellow, even after our searching has ended.

3. Next we have the `search_for()` function that does the actual searching. The code is as follows:

```
def search_for(needle, cssnstv, textPad, t2, e) :
  textPad.tag_remove('match', '1.0', END)
  count =0
  if needle:
    pos = '1.0'
    while True:
      pos = textPad.search(needle, pos, nocase=cssnstv,
      stopindex=END)
    if not pos: break
      lastpos = '%s+%dc' % (pos, len(needle))
      textPad.tag_add('match', pos, lastpos)
      count += 1
      pos = lastpos
  textPad.tag_config('match', foreground='red',
    background='yellow')
  e.focus_set()
  t2.title('%d matches found' %count)
```

The description of the code is listed as follows:

❑ This part of code is the heart of the search function. It searches through the entire document using the `while True` loop, breaking out of the loop only if no more text items remain to be searched.

❑ The code first removes any previous search-related `match` tags as we do not want to append the results of the new search to previous search results. The function uses the `search()` method provided in Tkinter on the Text widget. The `search()` function takes the following arguments:

```
search(pattern,  index,  stopindex=None,  forwards=None,
backwards=None, exact=None, regexp=None, nocase=None, count=None)
```

The method returns the starting position of the first match. We store it in a variable with the name `pos` and also calculate the position of the last character in the matched word and store it in the variable `lastpos`.

❑ For every search match that it finds, it adds a tag named `match` to the range of text starting from the first position to the last position. After every match, we set the value of `pos` to be equal to `lastpos`. This ensures that the next search starts after `lastpos`.

❑ The loop also keeps track of the number of matches using the count variable.

❑ Outside the loop, the tag `match` is configured to be of a red font color and with a background of yellow. The last line of this function updates the title of the **Find** window with the number of matches found.

In the case of event bindings, interaction occurs between your input devices (keyboard/mouse) and your application. In addition to event binding, Tkinter also supports protocol handling.

The term "protocol" means the interaction between your application and the window manager. An example of a protocol is `WM_DELETE_WINDOW`, which handles the `close` window event for your window manager. Tkinter lets you override these protocols handlers by mentioning your own handler for the root or Toplevel widget. To override our window exit protocol, we use the following command:

```
root.protocol("WM_DELETE_WINDOW", callback)
```

Once you add this command, Tkinter bypasses protocol handling to your specified callback/handler.

Objective Complete – Mini Briefing

Congratulations! In this iteration, we have completed coding the Select All and Find functionality into our program.

More importantly, we have been introduced to indexing and tagging—two very powerful concepts associated with many Tkinter widgets. You will find yourself using these two concepts all the time in your projects.

Classified Intel

In the previous code, we used a line that reads: `t2.transient(root)`. Let's understand what it means here.

Tkinter supports four types of Toplevel windows:

- ▶ **Main Toplevel window**: These are the ones that we have constructed so far.

- ▶ **Child Toplevel window**: These are the ones that are independent of the root. The child Toplevel behaves independently of its root but it gets destroyed if its parent is destroyed.

- ▶ **Transient Toplevel window**: This always appears on top of its parent. The transient window is hidden if the parent is minimized and it is destroyed if the parent is destroyed.

- ▶ **Undecorated Toplevel window**: A Toplevel window is undecorated if it does not have a window manager decoration around it. It is created by setting the `overrideredirect` flag to `1`. An undecorated window cannot be resized or moved.

See the code in `2.05.py` for a demonstration of all these four types of Toplevel windows.

Working with forms and dialogs

The goal for this iteration is to complete the functioning of the **File** menu options of **Open**, **Save**, and **Save As**.

Prepare for Lift Off

We regularly use the **Open** and **Save** dialogs. They are common across many programs. We know how these menu items behave. For instance, when you click on the **Open** menu, it opens up a dialog form that lets you traverse to the location of the file you want to open. When you select a particular file and click on **Open**, it opens up in your editor. Similarly, we have the **Save** dialog.

While we can implement these dialogs using standard Tkinter widgets, it turns out that they are so commonly used that a specific Tkinter module called `tkFileDialog` has been included in the standard Python distribution. We will not try to reinvent the wheel and in the spirit of less coding, we will use the `tkFileDialog` module to implement Open and Save functionality for our text editor as shown in the following screenshot:

To use the module, we simply import it into the current namespace as given in the code file of `2.06.py`:

```
import tkFileDialog
```

You can specify the following additional options for `tkFileDialog`:

File dialog	Configurable options	Description
`askopenfile` `(mode='r', **options)`	`parent`, `title`, `message`, `defaultextension`, `filetypes`, `initialdir`, `initialfile`, and `multiple`	Asks for a filename to open, and then it returns the opened file
`askopenfilename` `(**options)`	`parent`, `title`, `message`, `defaultextension`, `filetypes`, `initialdir`, `initialfile`, and `multiple`	Asks for a filename to open but returns nothing
`asksaveasfile` `(mode='w', **options)`	`parent`, `title`, `message`, `defaultextension`, `filetypes`, `initialdir`, `initialfile`, and `multiple`	Asks for a filename to save as, and it returns the opened file
`asksaveasfilename` `(**options)`	`parent`, `title`, `message`, `defaultextension`, `filetypes`, `initialdir`, `initialfile`, and `multiple`	Asks for a filename to save as but returns nothing
`askdirectory` `(**options)`	`parent`, `title`, `initialdir`, `must` `exist`	Asks for a directory, and it returns the filename

Engage Thrusters

1. Let us now develop our Open function using `tkDialogBox` (refer to code `2.07.py`):

```python
import tkFileDialog
import os

def open_file():
  global filename
  filename =   tkFileDialog.askopenfilename(defaultextension=".
txt",filetypes =[("All Files","*.*"),("Text Documents","*.txt")])
```

```
if filename == "": # If no file chosen.
  filename = None # Absence of file.
else:
  root.title(os.path.basename(filename) + " - pyPad") #
  #Returning the basename of 'file'
  textPad.delete(1.0,END)
  fh = open(filename,"r")
  textPad.insert(1.0,fh.read())
  fh.close()
```

We then modify the **Open** menu to add a `command` callback to this newly-defined method:

```
filemenu.add_command(label="Open", accelerator='Ctrl+O',
compound=LEFT, image=openicon, underline =0, command=open_file)
```

The description of the code is listed as follows:

- ❑ We import the `tkfileDialog` and `os` modules into the current namespace.

- ❑ We define our function `open_file()`.

- ❑ We declare a variable in the global scope to keep track of the filename of the opened file. This is required to keep track of whether or not a file has been opened. We need this variable in the global scope, as we want this variable to be available to other methods such as `save()` and `save_as()`. Not specifying it as global would mean that it is only available within the function. So our `save()` and `save_as()` functions would not be able to check if a file is already open in the editor.

- ❑ We use `tkFileDialog.askopenfilename` to fetch the filename of the opened file. If the user cancels opening the file or if no file is chosen, the filename returned is `None`. In that case we do nothing.

- ❑ If, however, `tkFileDialog` returns a valid filename, we isolate the filename using the `os` module and add it as a title of our root window.

- ❑ If the Text widget already contains some previous text, we delete it all.

- ❑ We then open the given file in read mode and insert all its content into the text area.

- ❑ After this we close the file handle `fh`.

- ❑ Finally, we add a `command` callback to our **File | Open** menu item.

This completes the coding of **File | Open**. If you now go and click on **File | Open** and select a text file and click on **Open**, the text area will be populated with the content of the text file.

Use of global variables is generally considered a bad programming practice because it is very difficult to understand a program that uses lots of global variables.

A global variable can be modified or accessed from many different places in the program, and it therefore becomes difficult to remember or work out every possible use of the variable.

A global variable is not subject to any access control, which may pose security hazards in certain situations, say when this program is to interact with a third party code.

However, when you work on programs in the procedural style like this one, global variables are sometimes unavoidable.

An alternative approach to programming involves writing code in a class structure (also called **object-oriented programming**), where a variable can only be accessed by members of predefined classes. We will see a lot of examples of object-oriented programming in the next project.

2. Next we will see how to save a file. There are two components for saving a file:

   ❑ Save File

   ❑ Save As

If the text pad already contains a file, we do not prompt the user for a filename. We simply overwrite the contents of the existing file. If there is no filename associated with the current content of the text area, we prompt the user with a **Save As** dialog. Moreover, if the text area has an open file, and the user clicks on **Save As**, we still prompt them with a **Save As** dialog to allow them to write the contents to a different filename.

The code for Save and Save As is as follows (see the code in 2.07.py):

```
#Defining save method
def save():
  global filename
  try:
    f = open(filename, 'w')
    letter = textPad.get(1.0, 'end')
    f.write(letter)
    f.close()
  except:
    save_as()


#Defining save_as method
def save_as():
  try:
```

```
    # Getting a filename to save the file.
    f = tkFileDialog.asksaveasfilename(initialfile =
        'Untitled.txt', defaultextension=".txt",filetypes=[("All
        Files","*.*"),("Text Documents","*.txt")])
    fh = open(f, 'w')
    textoutput = textPad.get(1.0, END)
    fh.write(textoutput)
    fh.close()
    root.title(os.path.basename(f) + " - pyPad")
except:
    pass


filemenu.add_command(label="Save", accelerator='Ctrl+S',
compound=LEFT, image=saveicon, underline=0, command=save)
filemenu.add_command(label="Save as", accelerator='Shift+Ctrl+S',
command=save_as)
```

The description of the code is listed as follows:

- The `save` function first tries to locate if a file is open in the text area using a `try` block. If a file is open, it simply overwrites the content of the file with the current content of the text area.

- If there is no filename associated with the text area, it simply passes the work to our `save_as` function.

- The `save_as` function opens a dialog using `tkFileDialog.asksaveasfilename` and tries to get the filename provided by the user for the given file. If it succeeds, it opens the new file in the write mode and writes the content of text into this new filename. After writing, it closes the current file handler and changes the title of the window to reflect the new filename.

- To obtain the new filename, our `save_as` function makes use of the `os` module. We, therefore, need to import the `os` module into our namespace before we can use it to extract the current filename.

- If the user does not specify a filename or if the user cancels the `save_as` operation, it simply ignores the process by using a `pass` command.

- Finally, we add a `command` callback from our existing **Save** and **Save As** menu items to invoke these two functions.

We are now done adding Save and Save As functionality to our code editor.

3. While we are at it, let's complete our functionality of **File | New**. The code is simple. For this see the code in 2.07.py:

```
def new_file():
  root.title("Untitled")
  global filename
  filename = None
  textPad.delete(1.0,END)

filemenu.add_command(label="New", accelerator='Ctrl+N',
compound=LEFT, image=newicon, underline=0, command=new_file )
```

The description for this code is listed as follows:

❑ The new_file function begins by changing the title attribute of the root window to Untitled.

❑ It then sets the value of the global variable filename to None. This is important because our save and save_As functionality uses this global variable name to track whether or not the file exists or is new.

❑ Our function then deletes all the content of the Text widget, creating a fresh document in its place.

❑ Finally, we add a command callback to function from our **File | New** menu item.

This completes our coding of **File | New** into our code editor.

Objective Complete – Mini Briefing

In this iteration, we completed coding functionality for the **New**, **Open**, **Save**, and **Save As** submenus, present under the **File** menu, for our editor.

More importantly, we saw how to use the tkFileDialog module to achieve certain commonly-used features in our program. We also saw how we could use indexing to achieve a wide variety of tasks for our programs.

Working with message boxes

In this iteration, let's complete our code for the **About** and **Help** menus. The functionality is simple. When a user clicks on the **Help** or **About** menu, it pops up a message window and waits for the user to respond by clicking on a button. While we can easily code new Toplevel windows to show our **About** and **Help** popup windows, we will instead use a module called tkMessageBox to achieve this functionality. This is because the module provides an efficient way to handle this and similar functionalities with minimal coding.

We will also complete coding the **Exit** button functioning in this iteration. Currently, when a user clicks on the **Close** button, the window is simply closed. We want to ask the user if they really want to quit or have they clicked on the **Close** button accidentally.

Prepare for Lift Off

The tkMessageBox module provides ready-made message boxes to display a wide variety of messages in your applications. Some of these functions are showinfo, showwarning, showerror, askquestion, askyesno, askokcancel, and askretryignore. These are illustrated, when in use, in the following screenshot:

To use the module, we simply import it into the current namespace as shown in the following command:

```
import tkMessageBox
```

A demonstration of commonly-used functions of tkMessageBox is illustrated in 2.08.py. Some common usage patterns are mentioned as follows:

```
tkMessageBox.showwarning("Beware", "You are warned")
tkMessageBox.showinfo("FYI", "This is FYI")
tkMessageBox.showerror("Err..", "its leaking.")
tkMessageBox.askquestion("?", "Can you read this ?")
tkMessageBox.askokcancel("OK", "Quit Postponing ?")
tkMessageBox.askyesno("Yes or No", " What Say ?")
tkMessageBox.askretrycancel("Retry", "Load Failed")
```

Using this module to display messages has the following advantages:

- Minimal coding yields functional features
- The messages can easily be configured
- Messages are presented with icons
- It presents a standardized view of common messages on each platform

Engage Thrusters

1. Let us now code the `about` and `help` functions for our code editor. The use case is simple. When a user clicks on the **About** menu, it pops up a message with the **OK** button. Similarly, when the user clicks on the **Help** button, they are also prompted with a message with the **OK** button.

   To achieve these functionalities, we include the following code in our editor. (See the code in `2.09.py`)

```
import tkMessageBox
def about(event=None):
   tkMessageBox.showinfo("About","Tkinter GUI Application\n
     Development Hotshot")


def help_box(event=None):
   tkMessageBox.showinfo("Help","For help refer to book:\n
   Tkinter GUI Application\n Development Hotshot ",
     icon='question')


aboutmenu.add_cascade(label="Help", command=help_box)
```

2. Next, we will look at adding the Quit Confirmation feature. When the user clicks on **File | Exit**, it prompts an `Ok-Cancel` dialog to confirm the quit action.

```
def exit_editor(event=None):
   if tkMessageBox.askokcancel("Quit", "Do you really want to
   quit?"):
     root.destroy()
root.protocol('WM_DELETE_WINDOW', exit_command) # override close
filemenu.add_command(label="Exit", accelerator='Alt+F4',
command=exit_editor)
```

   The description of the code is listed as follows:

   - First we import `tkMessageBox` into our current namespace.
   - We then define our `about` function to display a `showinfo` message box.
   - Similarly, we define our `help_box` function to display a `showinfo` message box.
   - We then define the `exit` command with an `askokcancel` box. If the user clicks on **OK**, the `exit` command destroys the root window to close the window.
   - We then override the close button protocol and redirect it to be handled by our definition of the `exit` command.
   - Finally, we add `command` callbacks to **About**, **Help**, and **Exit** menu items.

Objective Complete – Mini Briefing

In this iteration, we completed coding the functionality for the **File | Exit, About | About**, and **About | Help** menu items of our code editor. We also saw how to use the `tkMessageBox` module to display different message boxes for some commonly-used message formats.

The icon toolbar and View menu functions

In this iteration, we will add a few more functionalities to our text editor:

- ▶ Showing the shortcut icon toolbar
- ▶ Displaying line numbers
- ▶ Highlighting the current line
- ▶ Changing the color theme of the editor

In the process, we will see more usage of indexing and tagging.

Engage Thrusters

Let's start with a simple task first. In this step we add the shortcut icon toolbar to our editor. Recall that we have already created a frame to hold these toolbar icons. Let's add these icons now.

1. Let's start with adding a shortcut icon toolbar. While adding these icons, we have followed a convention. All icons have been placed in the `icons` folder. Moreover, the icons have been named exactly the same as the corresponding function that handles them. Following this convention has enabled us to loop through a list, simultaneously applying the icon image to each button and adding the `command` callback from within the loop.

   The code has been placed between the shortcut frame we created earlier to place these icons. The code is as follows (refer to the code in `2.10.py`):

   ```
   shortcutbar = Frame(root,  height=25, bg='light sea green')
   #creating icon toolbar
   ```

```
icons = ['new_file', 'open_file', 'save', 'cut', 'copy', 'paste',
'undo', 'redo', 'on_find', 'about']
for i, icon in enumerate(icons):
  tbicon = PhotoImage(file='icons/'+icon+'.gif')
  cmd = eval(icon)
  toolbar = Button(shortcutbar, image=tbicon, command=cmd)
  toolbar.image = tbicon
  toolbar.pack(side=LEFT)
shortcutbar.pack(expand=NO, fill=X)
```

The description of the code is listed as follows:

- ❑ We have already created a shortcut bar in our first iteration. Now we place our code between the lines where we created the frame and line and where we used the `pack` manager to display it.

- ❑ We create a list of icons, taking care to name them exactly as the name of icons.

- ❑ We then iterate through a loop with length equal to the number of items in the icons lists. In every loop, we create a Button widget, taking the corresponding image and adding the respective `command` callback.

- ❑ Before adding the `command` callback, we had to convert the string to an equivalent expression using the `eval` command. If we do not apply `eval`, it cannot be applied as an expression to our `command` callback.

This completes our coding of the shortcut icon toolbar. Now, if you run the code (code `2.10.py`), it should show you a shortcut icon toolbar at the top. Moreover, as we have linked each button to a callback, all these shortcut icons should work as they should.

2. Let us now work at showing line numbers on the left frame of the Text widget. This will require us to do a bit if tweaking of code at various places. So, before we start coding, let's take a look at what we are trying to achieve here:

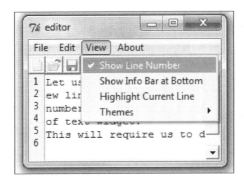

- The **View** menu has a menu item that lets the user choose whether or not to show the line numbers. We only want to show line numbers if the option is selected.

- If the option is selected, we need to display line numbers in the left frame that we created earlier.

- The line number should update every time a user enters a new line, deletes a line, cuts or pastes text from the line, performs an undo or redo operation, opens an existing file, or clicks on the new menu item. In short, the line number should be updated after every activity that may affect line numbers.

Therefore, we need to define a function called `update_line_number()`. This function should be called after every keypress, cut, paste, undo, redo, new, and open definitions to see if lines have been added or removed from the text area and accordingly update the line numbers. We achieve this using these two strategies (see the code in `2.10.py`):

- Bind any keypress events to our `update_line_number()` function:

  ```
  textPad.bind("<Any-KeyPress>", update_line_number)
  ```

- Add a call to our `update_line_number()` function in each of our definitions of cut, paste, undo, redo, new, and open

Finally, we define our `update_line_number()` function as follows:

```
def update_line_number(event=None):
  txt = ''
  if showln.get():
    endline, endcolumn = textPad.index('end-1c').split('.')
    txt = '\n'.join(map(str, range(1, int(endline))))
  lnlabel.config(text=txt, anchor='nw')
```

The description of the code is listed as follows:

- Recall that we have assigned a variable `showln` to our menu item earlier:

  ```
  showln = IntVar()
  showln.set(1)
  viewmenu.add_checkbutton(label="Show Line Number",
  variable=showln)
  update_line_number
  ```

- We first mark the text configuration of label as blank.

- If the `showline` option is set to `1` (that is to say, it has been tick-marked in the menu item), we calculate the last line and last column in the text.

- ❑ We then create a text string consisting of numbers from 1 to the number of the last line, each number separated by a line break, \n. This string is then added to the left label using the `textPad.config()` method.

- ❑ If **Show Line Number** is unchecked in the menu, the variable text remains blank, thereby displaying no line numbers.

- ❑ Finally, we update each of our previously defined cut, paste, undo, redo, new, and open functions to invoke the `update_line_number()` function at their end.

We are now done adding the line number functionality to our text editor.

You may have noticed an `event=None` argument in our function definition previously given. We need to specify this here, because this function can be invoked from two places:

- ▶ From the event binding (we bound it to the `<Any-KeyPress>` event)
- ▶ From other functions such as cut, copy, paste, undo, redo, and more

When the function is invoked from other functions, no arguments are passed. However, when the function is invoked from an event binding, the event object is passed as parameter. If we do not specify the `event=None` argument and the function is invoked from an event binding, it will give the following error:

```
TypeError: myfunction() takes no arguments (1 given)
```

3. Last in this iteration, we will implement a feature where the user can select to add a highlight on the current line. (See the code in `2.10.py`)

The idea is simple. We need to locate the line of the cursor and add a tag to the line. And finally, we need to configure that tag to appear with a different color background to highlight it.

Recall that we have already provided a menu choice to our user to decide whether or not to highlight the current line. We now add a `command` callback from this menu item to a function that we define as `toggle_highlight`:

```
hltln = IntVar()
viewmenu.add_checkbutton(label="Highlight Current Line",
onvalue=1, offvalue=0, variable=hltln, command=toggle_highlight)
```

We define three functions to handle this for us:

```
#line highlighting
def highlight_line(interval=100):
```

```
textPad.tag_remove("active_line", 1.0, "end")
textPad.tag_add("active_line", "insert linestart", "insert
lineend+1c")
textPad.after(interval, toggle_highlight)

def undo_highlight():
  textPad.tag_remove("active_line", 1.0, "end")

def toggle_highlight(event=None):
  val = hltln.get()
  undo_highlight() if not val else highlight_line()
```

The description of the code is given as follows:

- ❑ Every time a user checks/unchecks the **View | Highlight Current Line**, it invokes our function `toggle_highlight`. This function checks if the menu item is checked. If it is checked, it invokes the `highlight_line` function, otherwise, if the menu item is unchecked, it invokes the undo highlight function.

- ❑ Our `highlight_line` function simply adds a tag called `active_line` to our current line, and after every one second it calls the toggle highlight function to check whether the current line should still be highlighted.

- ❑ Our `undo_highlight` function is invoked when the user unchecks highlighting in the **View** menu. Once invoked, it simply removes the `active_line` tag from the entire text area.

- ❑ Finally, we configure our tag named `active_line` to be displayed with a different background color:

  ```
  textPad.tag_configure("active_line", background="ivory2")
  ```

In our code, we used the `.widget.after(ms, callback)` handler. Methods like this that let us perform some periodic actions are called **alarm handlers**. Some commonly used Tkinter alarm handlers include:

- ▶ `after(delay_ms, callback, args...)`: Registers an alarm callback to be called after given number of millisecond

- ▶ `after_cancel(id)`: Cancels the given alarm callback

- ▶ `after_idle(callback, args...)`: Calls back only when there are no more events to process in the mainloop, that is, after the system becomes idle

4. The info bar is simply a small area at the bottom-right corner of our Text widget, which displays the current line number and column number of the position of the cursor as shown in the following screenshot:

The user can choose to show/hide this info bar from the view menu; refer to the code in 2.11.py. We begin by creating a Label widget within the Text widget and pack it in the southeast corner.

```
infobar = Label(textPad, text='Line: 1 | Column: 0')
infobar.pack(expand=NO, fill=None, side=RIGHT, anchor='se')
```

In many ways, this is similar to displaying the line numbers. Here, too, the positions must be calculated after every keypress or after events such as cut, paste, undo, redo, new, open, or activities that lead to a change in cursor positions. Because this is so similar to our line number code, we will use the existing bindings and existing function update_line_number() to update this. To do this, we simply add two lines to our existing definition of the update_line_number() function:

```
currline, curcolumn = textPad.index("insert").split('.')
infobar.config(text= 'Line: %s | Column: %s' %(currline,
curcolumn))
```

This keeps updating the label with the line and column of the current cursor position.

Finally, if the user unchecks the option from the **View** menu, we need to hide this widget. We do this by defining a function called show_info_bar, which depending upon the user-selected choice, either applies pack or pack_forget to the infobar label.

```
def show_info_bar():
  val = showinbar.get()
  if val:
    infobar.pack(expand=NO, fill=None, side=RIGHT,
      anchor='se')
  elif not val:
    infobar.pack_forget()
```

This function is then connected to the existing menu item using a `command` callback:

```
viewmenu.add_checkbutton(label="Show Info Bar at Bottom",
variable=showinbar ,command=show_info_bar)
```

5. Recall that while defining our **Themes** menu, we defined a color scheme dictionary containing the name and hexadecimal color codes as a key-value pair. Actually, we need two colors for each theme, one for the background and other for our foreground color. Let's modify our color definition to specify two colors separated by the dot character (.). Refer to code `2.11.py`:

```
clrschms = {
'1. Default White': '000000.FFFFFF',
'2. Greygarious Grey': '83406A.D1D4D1',
'3. Lovely Lavender': '202B4B.E1E1FF' ,
'4. Aquamarine': '5B8340.D1E7E0',
'5. Bold Beige': '4B4620.FFF0E1',
'6. Cobalt Blue': 'ffffBB.3333aa',
'7. Olive Green': 'D1E7E0.5B8340',
}
```

Our theme choice menu has already been defined earlier. Let us now add a `command` callback to handle the selected menu:

```
themechoice= StringVar()
themechoice.set('1. Default White')
for k in sorted(clrschms):
  themesmenu.add_radiobutton(label=k, variable=themechoice,
  command=theme)
  menubar.add_cascade(label="View", menu=viewmenu)
```

Finally, let's define our `theme` function to handle the changing of themes:

```
def theme():
  global bgc,fgc
  val = themechoice.get()
  clrs = clrschms.get(val)
  fgc, bgc = clrs.split('.')
  fgc, bgc = '#'+fgc, '#'+bgc
  textPad.config(bg=bgc, fg=fgc)
```

The function is simple. It picks up the key-value pair from our defined color scheme dictionary. It splits the color into its two components and applies one color each to the Text widget foreground and background using `widget.config()`.

Now if you select a different color from the **Themes** menu, the background and foreground colors change accordingly.

Objective Complete – Mini Briefing

We completed coding our shortcut icon toolbar and all functionality of the **View** menu in this iteration. In the process we learned how to handle the Checkbutton and Radiobutton menu items. We also saw how to make compound buttons, while reinforcing several Tkinter options covered in previous sections.

Event handling and the context menu

In this last iteration, we will add the following features to our editor:

- ▸ Event handling
- ▸ The context menu
- ▸ The title bar icon

Engage Thrusters

Let us complete our editor in this final iteration.

1. First we will add the event handling features. We have added the accelerator keyboard shortcuts to a large number of our menu items. However, merely adding accelerator keys does not add the required functionality. For example, pressing the keys *Ctrl* + *N* should create a new file, but simply adding it as an accelerator does not make it functional. Let's add these event handling features into our code.

 Note that all our functionality is already complete. Now we simply need to map the events to their related callbacks. (Refer to the code in 2.12.py.)

```
textPad.bind('<Control-N>', new_file)
textPad.bind('<Control-n>', new_file)
textPad.bind('<Control-O>', open_file)
textPad.bind('<Control-o>', open_file)
textPad.bind('<Control-S>', save)
textPad.bind('<Control-s>', save)
textPad.bind('<Control-A>', select_all)
textPad.bind('<Control-a>', select_all)
textPad.bind('<Control-f>', on_find)
textPad.bind('<Control-F>', on_find)
textPad.bind('<KeyPress-F1>', help_box)
```

Simply adding these lines takes care of our event bindings. However, this introduces a new issue for us. We have already discussed that event bindings pass the event object as a parameter to the bound callback. None of our previous functions are equipped to handle the incoming parameters. To do that we need to add the `event=None` parameter.

Adding this optional argument allows us to use these functions with or without the event parameter.

Alternatively, you can also add `textPad.bind (event, lambda e: callback())` to ignore the `event` argument altogether.

Now you can access these functions using your keyboard shortcuts.

Note that we did not bind keyboard shortcuts for cut, copy, and paste. This is because the Text widget comes with automatic binding for these events. If you add bindings for these events, it will cause cut, copy, and paste events to take place twice; once from the built-in widget and once from your own defined event handler.

2. Next we will add the context menu. But before that, we need to understand what a context menu is.

The menu that pops up on the right-mouse-button click at the location of the mouse cursor is called the **context menu** or the **o**. This is shown in the following screenshot:

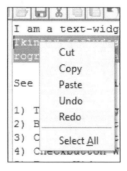

Let's code this feature in our text editor. We first define our context menu:

```
cmenu = Menu(textPad)
for i in ('cut', 'copy', 'paste', 'undo', 'redo'):
  cmd = eval(i)
  cmenu.add_command(label=i, compound=LEFT, command=cmd)
  cmenu.add_separator()
  cmenu.add_command(label='Select All', underline=7,
    command=select_all)
```

We then bind the right-click of a mouse with a callback named `popup`:

```
textPad.bind("<Button-3>", popup)
```

Finally, we define the method `popup`:

```
def popup(event):
    cmenu.tk_popup(event.x_root, event.y_root, 0)
```

3. As a final touch to our application, we add a title bar icon for our editor using the following code:

```
root.iconbitmap('icons/pypad.ico')
```

Objective Complete – Mini Briefing

In this iteration we added support for event handling, and added a contextual menu and title bar icon to our editor program.

Mission Accomplished

We have completed coding our editor in seven iterations. We started by placing all widgets on our Toplevel window. We then leveraged some built-in features of the Text widget to code some functionality. We learned some very important concepts of indexing and tagging, which you will find yourself using frequently in Tkinter projects.

We also saw how to use the `tkfileDialog` and `tkMessageBox` modules to quickly code some common features in our programs.

Congratulations! You have now completed coding your text editor.

A Hotshot Challenge

Here's your Hotshot challenge:

▶ Your goal is to turn this text editor into a Python code editor. Your editor should allow the opening and saving of the `.py` file extension.

▶ If the file has a `.py` extension, your editor should implement syntax highlighting and tab indenting.

▶ While this can be easily done with external libraries, you should try to implement these features on your own using built-in Tkinter options that we have seen so far. For hints you can look at the source code of Python's built-in editor IDLE, which is written in Tkinter.

Project 3

Programmable Drum Machine

We built a text editor in the last project. In the process, we looked at some common Tkinter widgets such as Menu, Buttons, Label, and Text. Now, let us now do some music. Let us build a cross-platform drum machine using Tkinter and some other Python modules.

Mission Briefing

In this project, we will build a programmable drum machine. The graphical user interface of the drum machine is based on Tkinter. You will be able to create an unlimited number of beat patterns using an unlimited number of drum samples. You can then store multiple riffs in a project and playback or edit the project later on.

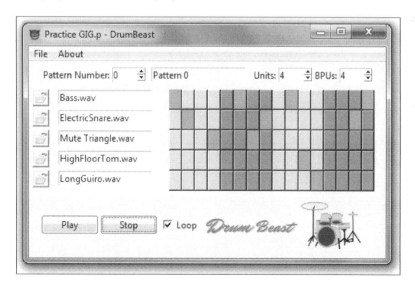

To create your own drum beat patterns, simply load some drum samples using the buttons on the left. You can change the units that constitute a beat pattern, which in turn decides the tempo of the rhythm. You can also decide the number of beats per units. Most western beats have four beats per unit, waltz would have three beats per unit, and some Indian and Arabic rhythms that I composed on this machine had 3 to 16 beats per unit!

Why Is It Awesome?

Don't be misled by the small size of the GUI. This is a powerful drum machine that can match features offered by some large commercial drum machine programs. By the end of this project, you should be in a position to extend it to outdo some of the commercial drum programs out there.

Some of the key features of the machine include:

- ▶ Large number of beats
- ▶ Large number of patterns to accompany songs
- ▶ Variable number of beats per pattern
- ▶ Use of 16 bit, 44100 kHz WAV samples (mono or stereo)
- ▶ Support for various file formats
- ▶ Ability to save projects comprising of several patterns

A few drum samples are provided in the `Loops` subdirectory; however, you can load any other drum sample. You can download a large number of samples for free from the Internet.

In the process of developing this program, we tweak Tkinter further and take a look at several important concepts and ideas that are normally encountered in GUI programming.

Your Hotshot Objectives

Some of the key objectives for taking up this project include:

- ▶ Understanding how Tkinter is normally applied in context of OOP
- ▶ Working with a few more Tkinter widgets such as Spinbox, Button, Entry, and Checkbutton
- ▶ Working with the `grid` geometry manager
- ▶ Working with ttk-themed widgets
- ▶ Understanding threaded programming in relation to Tkinter
- ▶ Working with other common modules from the Python standard library
- ▶ Object persistence with the `pickle` module

Apart from these key concepts, we discuss several other vital nuggets of GUI programming in the course of the project.

Mission Checklist

In this project, we will use some more built-in libraries from the standard Python distribution. This includes `Tkinter`, `ttk`, `tkFileDialog`, `tkMessageBox`, `os`, `time`, `threading`, `wave`, and `pickle` modules.

To verify that these modules do exist, simply run the following statement in the IDLE interactive prompt:

```
>>> import Tkinter, ttk, os, time, threading, wave, pickle, tkFileDialog,
tkMessageBox
```

This should not cause an error as the standard Python distribution comes with these modules built into the distribution.

Other than this, you need to add an extra Python module called `pymedia`.

The `pymedia` module can be downloaded at `http://pymedia.org/`.

After you have installed the module, you can verify it by importing it:

```
>>> import pymedia
```

If no errors are reported, you are ready to program the drum machine. Let's start!

Setting up the GUI in OOP

The text editor program that we developed as our previous project was set up in procedural code. While it offered some benefit of quick coding, it essentially ran as a single process.

We started encountering global variables. The function definitions needed to be defined above the code that called them and most importantly the code was not reusable.

Therefore, we need some way to ensure that our code is more reusable. This is why programmers prefer to use **Object Oriented Programming (OOP)** to organize their code into classes.

OOP is a programming paradigm that shifts the focus onto the objects we want to manipulate rather than the logic required to manipulate them.

This is in contrast to procedural programming that views a program as a logical procedure that takes input, processes it, and produces some output.

OOP provides several benefits such as data abstraction, encapsulation, inheritance, and polymorphism. In addition, OOP provides a clear modular structure for programs. Code modification and maintenance is easy as new objects can be created without modifying the existing ones.

Let us build our drum program using OOP to illustrate some of these features.

Prepare for Lift Off

An indicative OOP structure for our drum program could be as follows (see the code in `3.01.py`):

```python
from Tkinter import *
class DrumMachine():
  def app(self):
    self.root = Tk()
    # all other code are called from here
    self.root.mainloop()

if __name__ == '__main__':
  dm = DrumMachine()
  dm.app()
```

The description of the code is listed as follows:

- We create a class called `DrumMachine` and define a method `app()` to initialize the Toplevel window
- If the program is run as a standalone program, a new object is created and the `app` method is called to create the Toplevel window
- This code creates a blank Toplevel window

Now that we have our Toplevel window ready, let us add some widgets to it. In this iteration we will lay the top bar, left bar (the area that lets us upload drum samples), the right bar (that has buttons to define the beat patterns), and play bar at the bottom (which has a **Play** button, a **Stop** button, and a **Loop** check button).

The four areas have been demarcated in different squares to group widgets into separate frames, as shown in the following screenshot:

Engage Thrusters

1. First we will create the top bar. The top bar is one that holds the Spinbox widgets, which lets the user change the units and beats per unit in a rhythm pattern. These two together decide the tempo and the cyclical pattern of a rhythm as follows (see the code in `3.02.py`):

```
def create_top_bar(self):
    top_bar_frame = Frame(self.root)
    top_bar_frame.config(height=25)
    top_bar_frame.grid(row=0, columnspan=12, rowspan=10, padx=5,
    pady=5)
    Label(top_bar_frame, text='Units:').grid(row=0, column=4)
    self.units = IntVar()
    self.units.set(4)
    self.bpu_widget = Spinbox(top_bar_frame, from_=1, to=10,
    width=5, textvariable=self.units)
    self.bpu_widget.grid(row=0, column=5)
    Label(top_bar_frame, text='BPUs:').grid(row=0, column=6)
    self.bpu = IntVar()
    self.bpu.set(4)
    self.units_widget = Spinbox(top_bar_frame, from_=1, to=8,
    width=5, textvariable=self.bpu)
    self.units_widget.grid(row=0, column=7)
```

The description of the code is listed as follows:

- We first create a new method in order to create the top bar. We add a frame `top_bar_frame` for the top bar and then add two spin boxes to keep track of the units and beats per unit values. We do not add `command` callbacks now. The callbacks will be added later.

- We define two Tkinter variables `self.units` and `self.bpu` to hold the current value of both the Spinbox widgets. This is defined as an object variable (`self`) because we will need these variables outside the scope of this method.

- The widgets are placed using the `grid` geometry manager.

2. Next we will create the left bar. The left bar is one that will let the user load drum samples. Each row in the left bar allows for loading one unique drum sample. The drum samples are normally small `.wav` or `.ogg` file samples for different drums such as bass, snare, tom, bell, claves, or samples that the user decides.

   The buttons on the left bar will open an upload file. When the user uploads a drum sample, the name of the drum sample will automatically populate the Entry widget adjacent to that button.

Thus, each row has a Button and an Entry widget (refer to the code in `3.02.py`):

```
MAX_DRUM_NUM = 5
def create_left_pad(self):
  '''creating actual pattern editor pad'''
  left_frame = Frame(self.root)
  left_frame.grid(row=10, column=0,
    columnspan=6, sticky=W+E+N+S)
  tbicon = PhotoImage(file='images/openfile.gif')
  for i in range(0, MAX_DRUM_NUM):
    button = Button(left_frame, image=tbicon)
    button.image = tbicon
    button.grid(row=i, column=0, padx=5, pady=2)
    self.drum_entry = Entry(left_frame)
    self.drum_entry.grid(row=i, column=4, padx=7, pady=2)
```

The description of the code is listed as follows:

- The maximum number of drum samples that can be loaded is defined as a constant `MAX_DRUM_NUM`

- We create another frame called `left_frame` to hold various widgets in this area

- Iterating over a loop, we create Button and Entry widgets for as many drum samples as we need to allow the user to load

3. Next we will create the right bar. The right bar is the area that lets the user define the beat pattern. This area consists of a series of buttons. The number of row of buttons is equal to the number of drum samples that can be loaded. The number of columns of buttons is decided by the number of units and number of beats per unit selected by the user from the spin boxes in the top bar. The number of columns of buttons is equal to product of the number of units and beats per unit.

    We are not connecting the spin boxes with the buttons right now. For now, let us place buttons in four columns for each individual drum sample that can be loaded as follows (refer to the code in `3.02.py`):

```
def create_right_pad(self):
  right_frame = Frame(self.root)
  right_frame.grid(row=10, column=6,sticky=W+E+N+S, padx=15,
  pady=2)
  self.button = [[0 for x in range(4)] for x in
    range(MAX_DRUM_NUM)]
  for i in range(MAX_DRUM_NUM):
    for j in range(4):
      self.button[i][j] = Button(right_frame, bg='grey55')
      self.button[i][j].grid(row=i, column=j)
```

The description of the code is listed as follows:

- ❑ We create another frame `right_frame` to hold these buttons.

- ❑ Using list comprehension, we create an empty list of size 4 `*MAX_DRUM_NUM`.

- ❑ For now, we simply add four columns of buttons to occupy the place. The number of rows of buttons are kept equal to the maximum number of drum samples, to have one row of buttons corresponding to each sample.

There is reason behind grouping widgets into different methods.

For example, we have created the left pad and the right pad using two separate methods `create_left_pad` and `create_right_pad`. If we had defined these two groups of widgets within the same method, the user would have to reload the drum samples every time the left buttons changed due to changes in BPU and units. This would have been counterproductive for the end user.

As a rule of thumb, it is always advisable to keep related widgets within a single method. However, the deciding class structure is more of an art than science to be learned and refined over a lifetime.

4. Next we will create the play bar. The play bar at the bottom includes the **Play** button, the **Stop** button, and a **Loop** check button. Refer to the code in `3.02.py`, as shown in the following code:

```
def create_play_bar(self):
  playbar_frame = Frame(self.root, height=15)
  ln = MAX_DRUM_NUM+10
  playbar_frame.grid(row=ln, columnspan=13, sticky=W+E, padx=15,
  pa dy=10)
  button = Button( playbar_frame, text ='Play')
  button.grid(row= ln, column=1, padx=1)
  button = Button( playbar_frame, text ='Stop')='Stop')
  button.grid(row= ln, column=3, padx=1)
  loop = BooleanVar()
  loopbutton = Checkbutton(playbar_frame, text='Loop',
    variable=loop)
  loopbutton.grid(row=ln, column=16, padx=1)
```

The description of the code is listed as follows:

- The code is pretty self-explanatory. It creates a frame `playbar_frame` and puts two buttons and one check button within the frame.

- A Tkinter `BooleanVar()` is created to track the status of Checkbutton.

5. Now that we have created all the widgets, its now time to actually display them by explicitly calling the methods that created them. We do that within the main loop of our program as follows (refer to the code in `3.02.py`):

```
def app(self):
  self.root = Tk()
  self.root.title('Drum Beast')
  self.create_top_bar()
  self.create_left_pad()
  self.create_right_pad()
  self.create_play_bar()
  self.root.mainloop()
```

Rather than defining a separate method `app()` to run our main loop, we could also have run the main loop by creating an initialization method called `__init__`.

In that case, we would not have to call the `app()` method explicitly to run the program. However, in case someone ever needs to use this class in another program, it would have needlessly created a GUI.

Calling the `mainloop` function explicitly from the `app()` method leaves us room to use the code as a library for some other program.

Objective Complete – Mini Debriefing

This completes our first iteration. In this iteration we have managed to create the basic structure of our drum program. This includes creating the top, left, right, and bottom frames that holds different widgets as per the requirement of the drum program.

We have also seen one of the most common ways of structuring the Tkinter GUI program in an object-oriented style of programming.

Completing the pattern editor

In the preceding iteration, we coded a dummy `create_right_pad` with four columns of buttons. However, in the scheme of our program, the number of columns of buttons depends upon the choice of **Units** and beats per units (**BPU**) values selected by the end user.

The number of columns of buttons should be equal to:

Number of Units x BPU

Furthermore, to demarcate each unit, each consecutive unit of buttons should be displayed in different colors. Moreover, when a button is clicked, its color should change to track the user-defined pattern, as shown in the following screenshot:

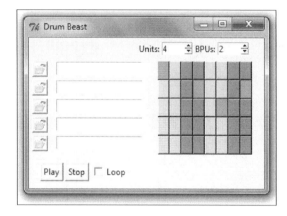

Let us add these three features to our drum editor.

Engage Thrusters

1. First, we will start by connecting buttons to the **Units** and **BPU** Spinbox widgets. The code is simple. We add `command` callbacks from both the Spinbox widgets in the top bar to call our `create_right_pad` method. Refer to the code in `3.03.py`:

```
self.units_widget = Spinbox(topbar_frame, from_=1, to=8, width=5,
textvariable=self.units, command= self.create_right_pad)
self.bpu_widget = Spinbox(topbar_frame, from_=1, to=10, width=5,
textvariable=self.bpu, command= self.create_right_pad)
```

We then modify our existing `create_right_pad` method as follows, and in code `3.03.py`:

```
def create_right_pad(self):
  bpu = self.bpu.get()
  units = self.units.get()
  c = bpu * units
  right_frame = Frame(self.root)
  right_frame.grid(row=10, column=6,sticky=W+E+N+S, padx=15,
  pady=2)
  self.button = [[0 for x in range(c)] for x in
    range(MAX_DRUM_NUM)]
  for i in range(MAX_DRUM_NUM):
    for j in range(c):
      color = 'grey55' if (j/bpu)%2 else 'khaki'
      self.button[i][j] = Button(right_frame,  bg=color,
        width=1, command=self.button_clicked(i,j,bpu))
      self.button[i][j].grid(row=i, column=j)
```

The description of the code is listed as follows:

- Within our frame `right_frame`, we iterate through a double-nested loop creating a two-dimensional matrix where the number of rows is equal to the constant `MAX_DRUM_NUM`, while the number of columns is equal to the product of **Units** and **BPU**.

- The color of each button is configured to either `grey55` or `khaki` depending on whether the factor `j/bpu` is even or odd.

- Now if you run the code (code `3.03.py`), you will find the number of buttons changing as per selections you make in the units and bpu spin boxes. Moreover, each unit will be colored alternately in khaki and gray colors.

- Notice how we have defined the `grid` geometry position of buttons in terms of variables `i` and `j`.

2. Now that the buttons respond to change in units and bpu, it is time that we change these buttons into toggle buttons. When a user clicks on any of the buttons, the color of the button should change to green. When the button is clicked again, the color reverts to its original color. We need this feature to define beat patterns.

   We first add a `command` callback to our buttons, passing the button's row, column, and bpu as arguments to a new method `button_clicked` (refer to the code in `3.03.py`), as shown in the following code:

```
self.button[i][j] = (Button(right_frame, bg='grey55', width=1,
command=self.Button_clicked(i,j,bpu)))
```

We then define the `button_clicked` method as follows:

```
def button_clicked(self,i,j,bpu):
  def callback():
    btn = self.button[i][j]
    color = 'grey55' if (j/bpu)%2 else 'khaki'
    new_color = 'green' if btn.cget('bg') != 'green' else
      color
    btn.config(bg=new_color)
  return callback
```

The description of the code is listed as follows:

- ❏ Our method `button_clicked` takes three arguments: `i`, `j`, and `bpu`.
- ❏ The variables `i` and `j` let us track which button is clicked. However, note that the `command` callback `self.Button_clicked(i,j,bpu)` makes a reference to `i` and `j` when the button is not yet created. In order to track the button that is clicked by the user, we enclose a separate `callback()` function within our `self.button_clicked` function, which then returns a callback. Now our method will return a different value of `i` and `j` for each button record.
- ❏ The `bpu` argument is needed to calculate the original color of the button. This is needed to revert the color of button back to its original color if the button is toggled. Before we change the color of the button to green, we store its original color in a variable `color`.

Objective Complete – Mini Debriefing

We have now completed coding the right drum pad. In the process we have created a two-dimensional list of buttons `self.button`, where `self.button[i][j]` refers to the button at the *i*th row and *j*th column.

Each of these buttons can be toggled on or off to represent whether or not a drum sample is to be played for that particular button.

When a button is on, its color changes to green. If it is switched off, it reverts to its original color. This structure can be easily used to define a beat pattern.

In the process, we have seen more advanced usage of the Spinbox and Button widget.

Loading drum samples

Our main objective is to play sound files, in the order of a beat pattern decided by the user. To do this we need to add sound files to the drum machine.

Our program does not have any preloaded drum files. Instead, we want to let the user select from a wide variety of drum files. Thus, besides the normal drum, you can play a Japanese tsuzumi, an Indian tabla, Latin American bongo drums, or just about any other sound that you want to add to your rhythm. All you need is a small .wav or .ogg file containing that sound's sample.

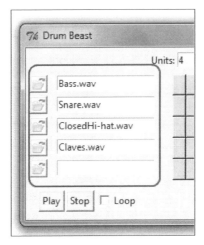

Let us code the ability to add this drum sample to our program.

The drum sample is to be loaded on the left bar, as shown in the preceding screenshot. We have already created buttons with folder icons to the left-hand side of our drum pad. The desired functionality is simple.

When a user clicks on any of the left buttons, they should open a file dialog letting the user choose a .wav or .ogg file. When the user selects the file and clicks on **Open**, the Entry widget next to that button should be populated with the name of the file. Further, the location of the drum sample file should be added to a list for playing it later.

Engage Thrusters

1. First we will import the required modules. To open the sound file, we will use the `tkFileDialog` module. We will also use the `tkMessageBox` module to display certain pop-up messages. We will also need to extract the filename of the given sound sample using the `os` module. Let us begin by importing the three modules (given in the following code) into our current namespace (refer to the same code present in `3.04.py`):

```
import tkFileDialog
import tkMessageBox
import os
```

2. Next, we will add Attributes to track the loaded samples. The user will invariably load more than one drum sample. Therefore, we need to track the Entry widget where the drum sample was loaded, the location of each of the drum samples, and a number indicating the current drum number. Accordingly, we create two lists called `self.widget_drum_name` and `self.widget_drum_file_name` to store the Entry widget instance and file location respectively.

   We also declare a variable `self.current_drum_no` to track the current drum number.

   We choose to initialize these variables and list under our initialization method `__init__` (refer to the code in `3.04.py`):

```
def __init__(self):
    self.widget_drum_name = []
    self.widget_drum_file_name = [0]*MAX_DRUM_NUM
    self.current_drum_no = 0
```

   We then modify our `create_left_pad` method to include a line that appends a list of all drum Entry widgets in our newly-created list `self.widget_drum_name`:

```
self.widget_drum_name.append(self.drum_entry)
```

3. We then add a `command` callback to the buttons in our `create_left_pad` method to load drum samples, as shown in the following code snippet:

```
button = Button(left_frame, image=tbicon, command=
self.drum_load(i))
```

4. Finally, we code our `drum_load` method as follows (refer to the code in `3.04.py`):

```
def drum_load(self, drum_no):
  def callback():
    self.current_drum_no = drum_no
    try:
      file_name = tkFileDialog.askopenfilename(
        defaultextension=".wav", filetypes=[("Wave
        Files","*.wav"),("OGG
        Files","*.ogg")])Files","*.ogg")])
      if not file_name: return
      try:
        delself.widget_drum_file_name[drum_no]
      except: pass
      self.widget_drum_file_name.insert(drum_no,
      file_name)
      drum_name = os.path.basename(file_name)
      self.widget_drum_name[drum_no].delete(0, END)
      self.widget_drum_name[drum_no].insert(0, drum_name)
    except:
      tkMessageBox.showerror('Invalid', "Error loading
      drum samples")
  return callback
```

The description of the code is listed as follows:

- We define a callback function within our function because we need to track several drum samples.

- To track the widget, through which a sound sample has been loaded, we set the `self.current_drum_no` value to be equal to the `drum_num` value received as an argument from the button `command` callback.

- In a `try` block, we use `tkFileDialog.askopenfilename` to get the filename of the drum sample. We then check whether a filename already exists in our filename list. If it does, we delete it.

- Using `os.path.basename` from the `os` module, we obtain the filename from the file path and insert it into corresponding Entry widget.

- If `askopenfilename` fails, we use `tkMessageBox.showerror` to display a custom error message.

Objective Complete – Mini Debriefing

In this iteration, we imported modules to handle dialogs and message boxes. We then added attributes to track drum samples. Finally, we added `command` callbacks to buttons which when clicked open a dialog for the user to select drum samples.

Our code is now capable of loading drum samples and storing all necessary records that we will require to play beat patterns.

Next, let us turn our attention to playing the beat samples as per a user-defined pattern.

Playing the drum machine

Now that we have a mechanism to load drum samples and a mechanism to define beat patterns in place, let us add the ability to play these beat patterns. In many ways, this is the core of our program.

Let us first understand the functionality that we want to achieve here. Once the user has loaded one or more drum sample and has defined a beat pattern using the toggle buttons, we need to scan each column of the pattern to see if it finds a green button. If it finds one, our code should play the corresponding drum sample before moving ahead. Moreover, green buttons on the same column should play almost together, while there should be some time gap between each successive column, which would define the tempo of the music.

Prepare for Lift Off

We will use the `pymedia` module to play the sound files. The `pymedia` module can play a wide variety of sound formats such as `.wav`, `.ogg`, `.mp3`, `.avi`, `.divx`, `.dvd`, and `.cdda` on multiple operating systems.

Without getting into the details of how pymedia plays the sound files, the official documentation tells us that we can play audio files using the following code sample:

```
import time, wave, pymedia.audio.sound as sound
f= wave.open( 'YOUR FILE NAME', 'rb' )
sampleRate= f.getframerate()
channels= f.getnchannels()
format= sound.AFMT_S16_LE
snd= sound.Output( sampleRate, channels, format )
s= f.readframes( 300000 )
snd.play( s )
```

If you run this piece of code as an independent script and supply the file location of a supported audio file in place of `'YOUR FILE NAME'`, this should play the media file on your computer.

Using this code sample, we will implement the play functionality for our drum machine.

Engage Thrusters

1. Let us first import all of the necessary modules into our namespace (refer to the code in `3.05.py`):

```
import time
import wave
import pymedia.audio.sound as sound
```

2. Next, we will define the `play_sound` method as follows:

```
def play_sound(self, sound_filename):
  try:
    self.s = wave.open(sound_filename, 'rb')
    sample_rate = self.s.getframerate()
    channels = self.s.getnchannels()
    frmt = sound.AFMT_S16_LE
        self.snd= sound.Output(sample_rate, channels, frmt)
        s = self.s.readframes(300000)
    self.snd.play(s)
  except:
    pass
```

This method simply takes the API provided by `pymedia` and wraps it into a method that takes a filename and plays it.

3. Let us now define the `play` method that actually plays the beat samples:

```
def play(self):
  for i in range(len(self.button[0])):
    for item in self.button:
      try:
        if item[i].cget('bg') == 'green':
        if not self.widget_drum_file_name
            [self.button.index(item)]:continue
        sound_filename = self.widget_drum_file_name
            [self.button.index(item)]
         self.play_sound(sound_filename)
      except: continue
      time.sleep(3/4.0)
```

The description of the code is listed as follows:

- ❑ We loop through all of the buttons scanning each column before moving to the next column. For every button, we use `widget.cget()` to check to see if its color is green.

- ❑ If the color is green, we check if there is a corresponding drum sample loaded. If not, we ignore the green button and move to the next item in the loop using `continue`.

- ❑ If the color is green and there is a corresponding drum sample loaded, we use the previously-defined `pymedia` wrapper method for playing audio to play that sample.

- ❑ Before moving to the next column the code is made to sleep for a small interval. If the code is not made to sleep for a small duration, the program would play all the samples at a very rapid succession.

- ❑ We have chosen to make the code sleep for a time period of one-eighth of a second. You can change this sleep time to vary the tempo.

Objective Complete – Mini Debriefing

In this iteration, we added the capability to play the loaded drum samples.

Our drum machine is now operational. You can load drum samples, define beat patterns, and when you click on the **Play** button, the drum machine plays that beat pattern!

In this example, we decided whether or not to play a drum sample based on the color of the button. This has been used here for demonstration purposes. However, it is not a good practice to mix logic with appearance. A better idea would be to implement a data structure for buttons that would keep track of button state as "clicked" or "not-clicked", and then play the audio based on this button's state. Implementation of this dual button states is left as an exercise for you to explore.

Classified Intel

In our previous code, we used `widget.cget()` to fetch the current value of the button's bg option to check if it is green. You can use `w.cget(key)` to return the current value of a widget option. Also, note that `cget()` always returns the value as a string even if you give a nonstring value when configuring the widget option.

Similar to `widget.cget()` method, Tkinter offers a wide variety of methods for all its widgets. For a list of basic widget methods, refer to the *The basic widget methods* section in *Appendix B, Quick Reference Sheets*.

If you want to know all of the options configured for a particular widget, you may use the `widget.config()` method instead, as follows: (See the code in `3.06.py`)

```
from Tkinter import *
root = Tk()
widget = Button(root, text="#", bg='green')
widget.pack()
print widget.config()
print widget.config('bg')
root.mainloop()
```

This code will print a dictionary showing all the key-value pairs for widget options and their values listed as tuples. For example, in the preceding code the line `print widget.config('bg')` prints a tuple:

```
('background', 'background', 'Background', <border object at
022A1AC8>, 'green')
```

Tkinter and threading

Our drum machine plays patterns in the way that we want it to. However, there is a small problem. The `play` method blocks the main loop of our Tkinter program. It does not relinquish control back to the main loop until it is done playing all of the sound samples.

This means that if you now want to click on the **Stop** button or change some other widget, you will have to wait for the `play` loop to complete.

You might have noticed that when you hit the **Play** button, it remains pressed for the time the sound loops are being played. During that time you cannot access any other widget in the Toplevel window.

This clearly is a glitch. We need some method to confer back the control to Tkinter main loop while the play is still in progress.

Prepare for Lift Off

One of the simplest ways that we can achieve this is to use the `root.update()` method within our `play` loop. This updates the `root.mainloop()` method after each sound sample is played (see the commented code in `3.07.py`).

However, this is an inelegant method because the control is passed to the main loop with some staggering experienced in the GUI. Thus, you may experience a slight delay in responses of other widgets in the Toplevel.

Further, if some other event causes the method to be called, it could result in a nested event loop.

A better solution would be to run the `play` method from a separate thread. To do that let us employ the `threading` module of Python.

Engage Thrusters

1. Let us first import the `threading` module into our namespace (refer to the code in `3.07.py`):

    ```
    import threading
    ```

2. Now, let us create a method that calls the `self.play()` method to run in a separate thread. This redirects `play` through the threading model:

    ```
    def play_in_thread(self):
      self.thread = threading.Thread(None, self.play, None, (), {})
      self.thread.start()
    ```

3. Finally, change the `command` callback for the **Play** button in the `play_bar` method from the existing `self.play()` method to `self.play_in_thread()`:

    ```
    button=Button(playbar_frame, text ='Play', command= self.play_in_
    thread)
    ```

    Now if you load some drum samples, define the beat patterns, and hit the **Play** button, the sound will play in a separate thread without preventing the main loop from updating (refer to the code in `3.07.py`).

4. The next step would be that of coding the **Stop** button. The role of the **Stop** button is simple; it merely stops the currently playing pattern. To do that, we first add a `command` callback to the **Stop** button calling on a method `stop_play` as follows (see the code in `3.07.py`):

    ```
    button=Button(playbar_frame, text='Stop', command= self.stop_play)
    ```

    Then we define the `stop_play` method as follows:

    ```
    def stop_play(self):
      self.keep_playing = False
    ```

5. Our thread system now runs the `play` method from a separate thread. However, if the user clicks on the button more than once, this will spawn more threads, which will play the beat. To avoid this, the button should be configured with `state='disabled'`, and enabled again when the sequence finishes.

To disable the **Play** button when the program starts running, we add the following line to our `play_in_thread` method (refer to the code in `3.07.py`):

```
self.start_button.config(state='disabled')
```

Similarly, when the sequence finishes playing or the **Stop** button is clicked, we want to enable the **Play** button again. To enable it, we add the following line to our `play` and `stop_play` methods:

```
self.start_button.config(state='normal')
```

Tkinter and thread safety

Tkinter is not thread safe. The Tkinter interpreter is valid only in the thread that runs the main loop. Any call to widgets must ideally be done from the thread that created the main loop. Invoking widget-specific commands from other threads is possible (as we do here), but is not reliable.

When you call a widget from another thread, the events get queued for the interpreter thread, which executes the command and passes the result back to the calling thread. If the main loop is running but not processing events, it sometimes results in unpredictable exceptions.

The only change we make to our existing `play` method is to include the entire code in a `try-except` block. We do this because Tkinter is not thread safe and can cause some unwanted exceptions when dealing with the `play` thread. The best we can do here is ignore those cases using a `try-except` block.

mtTkinter – a thread-safe version of Tkinter

If you find yourself working on an inherently multithreaded project, you might consider looking at **mtTkinter**—a thread-safe version of Tkinter. For more information on mtTkinter, visit `http://Tkinter.unPythonic.net/wiki/mtTkinter`.

For more specialized multiprocessing needs you may also want to take a look at *multiprocessing module* or an *event model* such as **Twisted**.

6. The last step sees us code the **Loop** Checkbutton. The role of the **Loop** checkbox is simple. If the **Loop** checkbox is unchecked, the pattern plays only once. If it is checked, the pattern keeps playing in an endless loop. The pattern stops playing only if the **Loop** Checkbutton is unchecked or if the **Stop** button is pressed.

We add a `command` callback to the **Loop** checkbox:

```
loopbutton = Checkbutton(playbar_frame, text='Loop',
variable=loop, command=lambda: self.LoopPlay(loop.get())) )
```

We then define the `loop_play` method as follows:

```
def loop_play(self, xval):
    self.loop = xval
```

Equipped with these two variables, we modify our `play` method to keep playing while `self.keep_playing` is equal to `True` see the code in `3.07.py`).

If the value of `self.loop` is equal to `False`, we set the value of `self.keep_playing` equal to `False`, which breaks out of the play loop.

Objective Complete – Mini Debriefing

This completes the project iteration. In this round, we refined our `play` method to play the audio files from a separate thread.

We used Python's built-in threaded module to play the loops in separate thread. We looked at some of the threading-related limitations of Tkinter and some ways in which we can overcome those limitations.

We also coded for the **Stop** button and **Loop** checkbox functionality.

More beat patterns

Our drum program is now functional. You can load drum samples and define a beat pattern and our drum machine will play it out. Let us now extend our drum program so that we are able to create more than one pattern in the same program.

Rather than a single drum pattern, now we will have a list of patterns. While playing the patterns, a user will be able to switch between many different beat patterns. This will allow the drummer to add variations to the performance.

Engage Thrusters

1.   The first thing we need to do is add a Spinbox widget in the top bar (as shown in the following screenshot), which will keep count of the number of patterns. We also add an Entry widget next to the Spinbox widget to keep track of the pattern name, which is decided by the number selected in the spin box.

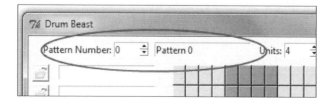

This is added to the `create_top_bar` method (refer to the code in `3.08.py`):

```
Label(top_bar_frame, text='Pattern Number:').grid(row=0, column=1)
self.patt = IntVar()
self.patt.set(0)
self.prevpatvalue = 0 # to trace last click
Spinbox(top_bar_frame, from_=0, to=9, width=5,
    textvariable=self.patt, command=self.record_pattern).grid(
    row=0, column=2)
self.pat_name = Entry(top_bar_frame)
self.pat_name.grid(row=0, column=3, padx=7,pady=2)
self.pat_name.insert(0, 'Pattern %s'%self.patt.get())
self.pat_name.config(state='readonly')
```

The description of the code is listed as follows:

- The pattern number is stored in a Tkinter integer variable as `self.patt`.

- The Entry widget that stores the corresponding pattern name is called `self.pat_name`. This widget is marked as "read only", as we do not want to allow the user to modify the name.

- The Spinbox widget has a `command` callback to a new method `record_pattern`.

2. Let us now code the `record_pattern` method. The role of this method is to keep track of the state of a given pattern. Thus, for every pattern it needs to track the pattern number, units, BPU, drum samples loaded, and the beat pattern defined by the user for that pattern number. We will store this information in a list named `self.pattern_list`.

   Our pattern spin box allows for adding 10 patterns. Therefore, we first initialize `self.pattern_list` as an empty list comprising of 10 empty spaces.

   We initialize it in our class `__init__` method as follows (also seen in the code `3.08.py`):

```
self.pattern_list = [None]*10
```

   Let us now code the `record_pattern` method:

```
def record_pattern(self):
  pattern_num, bpu, units = self.patt.get(),self.bpu.get(),
  self.units.get()
  self.pat_name.config(state='normal')
  self.pat_name.delete(0, END)
  self.pat_name.insert(0, 'Pattern %s'%pattern_num)
  self.pat_name.config(state='readonly')
  prevpval = self.prevpatvalue
```

```
self.prevpatvalue = pattern_num
c = bpu*units
self.buttonpickleformat =[[0] * c for x in range
  MAX_DRUM_NUM)]
for i in range(MAX_DRUM_NUM):
  for j in range(c):
    if self.button[i][j].config('bg')[-1] == 'green':
      self.buttonpickleformat[i][j] = 'active'
      self.pattern_list[prevpval] = {'df':
        self.widget_drum_file_name, 'bl':
        self.buttonpickleformat, 'bpu':bpu,
        'units':units}
self.reconstruct_pattern(pattern_num, bpu, units)
```

The description of the code is listed as follows:

- The first line simply fetches the value of the current pattern number, bout, and units for the pattern to be recorded.

- The next four lines of this code do one simple job. For every change in pattern, it simply updates the corresponding Entry widget with the new name of the pattern. Since the Entry widget is "read only", we first configure its state as normal to allow us to enter text into the Entry widget. We then delete anything that might already be written in the widget and enter the new pattern name with the Python string formatting of pattern_num'Pattern %s'%pattern_num. Finally, we restore the entry widget to a read only state.

- The next two lines keep track of the last Spinbox widget number.

- The next four lines of code actually record the state of the user-defined pattern in a two-dimensional list named self.buttonpickleformat. The list is first initialized to an empty two-dimensional matrix, taking into consideration the size of the pattern maker.

- The loop then goes through every single button in the current pattern. If the button is not selected (not green), it leaves the value as 0. If the button is selected (green), the value at the corresponding place is changed from 0 to active. Using this list we can then easily reproduce the user-defined pattern later on.

- Finally, all of this pattern-related data is stored as a list of the dictionary: self.pattern_list[prevpval] = {'df': self.widget_drum_file_name, 'bl': self.buttonpickleformat, 'bpu':bpu, 'units':units}

- ❑ The key df stores the list of drum filenames. The key bl stores the pattern defined by the button. The key bpu stores the BPU for that pattern, and the key units stores the units for that pattern.

- ❑ Now that all of these items for a pattern are stored as a dictionary, we can easily use the dictionary to reconstruct the pattern. The last line calls the method reconstruct_pattern(), which actually does the reconstruction for us.

3. Now that we have stored pattern records, we need some method to reconstruct those patterns on our drum board. We define a new method reconstruct_pattern to handle it, as shown in the following code see the code in 3.08.py):

```python
def reconstruct_pattern(self,pattern_num, bpu, units):
    self.widget_drum_file_name = [0]*MAX_DRUM_NUM
    try:
        self.df = self.pattern_list[pattern_num]['df']
        for i in range(len(self.df)):
            file_name = self.df[i]
            if file_name == 0:
                self.widget_drum_name[i].delete(0, END)
                continue
            self.widget_drum_file_name.insert(i,
              file_name)
            drum_name =
                os.path.basename(file_name)
            self.widget_drum_name[i].delete(0, END)
            self.widget_drum_name[i].insert(0, drum_name)
    except:
            for i in range(MAX_DRUM_NUM):
                try: self.df
                except:self.widget_drum_name[i].delete(0, END)
    try:
        bpu = self.pattern_list[pattern_num]['bpu']
        units = self.pattern_list[pattern_num]['units']
    except:
        return
    self.bpu_widget.delete(0, END)
    self.bpu_widget.insert(0, bpu)
    self.units_widget.delete(0, END)
    self.units_widget.insert(0, units)
    self.create_right_pad()
```

```
c = bpu * units
self.create_right_pad()
try:
    for i in range(MAX_DRUM_NUM):
        for j in range(c):
            if self.pattern_list[pattern_num]['bl'][i][j]
               == 'active':
                self.button[i][j].config(bg='green')
except:return
```

This code can be broken into three broad parts:

- ❑ Reconstructing drum sample uploads
- ❑ Reconstructing BPU and units
- ❑ Reconstructing beat patterns

Having reconstructed these three things, we can easily replay any beat pattern. A brief description of each of these is as follows:

- ❑ The list of drum filenames for a given pattern can easily be acquired from the key-value pair of the dictionary item `self.pattern_list[pattern_num]['df']`. We then iterate through items in this list and fill up the Entry widgets with each drum sample's filename.

- ❑ We then fetch the value of BPU and units from the dictionary keys `self.pattern_list[pattern_num]['bpu']` and `self.pattern_list[pattern_num]['units']`. We insert these values in their respective Spinbox widgets and then call the `create_right_pad()` method, which places the desired number of buttons on the right pad.

- ❑ In the last iteration, we fetch the value of dictionary key `self.pattern_list[pattern_num]['bl']`, which gives us the position of the green buttons. Iterating through a loop, we check if a particular button is to be set to `active`. If yes, we change the color of the button to green.

- ❑ Combined together, we can now load the previously recorded drum samples, set their **Units** and **BPU** values, and reconstruct the beat pattern as per previously set values.

- ❑ At each stage, the code checks if it cannot reconstruct a particular pattern because of invalid file markup. If it does find some invalid markup, it breaks out of the code using appropriate exception handling.

Hit the **Play** button and the drum machine will start rolling sound. Change the pattern number and define a new beat pattern. The new pattern will start playing. Revert to older patterns and the older patterns start playing again (refer to the code in `3.08.py`).

Objective Complete – Mini Debriefing

We've completed coding our drum machine to support the storing of multiple beat patterns, and the ability to play these patterns simply by changing the pattern number. This gives the user the ability to make different beats for the intro, verse, chorus, bridge, and other parts of a song.

In the process, we saw how to use Python's built-in data types to store custom data and to reproduce them in any required way.

Object persistence

In the preceding iteration, we added the capability to define multiple beat patterns. However, the beat patterns can be played only on a single script run. When the program is closed and restarted, all previous pattern data is lost.

We need a way to persist or store the beat patterns beyond a single program run. We need the ability to store values in some form of file storage and reload, play, and even edit the patterns. We need some form of object persistence.

Prepare for Lift Off

Python provides several modules for object persistence. The module that we will use for persistence is called the **pickle module**. This is a standard library of Python.

An object represented as a string of bytes is called **pickle** in Python. **Pickling**, also known as **object serialization**, lets us convert our object into a string of bytes. The process reconstructing of the object back from the string of bytes is called **unpickling** or **deserialization**.

More information about the `pickle` module is available at `http://docs.python.org/2/library/pickle.html`.

Let us illustrate it with a simple example:

```
import pickle
party_menu= ['Bread', 'Salad', 'Bordelaise','Wine', 'Truffles']
pickle.dump(party_menu, open( "mymenu.p", "wb" ) )
```

First, we serialize or pickle our list `PartyMenu` using `pickle.dump` and save it in an external file `mymenu.p`.

We later retrieve the object using `pickle.load`:

```
import pickle
menu= pickle.load( open( "mymenu.p", "rb" ) )
print menu # ['Bread', 'Salad', 'Bordelaise', 'Wine', 'Truffles']
```

Remember that in our previous iteration, we created a list, called `self.pattern_list`, where each item of the list is a dictionary that stores information about one single beat pattern.

If we need to reuse this information, we only need to pickle this `self.pattern_list`. Having saved the object, we can later easily unpickle the file to reconstruct our beat patterns.

Engage Thrusters

1. We first need to add three top menu items to our program, as shown in the following screenshot:

- ❏ **File | Load Project**
- ❏ **File | Save Project**
- ❏ **File | Exit**

While we are creating our menu items let us also add an **About** menu item:

- ❏ **About | About**

Here, we are particularly interested in saving the project (pickling), and loading the project back (unpickling). The code for menu items is defined in a separate method called `create_top_menu`, as shown in the following code (also refer to the code in `3.09.py`):

```
def create_top_menu(self):
  self.menubar = Menu(self.root)
  self.filemenu = Menu(self.menubar, tearoff=0 )
  self.filemenu.add_command(label="Load Project",
    command=self.load_project )
  self.filemenu.add_command(label="Save Project",
    command=self.save_project)
  self.filemenu.add_separator()
  self.filemenu.add_command(label="Exit",
    command=self.exit_app)
```

```
self.menubar.add_cascade(label="File",
    menu=self.filemenu)
self.aboutmenu = Menu(self.menubar, tearoff=0 )
self.aboutmenu.add_command(label="About",
    command=self.about)
self.menubar.add_cascade(label="About",
    menu=self.aboutmenu)
self.root.config(menu=self.menubar)
```

The code is self-explanatory. We have created similar menu items in our last two projects. Finally, to display this menu, we call this method from our `Main` method.

2. To pickle our object, we first import the `pickle` module into the current namespace as follows (see the code in `3.09.py`):

```
import pickle
```

The **Save Project** menu has a `command` callback attached to `self.save_project`, which is where we define the pickling process:

```
def save_project(self):
    self.record_pattern() #make sure last pattern is recorded
    file_name = tkFileDialog.asksaveasfilename(filetypes=[('Drum
    Beat File','*.bt')] , title="Save project as...")
    pickle.dump(self.pattern_list,open( file_name, "wb" ) "wb" ) )
    self.root.title(os.path.basename(filenamefile_name) + " -
    DrumBeast")
```

The description of the code is listed as follows:

❑   Recall that a pattern is added to `self.pattern_list` only when the pattern number is changed by the user. In situations where a user might have defined a beat pattern but may not have clicked on the pattern number's Spinbox widget, the pattern is not included in `self.pattern_list`. To make sure it is added, we first call `self.record_pattern` to capture this beat pattern.

❑   The `save_project` method is called when the user clicks on the **Save Project** menu, hence, we need to give the user an option to save the project in a file. We have chosen to define a new file extension (`.bt`) to keep track of our beat patterns.

❑   When the user specifies the filename with `.bt` extension, the data in the `self.pattern_list` object is dumped into the file using `pickle.dump`.

❑   Lastly, the title of the Toplevel window is changed to reflect the filename.

3. We are done pickling the object. Let us now code the unpickling process.

    The unpickling process is handled by a method `load_project`, which is called from the **Load Project** menu as follows:

```
def load_project(self):
  file_name = tkFileDialog.askopenfilename(filetypes=[('Drum Beat
  File','*.bt')], title='Load Project')
  if file_name == '':return
  self.root.title(os.path.basename(file_name) + " - DrumBeast")
  fh = open(file_name,"rb") # open the file in reading mode
  try:
    while True: # load from the file until EOF is reached
      self.pattern_list = pickle.load(fh)
  exceptEOFError:
    pass
  fh.close()
  try:
    self.Reconstruct_pattern(0,
      pattern_listself.pattern_list[0]['bpu'],
      pattern_listself.pattern_list[0]['units'])
  except:
    tkMessageBox.showerror("Error","An unexpected error
    occurred trying to reconstruct patterns")
```

The description of the code is listed as follows:

- ❑ When a user clicks on the **Load Project** menu, the first line of the method prompts him/her with an **Open File** window. When the user specifies a previously pickled file with a `.bt` extension, the filename is stored in a variable called `file_name`.

- ❑ If the filename returned is `none` because the user cancels the **Open File** dialog, nothing is done.

- ❑ If filename is supplied, the title of the Toplevel window is changed to add the filename. The file is then opened in read mode, and the contents of the file are read into `self.pattern_list` using `pickle.load`.

- ❑ The `self.pattern_list` now contains the list of beat patterns defined in the previous pickle. The file is closed and the first pattern of `self.pattern_list` is reconstructed in the drum machine. If there are more than one patterns defined in the serialized file, you can view each of the patterns simply by changing the pattern number Spinbox widget.

- ❑ Try playing any of the patterns, and you should be able to replay the pattern exactly as it was defined at the time of pickling.

Pickling, though great for serialization, is vulnerable to malicious or erroneous data. You may want to use pickle only if the data is from a trusted source, or if proper validation mechanisms are in place.

You may also find the json module useful for serializing objects in **JSON** and **ElementTree**, or **xml.minidom** libraries relevant for parsing XML data.

4. Now, let us complete coding our exit and about commands:

```
def about(self):
  tkMessageBox.showinfo("About", "About Info")

def exit_app(self):
  if tkMessageBox.askokcancel("Quit", "Really Quit?"):
    self.root.destroy()
```

And add this line to our app method to override the **Close** button of the Toplevel window:

```
self.root.protocol('WM_DELETE_WINDOW', self.exit_app)
```

This is self-explanatory. We have done similar coding in our previous project.

Objective Complete – Mini Debriefing

In this iteration, we used Python's built-in pickle module to pickle and unpickle the beat patterns defined by the user.

This now lets us save patterns defined by the user. We have also provided the ability to load, replay, and edit the project later.

Now, if you define one or more beat patterns in your program you can save the project with a .bt file extension. You can later load the project and start working on it from the place where you had last left it.

While we were dealing with the top menu we also completed the code for the **About** and **Exit** menu items.

ttk-themed widgets

We are almost done programming our drum machine. However, we would like to end this project by introducing you to the ttk-themed widgets.

Prepare for Lift Off

On many platforms such as Windows and X11, Tkinter does not bind to the native platform widgets. The Tk toolkit (and Tkinter) originally appeared on X-Window systems, hence, it adopted the motif look and feel, which was the de facto standard for GUI development on X-Window systems. When Tk was ported to other platforms, such as Windows and Mac OS, this Motif style started appearing out of place with the look of these platforms.

Due to this, some even argue that Tkinter widgets are rather ugly and do not integrate well with such desktop environments.

Another criticism of Tkinter is based on the fact that Tkinter mixes logic and styling by allowing both to be changed as widget options.

It was also criticized to lack any kind of theming support. While we saw an example of centralized styling via the option database, the method required styling to be done at the widget level. It does not allow for selective styling of two button widgets differently, as an example. This made it difficult for developers to implement visual consistency for similar groups of widgets while differentiating them from other groups of widgets. As a result of this, many GUI developers moved to Tkinter alternatives such as **wxPython**, **glade**, **PyQT**, and others.

With Tkinter 8.5, the makers of Tkinter have tried to address all these concerns by introducing the `ttk` module, which may be considered as an advance to the original Tkinter module.

Let us take a look at some of the features offered by the ttk-themed widgets module.

One of the first things that `ttk` does is that it provides a set of built-in themes that allows Tk widgets to look like the native desktop environment in which the application is running.

Additionally, it introduces six new widgets: Combobox, Notebook, Progressbar, Separator, Sizegrip, and Treeview to the list of widgets, in addition to supporting 11 core Tkinter widgets, which are Button, Checkbutton, Entry, Frame, Label, LabelFrame, Menubutton, PanedWindow, Radiobutton, Scale, and Scrollbar.

To use the `ttk` module, we first import it into the current namespace:

```
import ttk
```

You can display the `ttk` widgets as follows see the code in `3.10.py`):

```
ttk.Button(root, text='ttk Button').grid(row=1, column=1)
ttk.Checkbutton(root, text='tkCheckButton').grid(row=2, column=1)
```

For a comparison of displays between the normal Tkinter widgets and the counterpart ttk widgets, see the code in 3.10.py, which produces a window, as shown in the following screenshot. Notice how the widgets look like more native widgets on your platform.

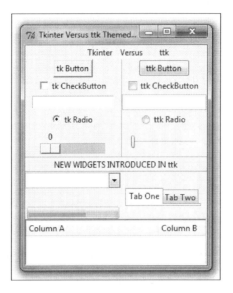

3.10.py also shows dummy examples of all the new widgets introduced in the ttk module.

You can even override the basic Tkinter widgets by importing ttk after Tkinter as follows:

```
from Tkinter import *
from ttk import *
```

This causes all widgets common to Tk and ttk to be replaced by ttk widgets.

This has the direct benefit of using the new widgets, which gives a better look and feel across platforms.

However, the disadvantage of this kind of import, is that you cannot distinguish the module from which the widget classes are imported. This is important because Tkinter and ttk widget classes are not completely interchangeable. In this case, an unambiguous solution is to import them, as shown in the following codeimport Tkinter as tk

```
import ttk
```

While most of the configuration options for Tkinter and ttk widgets are common, ttk-themed widgets do not support styling options such as `fg`, `bg`, `relief`, `border`, and more. This is purposefully removed from ttk in an attempt to keep logic and styling in different controls.

Instead, all styling-related options are handled by the respective style names. In a standard `ttk` module, each widget has an associated style name. You can retrieve the default style name of a widget using the `widget.winfo_class()` method.

For instance consider a ttk button:

```
>>> b = ttk.Button()
>>> b.winfo_class()
```

This prints **Tbutton**, which is the default style name for `ttk.Button`. For a list of default ttk style names for different widgets, refer to the *The ttk widgets* section in *Appendix B, Quick Reference Sheets*.

In addition to the default style, you can assign a custom style class to a widget or group of widgets. To set up a new style you use:

```
    x = ttk.Style()
```

To configure the style options for a default style, you use the command:

```
x.configure('mystyle.Defaultstyle', **styling options)
```

To use the new style on a widget you use the command:

```
ttk.Widget(root, style='mystyle.Defaultstyle')
```

Next we will discuss about ttk theming.

Style is used to control the appearance for individual widgets. Themes, on the other hand, control the appearance of the entire GUI. More simply put, a theme is a collection of styles. Grouping styles into themes lets the user switch designs for the entire GUI all at once. Like styles, all themes are uniquely identified by their name. The list of available themes can be obtained as follows:

```
>>> x = ttk.Style()
>>>x.theme_names()
('winnative', 'clam', 'alt', 'default', 'classic', 'xpnative')
```

To obtain the name of the currently active theme:

```
>>>x.theme_use()
'xpnative'
```

You can change to another theme using:

```
x.theme_use('yournewthemename')
```

Let us see various styling- and theming-related options of ttk through a dummy example (refer to the code in 3.11.py, which produces a window like the one shown in the following screenshot):

```
from Tkinter import *
import ttk
root= Tk()
x = ttk.Style()
x.configure('.', font='Arial 14', foreground='brown',
background='yellow')
x.configure('danger.TButton', font='Times 12', foreground='red',
padding=1)
ttk.Label(root, text='global style').pack()
ttk.Button(root, text='custom style', style='danger.TButton').pack()
# Different  styling for different widget states
x.map("s.TButton", foreground=[('pressed', 'red'), ('active', 'blue')])
ttk.Button(text="state style", style="s.TButton").pack()
# Overriding current theme styles
curr_theme = x.theme_use()
x.theme_settings(curr_theme, { "TEntry": { "configure":  {"padding":
2}, "map": {"foreground": [("focus", "red")]}  }})
ttk.Entry().pack()
root.mainloop()
```

The description of the code is listed as follows:

▸ The first three lines of code imports Tkinter and ttk, and sets up a new root window.

▸ The next line x = ttk.Style() is where you give a name x to your style.

- ▶ The next line configures a program-wide style configuration using `x.configure`. The dot character (.), which is the first argument of `configure`, means that this style would apply to the Toplevel window and to all its child elements. This is the reason why all of our widgets get to have a yellow background.

- ▶ The next line creates an extension (`danger`) to the default style (`TButton`). This is how you create custom styles, which are variations to a base default style.

- ▶ The next line creates a `ttk.label` widget. Since we have not specified any style for this widget, it inherits the global style specified for the Toplevel window.

- ▶ The next line creates a `ttk.button` widget and specifies it to be styled using our custom style definition of `'danger.TButton.'` This is why the foreground color of this button turns red. Notice how it still inherits the background color, yellow , from the global Toplevel style that we defined earlier.

- ▶ The next two lines of code demonstrate how ttk allows for styling different widget states. In this example we styled different states for a `ttk.button` widget to display in different colors. Go ahead and click on this second button to see how different styles apply to different states of a button. Here we use `map(style, query_options, **kw)` to specify dynamic values of style for changes in state of the widget.

- ▶ The next line fetches the current applicable theme. It then overrides some of the options for the theme's Entry widget using:

```
x.theme_settings('themename', ***options)
```

Now that we know how to make our widgets look more like native platform widgets, let us change the **Play** and **Stop** buttons for our drum machine to `ttk.button`. Let us also change the **Loop** check button from Tkinter Checkbutton to ttk Checkbutton.

Engage Thrusters

1. We first import `ttk` into our namespace and append `ttk` to the `play` and `stop` buttons as follows (see the code in `3.12.py`):

```
import ttk
```

2. We then simply modify the buttons and check button in the `create_play_bar` method as follows:

```
button = ttk.Button()
loopbutton = ttk.Checkbutton(**options)
```

 Note that these changes make the button and checkbutton look closer to the native widgets of your working platform.

Also, note that we cannot modify the Tkinter buttons that we have used in our pattern editor. This is because our code extensively plays on the button's background color to decide logic. The ttk buttons do not have the configurable `bg` option, hence, cannot be used for buttons in our right drum pad.

3. As a quick ending exercise let us add an image in the right-hand side of the play bar. Let us also add an icon for our Toplevel window (refer to the code in `3.12.py`):

To add an image we add this to our `create_play_bar` method:

```
photo = PhotoImage(file='images/sig.gif')
label = Label(playbar_frame, image=photo)
label.image = photo
label.grid(row=ln, column=35, padx=1, sticky=E)
```

To add a Toplevel icon, we add the following line to our `Main` method:

```
if os.path.isfile('images/beast.ico'):
    self.root.iconbitmap('images/beast.ico')
```

Objective Complete – Mini Debriefing

This concludes the last iteration of this project. In this iteration, we first saw how and why to use ttk-themed widgets to improve the look and feel of our programs.

We then used ttk buttons and ttk checkbuttons in our drum program to improve its look. We also saw the reasons why certain Tkinter buttons in our program could not be replaced by ttk buttons.

Mission Accomplished

We have come a long way in our experiments with Tkinter. In this project we made a highly-functional drum machine with loads of features.

In the process, we touched upon several vital concepts that go into the making of a GUI program with Tkinter.

To summarize, we touched upon the following vital concepts of Tkinter-based GUI programs:

▶ Structuring Tkinter program as classes and objects

▶ Working with more Tkinter widgets such as Spinbox, Button, Entry, and Checkbutton

▶ Using the `grid` geometry manager for structuring complex layout

- ▶ Understanding threaded programming in relation to Tkinter
- ▶ Working with other common modules from the Python standard library
- ▶ Object persistence with the `pickle` module
- ▶ Working with ttk-themed widgets

A Hotshot Challenge

The drum machine needs your attention. As a part of your Hotshot challenge, add the following features to your drum machine:

- ▶ The current application checks if the button is green in color to decide whether the button is in the pressed state. Modify the code so that this logic is not decided based on the color of the button, but by a separate variable that keeps track of the selected buttons.

- ▶ Add a tempo scale to your drum machine, which lets the user change the tempo of the beats using a slider.

- ▶ Add volume control for each drum sample, allowing the user to change the volume individually for each drum sample.

- ▶ Add a mute button for each drum sample. If the Checkbutton is clicked for a given drum sample, the sound is not played for that row. This way, a user can stop a complete row from playing without changing the patterns in that row.

- ▶ Add a time clock to your drum machine, which displays the time elapsed since the last press of the play button.

Project 4

Game of Chess

Let's now build a game of chess in Tkinter. You do not need to be a master at chess to build this game. If you have ever played chess and you know the basic rules that govern the chess pieces, you are ready to write this program.

If you have never played chess and do not know the basic rules, you would better start by reading those rules from the Internet before you start programming this application.

Mission Briefing

In its final form our chess game would look like the following screenshot:

Our chess game would enforce all standard rules applicable to the game of chess. Some advanced rules and features are left as an exercise for you to complete.

Why Is It Awesome?

In the process of building our chess application, we get introduced to the Tkinter Canvas widget, which is considered one of the most powerful and versatile features of Tkinter.

As you will see in the course of this project, the Canvas widget is a really powerful tool for a GUI programmer. It can be used to sketch compound objects using lines, rectangles, ovals, and polygons. It will also let you position images on the canvas with great accuracy.

In addition, the Canvas widget will let you place any other widget (such as labels, buttons, scale, and other widgets) on itself. This makes it an ideal container for accommodating widgets for a variety of different GUI programs.

In addition to learning about the Canvas widget, you will also get an insight on how to structure your data using Python built-in types. You will also be introduced to the concepts involved in selecting pertinent objects and structuring them into classes and modules at the right granularity.

As the application develops, we are also introduced to several other Python modules that you will often use in a variety of application development projects.

Your Hotshot Objectives

The following are the key objectives for this project:

> ▶ How to structure a program into its model and view components
> ▶ How to represent a problem domain in a desired notation
> ▶ Peeking into the versatility and power of the Tkinter Canvas widget
> ▶ Basic usage of canvas coordinates, object IDs and tags
> ▶ How to work with newer image formats not supported by the Tkinter photo image class
> ▶ Typical interaction of logic and presentation layers in a GUI program

Mission Checklist

We will need to process PNG images in our program. The Tkinter photo image class and other standard libraries of Python do not support PNG processing. We will use the **Python Imaging Library** (**PIL**) to render PNG files.

To install the PIL package visit:

```
http://www.pythonware.com/products/pil/
```

If you are working on windows x64 (64 bit)or MacOSX machine, you may instead need to install and work with Pillow, which is a replacement for the PIL, from:

```
http://www.lfd.uci.edu/~gohlke/pythonlibs/#pillow
```

After you have installed the package, go to your Python interactive prompt and type:

```
>>from PIL import ImageTk
```

If this executes without any error message, you are ready to make the chess application.

Structuring our program

All our previous projects have been structured as a single file. However, as programs grow in complexity, we need to break our programs into modules and class structures.

Development of large applications generally starts with recording the **software requirement specifications (SRS)**. This is generally followed by a graphical representation of constructs, such as class, composition, inheritance, and information hiding using several modeling tools. These tools can be flow charts, **unified modeling language (UML)**, data flow diagrams, Venn diagrams (for database modeling), and several other tools.

These tools are very useful when the problem domain is not very clear. However, if you have ever played the game of chess, you are very well acquainted with the problem domain. Furthermore, our chess program may be classified as a medium-sized program spanning a few hundred lines of code. Let us, therefore, bypass these visual tools and get to the actual program design.

Prepare for Lift Off

In this iteration, we decide an overall structure for our program.

In the true spirit of object-oriented programming (OOP), let's first list the kind of objects that we would encounter in our program. An intuitive look at a chessboard tells us that we have two sets of objects to handle:

- ▶ **Chessboard**: It is an 8 x 8 square board with alternatively colored squares
- ▶ **Chess pieces**: They are the king, queen, bishop, knight, rook, and pawns

As we proceed, we may or may not come across other objects. But we are sure to come across these two kinds of objects. So, without much further delay, let us create two files named `chessboard.py` and `pieces.py` in our project folder. (See *code folder 4.01*)

We will use these two files to define the respective classes to keep the logic associated with these two objects. Note that these files will not display the board or its pieces; it will instead keep all logic related to board and pieces. In programming parlance, this is broadly referred to as the **model**.

The actual display of board and pieces will be kept in a separate file, which will handle all views related to the program.

The rule of separating logic from presentation should be applied not only for deciding your file structure, but also when defining methods within your files.

Every time you write a method, try to separate its presentation from the logic. If you find a method mixing logic and presentation, refactor your code to separate the two. Avoid coupling the presentation and logic into the same method.

It is a good idea to keep the presentation layer (view) separate from logic (model). So, we will create a new file named `gui.py` to code all visible components of the program, including all our widgets. This file will be primarily responsible for generating the view.

In addition to the model and view files, many programs also keep a separate controller file to decouple behavioral aspects of a program from the logic (model) and presentation (view). This kind of structural segregation is named the **model-view-controller** (**MVC**) style of programming.

However, our chess program has just one event to handle: mouse click for moving chess pieces. Creating a separate controller for just one event can make the program more complex than it should be.

Given this limitation, we will handle the presentation (view) and event handling (controller) from a single class named `GUI`.

Now that we have our file structure ready, let us start our coding. To begin, let's code the GUI class for our chessboard, as shown in the following screenshot. Because this pertains to the view section, let's put this code in the gui.py file.

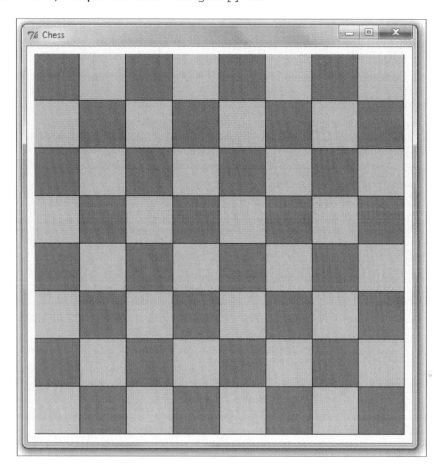

Engage Thrusters

Step 1 – creating the GUI class

We first create a GUI class and assign attributes such as rows, columns, colors of squares, and the dimension of each square in pixels. We initialize our GUI class to create the canvas on which we will draw our chessboard, as follows (see *code 4.01 gui.py*):

```python
from Tkinter import *
class GUI():
  rows = 8
  columns = 8
  color1 = "#DDB88C"
  color2 = "#A66D4F"
  dim_square = 64
  def __init__(self, parent):
      self.parent = parent
      canvas_width = self.columns * self.dim_square
      canvas_height = self.rows * self.dim_square
      self.canvas = Canvas(parent,
          width=canvas_width, height=canvas_height,
          background="grey")
      self.canvas.pack(padx=8, pady=8)
      self.draw_board()
```

The description of the code is listed as follows:

▶ We create a class, GUI, to handle the rendering of our view files. The init method of the GUI class is called immediately on object instantiation. The init method sets up a Canvas widget of the required size. This canvas will act as our container for all objects, such as chess square areas and eventually the chess pieces.

▶ We have used the Canvas widget as a container, because it provides us the ability to handle tasks based on precise location coordinates of events, such as click of the mouse button.

▶ The init method then calls the draw_board() method, which is responsible for creating square blocks of alternating colors similar to a chessboard.

Step 2 – creating the chessboard

Now, we draw the squares on the chessboard using the `canvas.create_rectangle` method, filling it alternating between the two colors we defined earlier.

```
def draw_board(self):
    color = self.color2
    for r in range(self.rows):
        color = self.color1 if color == self.color2
            else self.color2 # alternating between two
                colors
        for c in range(self.columns):
            x1 = (c * self.dim_square)
            y1 = ((7-r) * self.dim_square)
            x2 = x1 + self.dim_square
            y2 = y1 + self.dim_square
            self.canvas.create_rectangle(x1, y1, x2, y2,
            fill=color, tags="area")
            color = self.color1 if color == self.color2
                    else self.color2
```

The description of the code is listed as follows:

▸ To draw squares on the board we use the `canvas.create_rectangle()` method, which draws a rectangle given the x, y coordinates for the two diagonally opposite corners of the rectangle (coordinates of upper-left and lower-right edges).

▸ We will need to target the board. We, therefore, add a tag named `area` to each of the squares created on the board. This is similar to tagging of the text widget, as we had done in our text editor program.

Step 3 – creating Tkinter mainloop

Now, we will create Tkinter mainloop as follows:

```
def main():
    root = Tk()
    root.title("Chess")
    gui = GUI(root)
    root.mainloop()
if __name__ == "__main__":
    main()
```

The description of the code is listed as follows:

▸ Outside the class, we have a main method that sets the Toplevel window, starts Tkinter mainloop, instantiates a `GUI` object, and calls the `drawboard()` method.

The Tkinter Canvas widget lets you draw line, oval, rectangle, arc, and polygon shapes at a given coordinate specified location. You can also specify various configuration options, such as fill, outline, width, and several others for each of these shapes.

In addition, the Canvas widget has a huge list of methods and configurable options. For a complete list of canvas-related options, type the following into Python interactive shell:

```
>>> import Tkinter
>>> help(Tkinter.Canvas)
```

You can also access the documentation of Tkinter in your core Python installation directory. The documentation is located at `path\to\python\ installation\Doc\Python273`.

This is a compiled HTML help file. Within the help file, search for Tkinter, and you get a comprehensive reference with details of all widgets.

Objective Complete – Mini Debriefing

This completes our first iteration. In this iteration, we decided the class structure for our chess program. We created a `GUI` class and added attributes we would normally expect a chessboard to have.

We also got our first taste of the Canvas widget. We created a blank canvas, and then added square areas using the `canvas.create_rectangle` method to create our chessboard.

We also created out Tkinter mainloop and created an object out of the `GUI` class from within our mainloop. Now, if you run `code 4.01 gui.py`, you will see a chessboard.

Classified Intel

The Canvas widget comes with a rich set of methods and configurable options. However, there are three important things to note about the Canvas widget:

▸ It uses a coordinate system to specify position of objects on the widget. Coordinates are measured in pixels. The top-left corner of the canvas has coordinates (0,0).

▸ It offers methods to add images and to draw basic shapes, such as line, arc, ovals, and polygons.

▸ The objects drawn on the Canvas widget are usually handled through assigning them an ID or tag.

Structuring chessboard-and-pieces-related data

In our drum program, we had decided on a notation to describe a set of beat patterns. We could then store (pickle) that beat pattern notation and reproduce (unpickle) it later. The chess program is no different. It too needs a suitable notation for describing chess pieces and for locating their positions on the board.

Prepare for Lift Off

We can define our own notation for representing chess piece and their positions, but it turns out that there already exists a globally accepted, simple, compact, and standard notation for representing a chessboard. The notation is called **Forsyth-Edwards notation (FEN)** available at http://en.wikipedia.org/wiki/Forsyth-Edwards_Notation.

We might have decided to define our notation, but we preferred not to reinvent the wheel here.

The FEN record for starting position of a chess game is written as:

rnbqkbnr/pppppppp/8/8/8/8/PPPPPPPP/RNBQKBNR w KQkq - 0 1

The key things to note about the notation are as follows:

▶ The notation displays six records for a chess game. Each record is separated by a blank space.

▶ The first record shows the positions of pieces on a chessboard. Each row of the chessboard (rank) is represented in a section demarcated by the / symbol.

▶ Within the first record, each piece is identified by a single letter (pawn = p, knight = n, bishop = b, rook = r, queen = q and king = k).

▶ White pieces are represented using uppercase letters (PNBRQK), but black pieces are represented by lowercase letters (pnbrqk).

▶ Squares with no pieces on it are represented using digits 1 through 8 (the number of blank squares).

▶ The second record denotes the turn of a player. Letter w denotes white turn, and letter b denotes black turn.

▶ The third record KQkq indicates whether or not castling feature is available. If neither castle, this is -. Otherwise, this has one or more letters: K (white can castle kingside), Q (white can castle queenside), k (black can castle kingside), and/or q (black can castle queenside).

▸ The fourth record_captures En passant details for the game. We will not be implementing castling and En passant features in our game, so we can safely disregard these two records for now.

▸ The fifth record keeps track of half-move clock for the game. The half-move clock keeps track of number of turns played since the last pawn advance or last capture. This is used to determine if a draw can be claimed under the fifty-move rule.

▸ The sixth record tracks the full-move number, which is incremented by 1 after each move of black. This is used to track the overall length for which a game was played.

The notation as previously stated can be represented pictorially along x and y axis as follows:

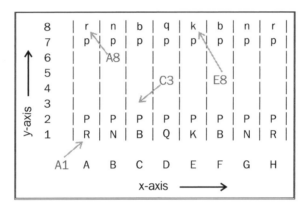

Using this notation, we can accurately represent any particular square on the chessboard.

The color of piece depends on whether the alphabet is in small letters (black) or capital letters (white).

Thus **A1** denotes the bottom and left-most square on the chessboard. Currently, it is occupied by a white rook. The **C3** position is currently empty, and **E8** has black king and **A8** has a black rook.

Following these rules, here is how the FEN notation would change after the following indicative turns played (`http://en.wikipedia.org/wiki/Forsyth-Edwards_Notation`):

After first move, `P` to `e4`:

`rnbqkbnr/pppppppp/8/8/4P3/8/PPPP1PPP/RNBQKBNR b KQkq e3 0 1`

After second move, `p` to `c5`:

`rnbqkbnr/pp1ppppp/8/2p5/4P3/8/PPPP1PPP/RNBQKBNR w KQkq c6 0 2`

After third move, N to f3:

```
rnbqkbnr/pp1ppppp/8/2p5/4P3/5N2/PPPP1PPP/RNBQKB1R b KQkq - 1 2
```

All our chessboard and piece related logic will use the preceding notation. It is, therefore, very important that we fully understand this notation before we proceed to code our game.

Now that we are clear about the preceding notation, let's apply the notation to represent our chessboard. The key idea here is that, given a FEN notation, we should be able to represent it on the board.

Engage Thrusters

Step 1 – creating a Piece superclass

Let's now first code the model code for `pieces.py` (see *code 4.02 pieces.py*) by creating a `Piece` super class as follows:

```
class Piece():
  def __init__(self, color):
     if color == 'black':
        self.shortname = self.shortname.lower()
     elif color == 'white':
        self.shortname = self.shortname.upper()
     self.color = color

  def ref(self, board):
   ''' Get a reference of chessboard instance'''
     self.board = board
```

The description of the code is listed as follows:

▸ We define a class, `Piece ()`. It's __init__ method, which takes a color as an argument. In accordance with our FEN notation, it changes the shortname to lowercase letter for black and uppercase letter for white. The color handling is done in the superclass, `Piece`, because it is a common feature for all chess pieces.

▸ We also define a method named `ref`. Its only purpose is to get an instance of the chessboard into the object namespace for the board and pieces to interact. We need this method, because our pieces will ultimately be interacting with the chessboard. Accordingly, we need a reference of the chessboard instance within the `Piece` class.

Step 2 – creating individual child classes for all pieces

We can create individual child classes for all pieces as follows:

```
class King(Piece):     shortname = 'k'
class Queen(Piece):    shortname = 'q'
class Rook(Piece):     shortname = 'r'
class Knight(Piece):   shortname = 'n'
class Bishop(Piece):   shortname = 'b'
class Pawn(Piece):     shortname = 'p'
```

The description of the code is listed as follows:

▶ We define classes for each of the pieces found on a chessboard. So, we have classes named King, Queen, Rook, Knight, Bishop, and Pawn. These classes are derived from the Piece super class.

▶ For now, these child classes merely define the shortname associated with them. We will later expand these child classes to define and enforce rules for movement of each of these pieces.

Step 3 – defining a method to return the piece instance

We will define a method to return the piece instance as follows:

```
import sys
SHORT_NAME = {'R':'Rook', 'N':'Knight', 'B':'Bishop',
'Q':'Queen', 'K':'King', 'P':'Pawn'}
def create_piece(piece, color='white'):
    if piece in (None, ''): return
    if piece.isupper(): color = 'white'
    else: color = 'black'
    piece = SHORT_NAME[piece.upper()]
    module = sys.modules[__name__]
    return module.__dict__[piece](color)
```

The description of the code is listed as follows:

▶ The code defines a dictionary with pieces shortname and full name as key-value pair.

▶ We then define a method piece which takes a piece shortname and returns the corresponding piece instance.

Step 4 – creating the Board class

Now that we have a basic model ready for pieces, let's code the model to deal with their placement on the chessboard. We code this in `chessboard.py`.(see *code 4.02 chessboard. py*) by creating a `Board` class as follows:

```
import pieces
import re
START_PATTERN = 'rnbqkbnr/pppppppp/8/8/8/8/PPPPPPPP/
RNBQKBNR w 0 1'
class Board(dict):
    y_axis = ('A', 'B', 'C', 'D', 'E', 'F', 'G', 'H')
    x_axis = (1,2,3,4,5,6,7,8)
    def __init__(self, patt = None):
        self.process_notation(START_PATTERN)
```

The description of the code is listed as follows:

▸ Our code begins with defining the starting pattern as per the FEN notation discussed earlier. We do not include the castle and En passant related notation, because we will not be coding that in our program.

▸ We then define our `Board` class as a subclass of built-in `dict` type. This is because we will store the pattern as a dictionary.

▸ We then define `x_axis` and `y_axis` for our chessboard as nonimmutable tuples.

▸ The `__init__` method of our class simply calls the `process_notation` method of the class.

Step 5 – displaying pieces on board for a given FEN notation

Pieces on `Board` for a given FEN notation can be displayed as follows:

```
def process_notation(self, patt):
    self.clear()
    patt = patt.split('')
        # expand_whitespaces blanks

def expand_whitespaces(match): return '' * int(match.group(0))
    patt[0] = re.compile(r'\d').sub(expand_whitespaces, patt[0])
    for x, row in enumerate(patt[0].split('/')):
        for y, alphabet in enumerate(row):
            if alphabet == '': continue
```

```
            xycoord = self.alpha_notation((7-x,y))
            self[xycoord] = pieces.piece(alphabet)
            self[xycoord].ref(self)
        if patt[1] == 'w': self.player_turn = 'white'
        else: self.player_turn = 'black'
```

The description of the code is listed as follows:

▶ The job of the `process_notation` method is to first expand the blank spaces represented by integers into actual spaces. It uses Python built-in regular expression module (`re`) to expand white spaces in a given FEN notation.

▶ The code, `expand_whitespaces`, does something that might be tricky for Python beginners. It replaces each digit by the corresponding number of whitespaces, so you can later assume that a whitespace is an empty square. It then converts the FEN notation into a string corresponding to x and y alphanumeric coordinate for every piece. For doing this, it calls another method named `alpha_notation`, which is defined in step 7.

▶ The final two lines keep a track of turns taken by the players.

Step 6 – checking if a given coordinate is on the board

Finally, let's end this iteration by defining a method to check if a given coordinate is on the board, as follows (see *code 4.02 chessboard.py*):

```
def is_on_board(self, coord):
    ifcoord[1] < 0 or coord[1] > 7
    or coord[0] < 0 or coord[0] >7:
        return False
    else: return True
```

Step 7 – generating alphabetic and numeric notation

We need a way to convert the x and y coordinates for a piece to its alphabetic equivalent notation for example, A1, D5, E3, and so on. We accordingly define the `alpha_notation` method as follows:

```
def alpha_notation(self,xycoord):
    if not self.is_on_board(xycoord): return
    return self.y_axis[xycoord[1]] +
        str(self.x_axis[xycoord[0]])
```

Similarly, we define a method that takes in an x,y coordinate as input and returns its equivalent numerical notation, as follows:

```
def num_notation(self, xycoord):
    return int(xycoord[1])-1,
        self.y_axis.index(xycoord[0])
```

Step 8 – checking places occupied on the board

Before every move, we will need to check all the places occupied by all the pieces of a given color. This is required not only to calculate valid moves, but to also ensure that move by some other piece does not cause a check on the king.

Accordingly, let's define a method to return a list of coordinates occupied by a given color (see *code 4.02 chessboard.py*) as follows:

```
def occupied(self, color):
    result = []
    for coord in self:
        if self[coord].color == color:
            result.append(coord)
            return result
```

Step 9 – handling errors and exceptions

For handling errors and exceptions, we define a custom exception class named ChessError, and all other exceptions will later be subclassed to it, as follows:

```
classChessError(Exception): pass
```

Objective Complete – Mini Debriefing

In this iteration, we created a basic Piece class and dummy child classes for each of the pieces found on the chessboard. The individual piece classes inherit from the parent Piece class. We handle color identification in the parent class because it is something we need to do for all child classes.

We then defined our Board class and added some methods that we will surely need every time we want to move a piece on the board.

We are yet to display those pieces on the board. We do that in the next iteration.

Adding pieces on the board

We now have a code that converts the FEN notation to its expanded coordinate-based representation. Now, let's code to actually display chess pieces on the board, based on a given FEN notation, as shown in the following screenshot:

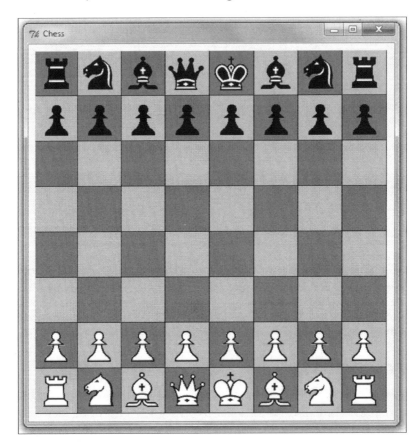

Prepare for Lift Off

We will use PNG images for displaying pieces on the board. We have provided PNG images for each piece in a folder named `pieces_image`. The images have been named by appending the shortname of each piece followed by the color of the piece. For instance, black queen is saved as `qblack.png`, and white knight is saved as `nwhite.png`.

We have chosen PNG over GIF because unlike GIF, PNG allows for alpha channels (variable transparency), automatic gamma correction on different platforms, and color correction.

However, the `TkinterPhotoImage` class does not support the PNG format. We, therefore, use the PIL to process PNG files.

Currently, the `TkinterPhotoImage` class supports images in GIF, PPM, XBM, and PGM formats only. None of these formats are in vogue currently. Unfortunately, support for new formats can only be added if the Tcl/Tk starts supporting those formats.

Up till then, you may find it handy to use the PIL, which supports most of the popular image formats including PNG, JPEG, GIF, TIFF, and BMP.

In addition to displaying images in Tkinter, the PIL module can also be used for image processing, such as size transformations, format conversions, thumbnail creation, and several other image manipulation requirements.

We will add code for displaying chess pieces in our view file, `gui.py`.

Engage Thrusters

Step 1 – importing PIL

Because we will use the PIL module to display PNG images for our pieces, we start by importing `ImageTk` from the PIL module as follows:

```
from PIL import ImageTk
```

Step 2 – defining method to draw pieces on chessboard

The code for adding pieces on the board is as follows (see *code 4.03: gui.py*):

```
def draw_pieces(self):
    self.canvas.delete("occupied")
    for xycoord, piece in self.chessboard.iteritems():
        x,y = self.chessboard.num_notation(xycoord)
        if piece is not None:
            filename = "../pieces_image/%s%s.png" %
            (piece.shortname.lower(), piece.color)
            piecename = "%s%s%s" % (piece.shortname, x, y)
            if (filename not in self.images):
                self.images[filename] =
                ImageTk.PhotoImage(file=filename)
            self.canvas.create_image(0,0, image=self.images[filename],
            tags=(piecename, "occupied"), anchor="c")
            x0 = (y * self.dim_square) + int(self.dim_square/2)
            y0 = ((7-x) * self.dim_square) + int(self.dim_square/2)
            self.canvas.coords(piecename, x0, y0)
```

The description of the code is listed as follows:

▶ We begin by importing `ImageTk` from the PIL module. We need this to handle PNG images.

▶ We define our `draw_pieces()` method, whose role is to draw the pieces on a board for a given FEN notation. Because the FEN notation is available to all class methods, we need not pass it as an argument.

▶ Recall that we have created an instance of the chessboard which produces a dictionary comprising of the coordinate-based location of a piece and the corresponding piece instance as the key-value pair.

▶ We loop through the dictionary using `iteritems()`, and break down the x and y coordinate string into corresponding x-and-y-based number notation.

▶ If there exists a piece for a given coordinate, we add it to the Canvas widget using `canvas.create_image()`.

▶ One of the most important things to note here is that we have added two tags to each of the pieces: the name of the piece and a static string name `occupied`. Tags are the most important tool that you can use to operate on objects within the Canvas widget.

▶ The next two lines create the x, y coordinate for a given board size.

▶ The final line of the method uses `self.canvas.coords` to place the piece at the calculated coordinate.

▶ Finally, we need to call our newly defined method. We do that from our `show()` method to invoke the pieces.

Let's wrap this iteration by analyzing the two canvas-related methods used here.

canvas.create_image(x, y, *options): The `create_image` method takes two arguments that specify x and y coordinates for positioning the image. After the coordinates, you may specify any number of option-value pairs. In our example, we have used the `anchor="c"` option to keep the image in the center.

canvas.coords(tag/id, x0, y0, x1, y1, ..., xn, yn): The `coords()` method decides or modifies the coordinates for items attached to a given tag or ID. If coordinates are not specified, it returns a tuple specifying the coordinates of the item referenced by given tag or ID. If coordinates are specified, then they replace the current coordinates for the named item. If the tag or ID is attached to multiple items, only the first item is used.

We will learn about the Canvas widget in greater detail as we progress. However, you may find it useful to look at the interactive help for the Canvas widget, or a list of available methods and configurable options.

Objective Complete – Mini Debriefing

Our code can now take a FEN notation and display the images for corresponding pieces on the chessboard. If you modify the FEN notation, the pieces on the chessboard will change their places accordingly.

In the process, we got acquainted with the basic features of the Canvas widget. We also saw two canvas-related methods to create image and to change the coordinates.

Finally, we saw how to overcome a Tkinter limitation on image handling by using the PIL module to handle formats not supported by Tkinter.

Enforcing rules for pieces' movement

Before we get these chess pieces to move on click of mouse, we need to know how many squares a given piece can move. We need to enforce rules for each of the chess pieces.

Prepare for Lift Off

Before we start coding the rules, let's quickly recap the rules of chess:

- ▶ King can move only one square in any direction: up, down, to the sides, and diagonally.

- ▶ Queen can move in any one straight direction: forward, backward, sideways, or diagonally; as far as possible as long as she does not move through any of her own pieces.

- ▶ Rook can move as far as it wants, but only forward, backward, and to the sides

- ▶ Bishop can move as far as it wants, but only diagonally.

- ▶ Knights are different from others. They must move two squares in one direction, and then one more move at a 90 degree angle, following the shape of *L*. Knights are also the only pieces that can jump over other pieces.

- ▶ Pawns move forward, but capture diagonally. Pawns can only move forward one square at a time, except for their very first move where they can move forward two squares. Pawns can only capture one square diagonally in front of them.

The bottom line here is that we need to track three common things for each of the piece:

- ▶ Its current position

- ▶ Allowed directions for movement

- ▶ Distance that a piece can move

Engage Thrusters

Step 1 – tracking moves available for all pieces from Pieces superclass

Because the preceding things can be tracked at a central place, let's define a method named moves_available in our superclass, Pieces (see *code 4.04: pieces.py*), for tracking moves available for all pieces as follows:

```
def moves_available(self, pos, diagonal, orthogonal,
                    distance):
    board = self.board
    allowed_moves = []
    orth = ((-1,0),(0,-1),(0,1),(1,0))
    diag = ((-1,-1),(-1,1),(1,-1),(1,1))
    piece = self
    beginningpos = board.num_notation(pos.upper())
    if orthogonal and diagonal:
        directions = diag+orth
    elif diagonal:
        directions = diag
    elif orthogonal:
        directions = orth

    for x,y in directions:
        collision = False
        for step in range(1, distance+1):
            if collision: break
            dest = beginningpos[0]+step*x,
                   beginningpos[1]+step*y
            if self.board.alpha_notation(dest) not in
                board.occupied('white') +
                board.occupied('black'):
                allowed_moves.append(dest)
            elif self.board.alpha_notation(dest) in
                board.occupied(piece.color):
                collision = True
            else:
                allowed_moves.append(dest)
                collision = True
    allowed_moves = filter(board.is_on_board, allowed_moves)
    return map(board.alpha_notation, allowed_moves)
```

The description of the code is listed as follows:

- ▶ The method accepts four arguments: the current position of a piece, two Boolean values representing whether or not diagonal and orthogonal movements are allowed for a piece, and the number of squares a piece can move at one time.

- ▶ Depending upon these arguments, the method collects all allowed moves for a given piece in a list, `allowed_moves`.

- ▶ Having collected all directions of movements, the code iterates through all locations to detect any possible collision. If collision is detected, it breaks out of the loop, else it appends the coordinate to `allowed_moveslist`.

- ▶ `collision = True` is our way to break out of the loop. We need to break out of the loop in two cases: when the destination is occupied, and when it is not occupied, and we have already appended that position into our list of possible moves.

- ▶ The second last line filters out those moves that fall out of the board, and the last line returns the equivalent board notations for all allowed moves.

[Having defined our `moves_available` method, we now simply need to call it from different pieces class.(see *code 4.04: pieces.py*).]

Step 2 – rules for the king, queen, rook and bishop class

King, queen, rook, and bishop pieces on the chessboard have relatively simple rules governing them. These pieces can capture only in the direction in which they move.

Moreover, they move in either orthogonal, diagonal, or a combination of these two directions. We have already coded `moves_available` in our superclass to handle these directions.

Accordingly, deciding their available moves is just a matter of passing the right arguments to our `moves_available` method.

```
class King(Piece):
    shortname = 'k'
    def moves_available(self,pos):
        return super(King, self).moves_available(pos.upper(), True,
                                                 True, 1)
class Queen(Piece):
    shortname = 'q'
    def moves_available(self,pos):
        return super(Queen,self).moves_available(pos.upper(), True,
                                                 True, 8)
```

```
class Rook(Piece):
    shortname = 'r'
    def moves_available(self,pos):
        return super(Rook, self).moves_available(pos.upper(),
                                                 False, True, 8)
class Bishop(Piece):
    shortname = 'b'
    def moves_available(self,pos):
        return super(Bishop,self).moves_available(pos.upper(), True,
                                                  False, 8)
```

Step 3 – rules for knight

Knight is a different beast because it does not move orthogonally or diagonally.
It can also jump over pieces.

Let's, therefore override the `moves_available` method from our `Knight` class.

The `Knight` class is defined as follows (see *code 4.04: pieces.py*):

```
class Knight(Piece):
    shortname = 'n'
    def moves_available(self,pos):
        board = self.board
        allowed_moves = []
        beginningpos = board.num_notation(pos.upper())
        piece = board.get(pos.upper())
        changes=((-2,-1),(-2,1),(-1,-2),(-1,2),(1,-2),(1,2),
                (2,-1),(2,1))
        for x,y in changes:
            dest = beginningpos[0]+x, beginningpos[1]+y
            if(board.alpha_notation(dest) not in
            board.occupied(piece.color)):
                allowed_moves.append(dest)
            allowed_moves = filter(board.is_on_board, allowed_moves)
        return map(board.alpha_notation, allowed_moves)
```

The description of the code is listed as follows:

▶ The method is quite similar to our previous super class method. However, unlike the super class method, the changes are represented to capture moves two squares in one direction, and then one more move at a 90 degree angle.

▶ Similarly, unlike the super class, we do not need to track collisions, because knights can jump over other pieces.

Step 4 – rules for pawn

Pawn too has a unique movement, in that it moves forward, but captures diagonally.

Let's similarly override the `moves_available` class from within the `Pawn` class as follows (see *code 4.04: pieces.py*):

```
class Pawn(Piece):
    shortname = 'p'
    def moves_available(self, pos):
        board = self.board
        piece = self
        if self.color == 'white':
            startpos, direction, enemy = 1, 1, 'black'
        else:
            startpos, direction, enemy = 6, -1, 'white'
        allowed_moves = []
        prohibited = board.occupied('white') +
                    board.occupied('black')
        beginningpos = board.num_notation(pos.upper())
        forward = beginningpos[0] + direction, beginningpos[1]
        # Can a piece move forward?
        if board.alpha_notation(forward) not in prohibited:
            allowed_moves.append(forward)
            if beginningpos[0] == startpos:
                # If pawn in starting pos allow a double move
                double_forward = (forward[0] + direction,
                                    forward[1])
                if board.alpha_notation(double_forward) not in
                            prohibited:
                    allowed_moves.append(double_forward)
        # Check for Capturing Moves Available
        for a in range(-1, 2, 2):
            attack = beginningpos[0] + direction, beginningpos[1]
                    + a
            if board.letter_notation(attack) in
                    board.occupied(enemy):
                allowed_moves.append(attack)
        allowed_moves = filter(board.is_on_board, allowed_moves)
        return map(board.alpha_notation, allowed_moves)
```

The description of the code is listed as follows:

▶ We first assign variables `startpos`, `direction`, and `enemy` depending on whether the pawn is black or white.

- ► Similar to our previous `moves_allowed` methods, this method also collects all allowed moves in a blank list, `allowed_moves`.

- ► We then collect a list of all prohibited moves by concatenating two lists of squares occupied by all black and white pieces.

- ► We define a list, `forward`, which holds the position of the one square immediately ahead of the current position of pawn.

- ► A pawn cannot move forward if there is a piece in front of it. If the forward position is not prohibited, the position is appended to our `allowed_moves` list.

- ► A pawn can move two places forward from its starting position. We check to see if the current position is the starting position, and if true, we append the double move to our `allowed_moves` list.

- ► A pawn can capture only diagonally adjacent pieces in front of it. We, therefore, assign a variable attack to track the diagonally adjacent positions on the board. If the diagonally adjacent square is occupied by an enemy, that position qualifies to be appended to our list, `allowed_moves`.

- ► We then filter our list to remove all positions which may fall off the board.

- ► The last line returns all allowed moves as a list of corresponding letter notations, as we had done in all our previous definitions.

Objective Complete – Mini Debriefing

In this iteration, we coded the logic for enforcing rules related to movement of chess pieces on the board.

The chessboard logic

Before we allow chess pieces to move on click of the mouse button, we must have a record of all possible movement options on the board. At every move, we also need to check that it is a legitimate turn for a given player, and that the proposed move should not cause a check on the king.

Now a check may occur on the king, not only from a piece that was moved, but from any other piece on the board as a consequence of such movement. Thus, after every move, we need to calculate the possible moves for all the pieces of the opponent.

Accordingly we will need two methods to:

▸ Keep track of all available moves for a player

▸ Verify if there is a check on the king

Let's add the code for the preceding methods into our Board class. (See *code 4.05: chessboard.py*)

Engage Thrusters

Step 1: Tracking all Available Moves

The code for keeping track of all available moves for a player is as follows:

```
def all_moves_available(self, color):
    result = []
    for coord in self.keys():
        if (self[coord] is not None) and self[coord].color == color:
            moves = self[coord].moves_available(coord)
            if moves: result += moves
    return result
```

The description of the code is listed as follows:

▸ We have already coded our moves_available method in the previous iteration. This method simply iterates through every item in the dictionary and appends the moves_available result for each piece of a given color in a list named result.

Step 2: Getting Current Position of King

Before we code the method to verify if a king is in check, we first need to know the exact position of the king. Let's define a method to get the current position of the king, as follows (see *code 4.05: chessboard.py*):

```
def position_of_king(self, color):
    for pos in self.keys():
        if is instance(self[pos], pieces.King) and
            self[pos].color == color:
            return pos
```

The preceding code simply iterates through all items in the dictionary. If a given position is an instance of the King class, it simply returns its position.

Step 3: Verifying if King is under Check

Finally, we define a method to verify if the king is under check from the opponent as follows:

```
def king_in_check(self, color):
    kingpos =  self.position_of_king(color)
    opponent = ('black' if color =='white' else 'white')
    for pieces in self.iteritems():
      if kingpos in self.all_moves_available(opponent):
        return True
      else:
        return False
```

The description of the code is listed as follows:

- ▸ We first obtain the current position of the king, and the color of the opponent.
- ▸ We then iterate through all possible moves for all pieces of the opponent. If the position of the king coincides with any position from all possible moves, the king is under check, and we return `True`, else we return `False`.

Objective Complete – Mini Debriefing

This completes our objectives for the iteration. We are now in a position to check for all available moves for a player at a given point in the game. We can also verify if a king is under check from the opponent team.

Making the chess functional

Now that we have all pieces and board-related validation rules in place, let's now add life to our chess. In this iteration, we will make our chess game fully functional.

In a game between two players, our chessboard would be like one shown in the following screenshot:

The objective for this iteration is to move pieces on click of the left mouse button. When a player clicks on a piece, our code should first check if it is a legitimate turn for that piece.

On the first click, the piece to be moved is selected, and all allowed moves for that piece are highlighted on the board. The second click should happen on the destination square. If the second click is done on a valid destination square, the piece should move from the source square to the destination square.

We also need to code the events of capturing of pieces and check on king. Other attributes to be tracked include list of captured pieces, halfmove clock count, fullmove number count, and history of all previous moves.

Engage Thrusters

Step 1 – updating the board for change in FEN notation

So far, we have the ability to take the original FEN notation and display it on board. However, we need a way that takes any FEN notation and updates the display on the board. We define a new method named `show()` to do this, as follows:

```python
def show(self, pat):
        self.clear()
        pat = pat.split(' ')
        def expand(match): return ' ' * int(match.group(0))
        pat[0] = re.compile(r'\d').sub(expand, pat[0])
        for x, row in enumerate(pat[0].split('/')):
            for y, letter in enumerate(row):
                if letter == ' ': continue
                coord = self.alpha_notation((7-x,y))
                self[coord] = pieces.create_piece(letter)
                self[coord].place(self)
        if pat[1] == 'w': self.player_turn = 'white'
        else: self.player_turn = 'black'
        self.halfmove_clock = int(pat[2])
        self.fullmove_number = int(pat[3])
```

Step 2 – binding mouse click event

The pieces need to move on click of the mouse. So, we need to track the mouse click event. We only need to track mouse clicks on the Canvas widget. Let us, therefore, add an event handler to our GUI class immediately after the code that created the Canvas widget in the init method as follows (see *code 4.06: gui.py, __init__ method*):

```python
self.canvas.bind("<Button-1>", self.square_clicked)
```

This will bind the left mouse click event to a new method, `square_clicked`. However, before we sit down and define this method, let's pause and think about the attributes we need to keep tracking our program.

Step 3 – adding attribute to track selected piece and remaining pieces

First of all, we need to track all pieces remaining on the board after every move. So we will create a dictionary pieces to keep track of this. We also need to track the name of the piece selected by the mouse click. We store that in an attribute, `selected_piece`. When a player clicks on a piece, we need to highlight all valid moves for that piece. We store all valid moves for that piece in a list named `focused`. Let's define these three attributes in our GUI class before defining any of the methods. We modify our GUI class to include these attributes as follows:

```
class GUI:
    pieces = {}
    selected_piece = None
    focused = None
    #other attributes from previous iterations
```

Step 4 – identifying square clicked

We will code our `square_clicked` method that gets called from the event handler we defined earlier.

The desired functionality of this method is twofold. We should be able to locate the coordinate of a piece being clicked. The first click should select a given piece. The second click should move the piece from the source square to the destination square.

The method is defined as follows(see *code 4.06: gui.py*):

```
def square_clicked(self, event):
    col_size = row_size = self.dim_square
    selected_column = event.x / col_size
    selected_row = 7 - (event.y / row_size)
    pos = self.chessboard.alpha_notation((selected_row,
        selected_column))
    try:
      piece = self.chessboard[pos]
    except:
      pass
    if self.selected_piece:
       self.shift(self.selected_piece[1], pos)
       self.selected_piece = None
       self.focused = None
       self.pieces = {}
       self.draw_board()
       self.draw_pieces()
    self.focus(pos)
    self.draw_board()
```

The description of the code is listed as follows:

- ▶ The first part of code calculates the coordinates for the piece clicked. Based on the calculated coordinates, it stores the corresponding letter notation in a variable named `pos`.

- ▶ It then tries to assign the variable piece to the corresponding piece instance. If there is no piece instance on the clicked square, it simply ignores the click.

- ▶ The second part of the method checks if this is the second click intended to move a piece to a destination square. If this is the second click, it calls the `shift` method, passing in the source and destination coordinates as its two arguments.

- ▶ If shift succeeds, it sets back all previously set attributes to their original empty values and calls our `draw_board` and `draw_pieces` method to redraw the board and pieces.

- ▶ If this is the first click, it calls a method named `focus` to highlight all available moves for the first click, followed by a call to draw the fresh board.

While coding the desired functionality for the `square_clicked` method, we called several new methods from within it. We need to define those new methods.

Step 5 – getting the source and destination position

We have called the `shift` method from the `square_clicked` method. The following shift code implemented is simply responsible for collecting the necessary arguments required for the shift operation.

In the spirit of keeping logic separate from presentation, we do not process shift-related rules in this view class. Instead, we delegate the `shift` method work from the GUI to Board class. Once the logic or validation for shift has been implemented, the visible part of the shift of pieces again takes place in the `draw_board` method of our GUI class.

Although this may seem like overkill at first, structuring logic and presentation in different layers is very important for code reuse, scalability, and maintainability.

The code is as follows:

```
def shift(self, p1, p2):
    piece = self.chessboard[p1]
    try:
        dest_piece = self.chessboard[p2]
    except:
        dest_piece = None
    if dest_piece is None or dest_piece.color != piece.color:
```

```
try:
    self.chessboard.shift(p1, p2)
except:
    pass
```

The code first checks if there exists a piece on the destination. If a piece does not exist at the destination square, it calls on a method, `shift`, from `chessboard.py`.

Step 6 – collecting list of moves to highlight

We have also called the focus method from `square_clicked` method. The purpose of this method is to collect all possible moves for a given piece in a list named `focused`. The actual focusing of available moves takes place in the `draw_board` method of our GUI class.

The code is as follows (see code 4.06: gui.py):

```
def focus(self, pos):
    try:
        piece = self.chessboard[pos]
    except:
        piece=None
    if piece is not None and (piece.color ==
                    self.chessboard.player_turn):
        self.selected_piece = (self.chessboard[pos], pos)
        self.focused = map(self.chessboard.num_notation,
                    (self.chessboard[pos].moves_available(pos)))
```

Step 7 – modifying draw_board to highlight allowed moves

In the `square_clicked` method, we called the `draw_board` method to take care of redrawing or changing the coordinates for our pieces. Our current `draw_board` method is not equipped to handle this, because we had designed it in the first iteration only to provide us with a blank board. Let's first modify our `draw_board` method to handle this, as follows (see *code 4.06: gui.py*):

```
highlightcolor ="khaki"
def draw_board(self):
    color = self.color2
    for row in range(self.rows):
     color = self.color1 if color == self.color2 else self.color2
     for col in range(self.columns):
        x1 = (col * self.dim_square)
        y1 = ((7-row) * self.dim_square)
        x2 = x1 + self.dim_square
        y2 = y1 + self.dim_square
```

```
        if(self.focused is not None and (row, col) in
            self.focused):
        self.canvas.create_rectangle(x1, y1, x2, y2,
            fill=self.highlightcolor, tags="area")
        else:
            self.canvas.create_rectangle(x1, y1, x2, y2,
            fill=color, tags="area")
            color = self.color1 if color == self.color2 else
            self.color2
    for name in self.pieces:
      self.pieces[name] = (self.pieces[name][0],
      self.pieces[name][1])
      x0 = (self.pieces[name][1] * self.dim_square) +
            int(self.dim_square/2)
      y0 = ((7-self.pieces[name][0]) * self.dim_square) +
            int(self.dim_square/2)
      self.canvas.coords(name, x0, y0)
    self.canvas.tag_raise("occupied")
    self.canvas.tag_lower("area")
```

The description of the code is listed as follows:

▸ The additions made to our existing `draw_board` method are highlighted in the preceding code. We first define an attribute named `highlightcolor`, and assign it a color.

▸ In essence, the code has been modified to handle the clicks. The first section of highlighted code fills a different color to highlight all available moves.

▸ The second section of highlighted code changes the coordinates of the piece instance to be located on new coordinates. Note the use of `canvas.coords(name, x0, y0)` to change the coordinates.

▸ The last two lines change the precedence of options specified by tags.

If an object on the canvas is tagged to multiple tags, options defined for tags at the top of the stack have higher precedence. You can, however, change the precedence of tags by using `tag_raise(name)` or `tag_lower(name)`.

For a complete list of canvas-related options, refer to interactive help for the Canvas widget using `help(Tkinter.Canvas)` in the command line.

Step 8 – defining attributes to keep game statistics

As a consequence of adding mobility to our pieces, we need to add the following new attributes to our `Board` class to keep game statistics, as follows (see *code 4.06: chessboard.py*):

```
Class Board(dict):
    #other attributes from previous iteration
    captured_pieces = { 'white': [], 'black': [] }
    player_turn = None
    halfmove_clock = 0
    fullmove_number = 1
    history = []
```

Step 9 – preshift validations

For that, we will code the `shift` method of our `Board` class, as follows (see *code 4.06: chessboard.py*):

```
def shift(self, p1, p2):
    p1, p2 = p1.upper(), p2.upper()
    piece = self[p1]
    try:
        dest = self[p2]
    except:
        dest = None
    if self.player_turn != piece.color:
        raise NotYourTurn("Not " + piece.color + "'s turn!")
    enemy = ('white' if piece.color == 'black' else 'black' )
    moves_available = piece.moves_available(p1)
    if p2 not in moves_available:
        raise InvalidMove
    if self.all_moves_available(enemy):
        if self.is_in_check_after_move(p1,p2):
            raise Check
    if not moves_available and self.king_in_check(piece.color):
        raise CheckMate
    elif not moves_available:
        raise Draw
    else:
        self.move(p1, p2)
        self.complete_move(piece, dest, p1,p2)
```

The description of the code is listed as follows:

- The code first checks if there exists a piece on the destination.

- It then checks if it is a valid turn for the player. If not, it raises an exception.

- It then checks if the move is proposed to occur to a valid location. If a player attempts to move a piece to an invalid location, it raises a corresponding exception.

- It then checks if there is a check on the king. To do that, it calls a method named `is_in_check_after_move`, which is defined as follows:

```
def is_in_check_after_move(self, p1, p2):
    temp = deepcopy(self)
    temp.unvalidated_move(p1,p2)
    returntemp.king_in_check(self[p1].color)
```

- This method creates a deep temporary copy of the object and tries to move the piece on the temporary copy. As a note, shallow copy of a collection is a copy of the collection structure, not the elements. When you do a shallow copy, the two collections now share the individual elements, so a modification at one place affects the other as well. In contrast, deep copies makes copy of everything, the structure as well as the elements. We need to create a deep copy of the board, because we want to check if the king makes a valid move before it actually moves and we want to do that without modifying the original object state in any way.

- After executing the move on the temporary copy, it checks if the king is in check to return `True` or `False`. If the king is in check on the temporary board, it raises an exception, not allowing such a move on our actual board.

- Similarly, it checks for possible occurrence of checkmate or draw and raises exceptions accordingly.

- If no exceptions are made, it finally calls a method named `move`, which actually executes the move.

Step 10 – actual movement of pieces

Actual movement of pieces can be coded as follows:

```
def move(self, p1, p2):
    piece = self[p1]
    try:
        dest = self[p2]
    except:
        pass

    del self[p1]
    self[p2] = piece
```

Step 11 – Post movement updates

After the move has actually been executed, it calls another method named `complete_move`, which updates game statistics as follows:

```
def complete_move(self, piece, dest, p1, p2):
    enemy = ('white' if piece.color == 'black' else 'black' )
    if piece.color == 'black':
        self.fullmove_number += 1
    self.halfmove_clock +=1
    self.player_turn = enemy
    abbr = piece.shortname
    if abbr == 'P':
        abbr = ''
        self.halfmove_clock = 0
    if dest is None:
        movetext = abbr +  p2.lower()
    else:
        movetext = abbr + 'x' + p2.lower()
        self.halfmove_clock = 0
    self.history.append(movetext)
```

The preceding method does the following tasks:

- Keeps track of statistics, such as number of moves, halfmove clock
- Changes the player's turn
- Checks if a pawn has been moved so as to reset the halfmove clock
- And finally, appends the last move to our history list

Step 12 – classes to handle exceptions and errors

Finally, we add the following empty classes for various exceptions raised by us:

```
class Check(ChessError): pass
classInvalidMove(ChessError): pass
classCheckMate(ChessError): pass
class Draw(ChessError): pass
classNotYourTurn(ChessError): pass
```

Objective Complete – Mini Debriefing

Let's summarize things that we did in this iteration

> ▸ We started by binding a mouse click event to a method named `square_clicked`.
>
> ▸ We added attributes to track selected piece and remaining pieces on the board.
>
> ▸ We then identified the square clicked, followed by collecting the source and destination position.
>
> ▸ We also collected a list of all possible moves for the selected piece, and then highlighted them.
>
> ▸ We then defined attributes to keep vital game statistics.
>
> ▸ We then did some preshift validations, followed by actual movement of pieces on the board.
>
> ▸ After a piece had been moved, we updated statistics about the game.
>
> ▸ We had defined several exceptions in this iteration. We simply defined empty classes to handle them silently.

Our chess game is now functional. Two players can now play a game of chess on our application.

Adding menu and an info frame

Though our game is fully functional, let's add two small features to it.

Let's add a top menu item by navigating to **File | New Game**. When clicked, it should reset the board to a new game.

Additionally, let's add a small frame at the bottom to display game-related information, such as the last move, next turn, check, draw, and checkmate.

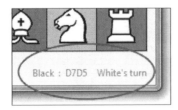

Engage Thrusters

Step 1 – creating top menu

Our Canvas widget was set up in the the __init__ method of our GUI class.

Let's modify it to include the top menu, as follows (see *code 4.06: gui.py*):

```
def __init__(self, parent, chessboard):
    self.chessboard = chessboard
    self.parent = parent
    self.menubar = Menu(parent)
    self.filemenu = Menu(self.menubar, tearoff=0)
    self.filemenu.add_command(label="New Game",
    command=self.new_game)
    self.menubar.add_cascade(label="File", menu=self.filemenu)
    self.parent.config(menu=self.menubar)
```

Step 2 – adding the bottom frame to display game statistics

Let's also add a bottom frame to display game statistics to the same __init__ method, as follows:

```
self.btmfrm = Frame(parent, height=64)
self.info_label = Label(self.btmfrm, text="  White to Start the
                        Game  ", fg=self.color2)
self.info_label.pack(side=RIGHT, padx=8, pady=5)
self.btmfrm.pack(fill="x", side=BOTTOM)
```

The modification to existing init method is highlighted. The code is self-explanatory. We have done similar things in all our previous projects.

Step 3 – starting a new game from File | New game menu

The **File | New game** menu item calls on our method, new_game(). The code for new_game() is as follows (see *code 4.06: gui.py*):

```
def new_game(self):
    self.chessboard.show(chessboard.START_PATTERN)
    self.draw_board()
    self.draw_pieces()
    self.info_label.config(text="White to Start the Game",
                           fg='red')
```

Step 4 – updating bottom label after every move

Finally, after every move, we want to update the label with details of the move and information about the next players turn. We also want to update the frame to display any error or exception that may have occurred during the move attempt. We accordingly modify the `shift` method of our `GUI` class to do this update for us as follows:

```python
def shift(self, p1, p2):
    piece = self.chessboard[p1]
    try:
        dest_piece = self.chessboard[p2]
    except:
        dest_piece = None
    if dest_piece is None or dest_piece.color != piece.color:
        try:
            self.chessboard.shift(p1,p2)
        exceptchessboard.ChessError as error:
            self.info_label["text"] = error.__class__.__name__
        else:
            turn = ('white' if piece.color == 'black' else 'black')
            self.info_label["text"] = '' + piece.color.capitalize() +"  :
"+ p1 + p2 + '' + turn.capitalize() + '\'s turn'
```

The description of the code is listed as follows:

▶   The modifications to our `shift` method are highlighted. We have simply included the `shift` method of our `Board` class in a try except block. If the shift is successful, the Label widget is updated to show the current move and the next players turn.

▶   If the shift is not successful, either because of invalid move or a check on the king, the corresponding error class name is displayed in the label with `error.__class__.__name__`.

Objective Complete – Mini Debriefing

This completes our goal for the iteration. The application now displays some useful information to the players during the course of a chess game.

We also added a **File | New menu** item, which can be used to reset the board to starting position.

Mission Accomplished

We now come to the end of the project.

So what is it that we have achieved here? Let's list all the key learning from this project:

- ▸ How to structure a program into its model and view components
- ▸ How to represent a problem domain in a desired notation
- ▸ Peek into the versatility and power of the Tkinter Canvas widget
- ▸ Basic usage of Canvas coordinates, object IDs and tags
- ▸ How to work with newer image formats
- ▸ Typical interaction of logic and presentation layers in a GUI program

Next project onwards, we take a look at different Tkinter widgets in greater detail.

A Hotshot Challenge

Here are the two hotshot challenges for you:

1. Add and implement the following menu items:

   - ❑ **File | Save**: Save a game state
   - ❑ **File | Open**: Loads a previously saved game
   - ❑ **Edit| Undo**: To let the players undo the turns played
   - ❑ **Edit |Redo**: To let the players redo any previous undo
   - ❑ **View | Moves History**: Opens a new Toplevel window to display the history of the game
   - ❑ **About| About**: Displays information about the game

2. Implement castling and En passant features in the game.

Project 5
Audio Player

Let's now build an audio media player!

Our application should have features offered by typical media players, such as play, pause, fast forward, rewind, next, mute, volume updates, and more. Our player should let the listener easily access individual media files or media library from his or her local drive.

In addition to this, our player should be able to scan entire directories for a song and accordingly, auto update the playlist with all supported formats. All this and more.

Let us start our project!

Mission Briefing

On completion our player will look as follows:

Our audio player will be capable of playing audio files in AU, MP2, MP3, OGG/Vorbis, WAV, and WMA formats. It will have all the controls that you would expect of a small media player.

We will use cross-platform modules to write our code. This will ensure that our player can play audio files on Windows, Mac OS X, and Linux platforms.

Why Is It Awesome?

In addition to getting to hear good music while testing our code, this project will introduce us to several new ideas related to GUI programming with Tkinter.

For one, we get to work with new sets of widgets, such as the Listbox, Progressbar, Scale, Radiobutton, and PMW Balloon widget.

We also take a look at the power of the Canvas widget in accommodating and precise positioning of other widgets within it.

Towards the end of the project, we take a look at a Tkinter extension named PMW. We also discuss some more Tkinter extensions that we do not use here, but are good to have in our GUI programming arsenal.

Though not a topic for this book, we also get a brief insight into the world of audio programming with Python, which necessarily looks at how to work with external libraries and API implementations.

Your Hotshot Objectives

Some of the key objectives outlined for this project include:

▶ Reinforcing our experiences and learning from previous projects
▶ Working with new set of widgets, such as Listbox, Scale, Progressbar, and Radiobutton
▶ Getting to know more of the Canvas widget
▶ Working with external APIs
▶ Getting to know about some common Tkinter extensions, such as PMW, WCK, Tix, and others
▶ Learning to refactor code at each stage of development

Mission Checklist

We will use the following additional libraries for this project:

Pyglet for audio manipulation

Window users can download and install binary packages for pyglet from:

`http://www.lfd.uci.edu/~gohlke/pythonlibs/#pyglet`

Mac OS X and Linux users should download and compile pyglet from the source ZIP file available at:

`http://www.pyglet.org/download.html`

When installing from source, you will also need to add the `AVbin.dll` to your current program directory. The link to the DLL file is also available at the preceding download page.

PMW Tkinter extension

We will be using **Python mega widgets (PMW)** Tkinter extension to code some widgets features not available in core Tkinter. PMW must be installed from the source package for all platforms. The package can be downloaded at:

`http://sourceforge.net/projects/pmw/files/Pmw/Pmw.1.3.3/`

 We use Version 1.3.3 in our application, and other versions of PMW may not be compatible with our code.

Additional font

This is an optional component meant only to augment our styling. We install a font to mimic the font of a digital clock. We have used the following font for this project:

`http://www.dafont.com/ds-digital.font`

After you have installed pyglet and PMW, execute the following command from your Python shell:

```
>>> import pyglet, Pmw
```

If the command executes without any error message, you are ready to code your media player.

Getting the audio to play

The first goal of our project is to add the ability to play the audio file. As usual, we will keep the audio related logic separate from our GUI section. Therefore, we create two separate files: `main-gui.py` and `player.py`. (See *code 5.01*)

Prepare for Lift Off

We first code a basic GUI, which includes a Play button (which toggles between play and stop functionality) and an Add File button. At the end of this iteration, we should be able to load a file, play it, and stop it. By the end of this section, our application will look like the following screenshot:

Engage Thrusters

Step 1 – creating the GUI class

Let's create the `GUI` class. The code for `main-gui.py` is as follows (see *code 5.01 main-gui.py*):

```
from Tkinter import *
import tkFileDialog
import player
class GUI:
    def __init__(self, player):
        self.player = player
        player.parent = self
        self.root = Tk()
        self.create_button_frame()
        self.create_bottom_frame()
        self.root.mainloop()
```

The description of the code is listed as follows:

- ▸ We create a class named `GUI`, and run the Tkinter mainloop from within its `__init__` method.

- ▸ We will separate the actual audio manipulation logic such as play, pause, rewind, forward, and others in a separate class to be defined later. However, because we want those functionalities to be available in this `GUI` class, we pass an object instantiated out of that `player` class as an argument to our `__init__` method.

- ▸ The line `self.player = player` within our `__init__` method ensures that the `player` class instance is available throughout the `GUI` class.

- ▸ Just like we want to access the properties and methods of the `player` class from this `GUI` class, we also want the methods and attributes of the `GUI` class to be available within our `player` class. We, therefore, use the line `player.parent = self` in the `__init__` method. This creates a reference to self so that all its methods can be assessed inside the `player` class using the syntax `parent.attribute` and `parent.method()`.

- ▸ With these two lines of code, we have ensured that all properties of the `GUI` class will be available in the `player` class and vice versa; all properties of the `player` class will be available in the `GUI` class.

Step 2 – creating the Play button and Add File button

For this, we add two methods: `create_button_frame` and `create_bottom_frame`. The `create_button_frame` method holds the Play button, and the `create_bottom_frame` method holds the Add File button, as follows:

```
def create_button_frame(self):
    buttonframe= Frame(self.root)
    self.playicon = PhotoImage(file='../icons/play.gif')
    self.stopicon = PhotoImage(file='../icons/stop.gif')
    self.playbtn=Button(buttonframe, text ='play',
                image=self.playicon, borderwidth=0,
                command=self.toggle_play_pause)
    self.playbtn.image = self.playicon
    self.playbtn.grid(row=3, column=3)
    buttonframe.grid(row=1, pady=4, padx=5)

def create_bottom_frame(self):
    bottomframe = Frame(self.root)
    add_fileicon = PhotoImage(file='../icons/add_file.gif')
```

```
add_filebtn=Button(bottomframe,
            image=add_fileicon, borderwidth=0, text='Add File',
            command=self.add_file)
add_filebtn.image = add_fileicon
add_filebtn.grid(row=2, column=1)
bottomframe.grid(row=2, sticky='w', padx=5)
```

The description of the code is listed as follows:

> ▸ Each of the two buttons is associated with a `TkinterPhotoImage` class icon. We have provided a set of icons in a separate folder named `icons`.

Step 3 – toggling between play and pause

The Play button has a command callback that toggles the button between play and stop functionality. The `toggle` method is defined as follows:

```
def toggle_play_pause(self):
    if self.playbtn['text'] =='play':
      self.playbtn.config(text='stop', image=self.stopicon)
      self.player.start_play_thread()
    elif self.playbtn['text'] =='stop':
      self.playbtn.config(text ='play', image=self.playicon)
      self.player.pause()
```

The description of the code is listed as follows:

> ▸ The method, `toggle_play_pause`, changes the icon alternatively between a play and pause icon. It also calls the `play` and `pause` methods of the `player` class to play and pause the songs.

Step 4 – add file dialog

The Add File button opens `tkFileDialog`, which associates the file opened with a class attribute named `currentTrack`, as follows:

```
def add_file(self):
    tfile = tkFileDialog.askopenfilename(filetypes=
            [('All supported', '.mp3 .wav .ogg'),
            ('All files', '*.*')])
    self.currentTrack = tfile
```

Step 5 – creating the Player class

Now, let's code the basic `player` class. For now, we will only add play and pause functionality to the class. The code for our `player` class is built upon the pyglet library.

Pyglet provides an object-oriented interface for developing rich media applications, such as games, audio and video tools, and others. It is a popular choice with Python programmers for media manipulation, because it has no external dependencies, supports a large number of formats, and is available on all major operating systems.

Before we proceed further, you might want to look at the API documentation of the pyglet player available at:

```
http://www.pyglet.org/doc/api/pyglet.media.Player-class.html
```

The documentation tells us that we can play an audio file using the following code:

```
myplayer= pyglet.media.Player()
source = pyglet.media.load(<<audio file to be played>>)
myplayer.queue(source)
myplayer.play()
pyglet.app.run()
```

We will use this code snippet to play the audio file. Accordingly, the code for our Player class is as follows(see *code 5.01 player.py*):

```
import pyglet
from threading import Thread
class Player():
    parent = None
    def play_media(self):
        try:
            self.myplayer= pyglet.media.Player()
            self.source = pyglet.media.load(self.parent.currentTrack)
            self.myplayer.queue(self.source)
            self.myplayer.play()
            pyglet.app.run()
        except:
            pass

    def start_play_thread(self):
        player_thread = Thread(target=self.play_media)
        player_thread.start()

    def pause(self):
        try:
            self.myplayer.pause()
            self.paused = True
        except: pass
```

The description of the code is listed as follows:

▸ We create a class named `Player` and initialize its parent class as `None`. Recall that in our GUI class, we have defined a reference `player.parent = self`, so as to be able to assess our GUI class properties from within our `player` class.

▸ We then define our `play_media` method, which is responsible for actually playing the sound. The method accesses the `currentTrack` attribute of the GUI class and tries to play it.

▸ Although this code can play audio files, pyglet requires running its own event loop to play the audio. This means it will return control to our GUI mainloop only after it has completed playing the entire sound, while freezing the Tkinter mainloop if run directly.

▸ We, therefore, need to call the play method in a separate thread. We use the threading module to define a new method named `start_play_thread`, which simply calls our `play_media` method in a separate thread, thus preventing freezing out of GUI.

▸ Lastly, we define the pause method, which pauses or stops the audio file being currently played. Pyglet does not differentiate between pause and stop functions. Therefore, we are typically stopping the audio using the pause command.

Step 6 – running the application

We finally run the application by creating an object out of our GUI class. Because this GUI class requires an object from the `player` class, we also instantiate a player object and pass it as an argument to our GUI class, as follows:

```
if __name__ == '__main__':
    playerobj = player.Player()
    app = GUI(playerobj)
```

The description of the code is listed as follows:

▸ The last section of code creates an object from the `player` class that we are yet to define. The `player` class will take care of all audio manipulation using pyglet.

▸ We first create an object out of the `player` class and pass it as an argument to the `__init__` method of our GUI class. This ensures that all attributes and methods of the `player` class are available within the GUI class using the syntax `player.attribute` and `player.method()`.

Objective Complete – Mini Debriefing

This completes our first iteration.

In this section, we created a GUI class, added a button that toggles between play and pause. We added another button to add a file using tkFileDialog.

We also created a Player class, which uses pyglet for playing audio files. The files are played in a separate thread to avoid freezing of the Tkinter mainloop while the audio is playing.

Finally, we ran our application by first creating a player object and passing it as an argument to another object created by our GUI class.

We now have a functional audio player, where you can load a single file using tkFileDialog. After loading, you can press the Play button and the audio file starts playing. You can stop the audio by clicking the Play button, which toggles alternatively between play and pause functions.

Adding a playlist

We now have the capability to play a single audio file, but what is an audio player if it does not allow for a playlist?

Let's add a playlist feature to our player. Once a playlist is added, we accordingly need to provide buttons to add files to the playlist, delete files from it, and add all supported files from a chosen directory and the ability to delete all items in the list at once.

At the end of this iteration, we will have a player that looks like the following screenshot:

Prepare for Lift Off

We will use Tkinter Listbox widget to provide a playlist. Let's look at some of the key features of the Listbox widget:

▸ You create a Listbox like you create any other widget as follows:

```
mylist = ListBox(parent, **configurable options)
```

▸ When you initially create the Listbox widget, it is empty. To insert one or more lines of text into the Listbox, you use the `insert()` method, which takes two arguments: an index of the position where the text is to be inserted and the actual string to be inserted as follows:

```
mylist.insert(0, "First Item")
mylist.insert(END, "Last Item")
```

▸ The `curselection()` method returns the index of all items selected in the list, and the `get()` method returns the list item for a given index as follows:

```
mylist.curselection() # returns a tuple of all selected
items
mylist.curselection()[0] # returns first selected item
mylist.get(1) # returns second item from the list
mylist.get(0, END) # returns all items from the list
```

▸ In addition, the Listbox widget has several other configurable options. For a complete Listbox widget reference, type the following into your Python interactive shell:

```
>>> import Tkinter
>>> help(Tkinter.Listbox)
```

Engage Thrusters

Step 1 – adding an empty Listbox widget

Let's first add an empty Listbox widget, as follows (see *code 5.02 main-gui.py*):

```
def create_list_frame(self):
    list_frame = Frame(self.root)
    self.Listbox = Listbox(list_frame, activestyle='none',
                    cursor='hand2', bg='#1C3D7D', fg='#A0B9E9',
                    selectmode=EXTENDED, width=60, height =10)
    self.Listbox.pack(side=LEFT, fill=BOTH, expand=1)
    self.Listbox.bind("<Double-Button-1>",
                    self.identify_track_to_play)
```

```
scrollbar = Scrollbar(list_frame)
scrollbar.pack(side=RIGHT, fill=BOTH)
self.Listbox.config(yscrollcommand=scrollbar.set)
scrollbar.config(command=self.Listbox.yview)
list_frame.grid(row=4, padx=5)
```

The description of the code is listed as follows:

▶ We create a new frame, `list_frame`, to hold our List widget.

▶ We create a Listbox widget within this frame and set some styling options, such as background color, foreground color, and mouse cursor. The styling of active line is set using the Listbox option, `activestyle`, which means that we do not want to underline the selected item.

▶ The `selectmode` option is configured as extended. See the following information box for a list of choices available and their meaning. We will use the EXTENDED select mode, because even though a single file can be played at once, we want to allow the user to select more than one file together at once for deletion.

▶ We add a scrollbar to the Listbox, similar to the way we did in our text editor project.

▶ We bind the double-click of mouse to another method named `identify_track_to_play`.

The Listbox widget offers four selection modes using the `selectmode` option as follows:

SINGLE: It allows only a single row to be selected at one time.

BROWSE (Default mode): It is similar to SINGLE but allows for moving the selection by dragging the mouse.

MULTIPLE: It allows for multiple selections by clicking on items one at a time.

EXTENDED: It allows for selection of multiple range of items using *Shift* and *Control* keys.

Step 2 – identify track to play

Our program was simpler in the first iteration, where we had only song to play. However, given a playlist, now we have to identify which song needs to be played from the given list.

The rule is simple. If a user clicks on a given song, it becomes our selected track. If the user has made no selection and hits the Play button, the first song in the playlist should be played. Put in code this would look like as follows (see *code 5.02 main-gui.py*):

```
def identify_track_to_play(self, event=None):
    try:
        indx = int(self.Listbox.curselection()[0])
```

```
      if self.Listbox.get(indx) == "":
        self.del_selected()
   except:
      indx = 0
      self.currentTrack =self.Listbox.get(indx)
   self.player.start_play_thread()
```

Step 3 – adding items to the list

Now that we have a Listbox and we can play any item by double-clicking on it, let's add methods to populate and remove items from the list.

However, even before we do any modifications to our list, let's first define an empty list named `alltracks` to keep track of all items in the playlist. We will need to update this list after any changes are done to the list, as follows(see *code 5.02 main-gui.py*):

```
alltracks = []
```

We had already created an `add file` method in the last section. Let's modify it slightly so that the file selected does not become the selected track, instead it gets added to the playlist, as follows (see *code 5.02 main-gui.py*):

```
def add_file(self):
    filename = tkFileDialog.askopenfilename(filetypes=
             [('All supported', '.mp3 .wav'),
              ('.mp3 files', '.mp3'), ('.wav files', '.wav')])
    if filename:
      self.Listbox.insert(END, filename)
    self.alltracks = list(self.Listbox.get(0, END))
```

The description of the code is listed as follows:

▶ The file selected through `tkFileDialog` is inserted at the end of the list box, and our attribute, `alltracks`, is updated with all elements in the Listbox widget.

▶ Notice that the `get()` method returns a tuple of all items. Because tuples are immutable, we explicitly convert the tuple into a list by using the `list` type declaration.

Step 4 – deleting items from the list

Let's add a new button to delete selected files. This is added to our existing `create_bottom_frame` method, as follows (see *code 5.02 main-gui.py*):

```
del_selectedicon = PhotoImage(file='../icons/del_selected.gif')
```

```
del_selectedbtn=Button(bottomframe, image=del_selectedicon, padx=0,
              borderwidth=0, text='Delete',
              command=self.del_selected)
del_selectedbtn.image = del_selectedicon
del_selectedbtn.grid(row=5, column=2)
```

This button has a command callback to a method named `del_selected`. The code for `del_selected` is as follows:

```
def del_selected(self):
    whilelen(self.Listbox.curselection())>0:
      self.Listbox.delete(self.Listbox.curselection()[0])
    self.alltracks = list(self.Listbox.get(0, END))
```

As usual, we update our `alltracks` list after deletion of items from the Listbox widget.

Now, you can make a selection from your list box and click on the Delete button to remove all selected items from the list box.

Step 5 – adding multiple items to the list

Adding individual audio files to a playlist can become tedious. We want to allow the users to select a directory, and our list should get populated with all supported media formats from that directory.

We, therefore, add a new button to allow for adding all media files from a given directory. This is also added to our existing `create_bottom_frame` method, as follows (see *code 5.02 main-gui.py*):

```
add_diricon = PhotoImage(file='../icons/add_dir.gif')
add_dirbtn=Button(bottomframe, image=add_diricon,
          borderwidth=0, padx=0, text='Add Dir',
          command=self.add_dir)
add_dirbtn.image = add_diricon
add_dirbtn.grid(row=5, column=3)
```

We need to use the `os` module to grab all supported types. Let's first import the `os` module into the current namespace, as follows:

```
import os
```

Now the associated command callback is as follows:

```
def add_dir(self):
    path = tkFileDialog.askdirectory()
    if path:
```

```
tfileList = []
for (dirpath, dirnames, filenames) in os.walk(path):
    for tfile in filenames:
        if tfile.endswith(".mp3") or tfile.endswith(".wav")
        or tfile.endswith(".ogg"):
            tfileList.append(dirpath+"/"+tfile)
for item in tfileList:
    self.listbox.insert(END, item)
self.alltracks = list(self.listbox.get(0, END))
```

The description of the code is listed as follows:

▸ The `add_dir` method first creates a temporary list, `tfilelist`.

▸ It then iterates through all filenames fetched through the `tkFileDialog.askdirectory()` method. If it encounters a supported file format, it appends the file to the temporary list.

▸ It then iterates through all items in the `tfilelist`, inserting them into our Listbox.

▸ It finally updates our `alltracks` attribute with all items in the newly modified list.

Step 6 – deleting all items

Finally, we add a button to delete all items from the playlist. The associated button is added to the `create_bottom_frame` method, as follows:

```
delallicon = PhotoImage(file='../icons/delall.gif')
delallbtn = Button(bottomframe, image=delallicon,
        borderwidth=0, padx=0, text='Clear All',
        command=self.clear_list)
delallbtn.image = delallicon
delallbtn.grid(row=5, column=4)
```

Now its associated command callback is as follows:

```
def clear_list(self):
    self.Listbox.delete(0, END)
    self.alltracks =list(self.Listbox.get(0, END))
```

Objective Complete – Mini Debriefing

This completes our second iteration.

In this iteration, we saw how to work with the Listbox widget. In particular, we learned to add Listbox, add items to he Listbox widget, select a particular item from the Listbox widget, and delete one or more items from it.

You now have a playlist where you can add and delete items.

The Listbox widget has an event binding for double-click of the mouse button on an item. This associated event callback selects the clicked item, and sends it across to be played on a separate thread.

In the process, we saw a list of common operations done on the Listbox widget.

Adding more controls to the player

Now that we have a playlist, we need to ensure that songs play in a queue. We also need to add a few more controls typically found in audio players, such as Next, Previous, Fast Forward, Rewind, and Mute buttons. We also need to provide a method to change the volume of playback.

At the end of this iteration, our player would have the following additional controls in the top-button frame:

The pyglet API documentation provides simple interfaces for all these controls. For your reference, the documentation is available at:

```
http://www.pyglet.org/doc/api/pyglet.media.Player-class.html
```

Let's begin by adding methods to handle these in our `Player` class.

Engage Thrusters

Step 1 – fast forwarding a track
We can fast forward a track as follows (see *code 5.03 player.py*):

```
FWDREWNDTIME = 20
#time to seek ahead or backwards in seconds
def fast_fwd(self):
```

```
    try:
       current_time = self.myplayer.time
       self.myplayer.seek(current_time+FWDREWNDTIME)
    except:pass
```

Step 2 – rewinding a track

We can rewind a track as follows:

```
def rewind(self):
    try:
       current_time = self.myplayer.time
       self.myplayer.seek(current_time-FWDREWNDTIME)
    except:pass
```

Step 3 – pausing a track

We can pause a track as follows:

```
def pause(self):
    try:
       self.myplayer.pause()
       self.paused = True
    except: pass
```

Step 4 – setting the volume of playback

We can set the volume of playback as follows:

```
def set_vol(self, vol):
    try:
       self.myplayer.volume = vol
    except:pass
```

Step 5 – muting and unmuting a track

We can mute and unmute a track as follows:

```
def mute(self):
    try:
       self.myplayer.volume = 0.0
       self.parent.volscale.set(0.0)
    except:pass

def unmute(self):
    self.set_vol(self.vol)
    self.parent.volscale.set(0.3)
```

We will not discuss the code here in detail. For coding these functionalities, we have used the API documentation for pyglet available at:

```
http://www.pyglet.org/doc/api/pyglet.media.Player-class.html
```

You can also access this documentation for the pyglet media player class by typing these two lines in your Python interactive shell:

```
>>> import pyglet
>>> help (pyglet.media.Player)
```

We have been indiscriminately using try/except blocks in this program to hide all errors emanating from the player class.

This might not be the best programming practice, but we ignore all player class errors so as not to deviate from our discussion on Tkinter.

In a normal case, you would handle all different kind of errors using different except blocks.

Step 6 – adding the control buttons

Now that we have the backend code to handle events, such as fast forward, rewind, volume change, mute, and others, it is simply time to add buttons for each of these controls to our GUI class. We link each of the buttons to its respective command callback.

So, we modify our create_button_frame widget to add buttons for these new controls.

We have added hundreds of buttons so far in our previous project. So, we do not reproduce the entire code here for sake of brevity. Rather, we simply show the implementation of the Previous Track button as one of its sample, and how it calls the associated command callback to the previous() method of the player class as follows (see *code 5.03 GUI.py*):

```
previcon = PhotoImage(file='../icons/previous.gif')
prevbtn=Button(buttonframe, image=previcon,
        borderwidth=0, padx=0, command=self.prev_track)
prevbtn.image = previcon
prevbtn.grid(row=3, column=1, sticky='w')
```

Step 7 – changing volume with the ttk Scale widget

In addition to these buttons, we also use the ttk Scale widget to allow the users to change the volume. The native Scale widget implementation in core Tkinter looks rather old fashioned and we instead settle for the ttk Scale widget, which has same set of configurable options as the core Tkinter Scale widget, as follows:

```
self.volscale = ttk.Scale(buttonframe, from_=0.0,
                to =1.0 , command=self.vol_update)
```

```
self.volscale.set(0.6)
self.volscale.grid(row=3, column=7, padx=5)
```

As per the pyglet documentation, the volume of playback must be specified as a float ranging from `0.0` (no sound) to `1.0` (maximum sound), and our `updateVolume` method uses this as the basis.

This has an attached callback to another method, `vol_update`, in the `GUI` class, which simply delegates the task to the `player` method to handle volume changes.

```
def vol_update(self, e):
    vol = float(e)
    self.player.set_vol(vol)
```

The description of the code is listed as follows:

> ▸ The pyglet `Player` class expects volume to be specified as a float, but the command here receives the new value of scale as a string. We, therefore, first convert it to float, and then pass it to the `set_vol` method of the `player` class.

Objective Complete – Mini Debriefing

This completes the second iteration where we added playback control features to our program.

This section was more about sticking to the API documentation of pyglet and trusting it as a blackbox to deliver what it says: namely, to be able to play and control audio.

We also saw how to use the ttk Scale widget in a practical demonstration of building our volume control.

Classified Intel

When it came to choosing an external implementation (as we did for audio API here), we first searched through the Python Standard Library at:

```
http://docs.python.org/library/
```

Because the Standard Library does not have a suitable package for us, we turned our attention to Python Package Index to see if there exists another high-level audio interface implementation. The Python package index lives at:

```
http://pypi.python.org/
```

Fortunately, we came across several audio packages. After comparing the packages against our needs and seeing how active its community was, we settled for pyglet. The same program could have been implemented with several other packages, though with varying levels of complexity.

In general, the lower you go down the protocol stack, the more complex your programs would get.

However, at lower layers of the protocol, you get a finer control over the implementation at the cost of increasing learning curves.

For instance, because the pyglet `player` class does not differentiate between pause and stop functionality, we had to altogether do away with the pause functionality and settle for a simpler implementation where pause and stop mean the same.

For a finer control of audio source, we will have to go deeper into the protocol stacks, which we will avoid for now, so as not to digress from our topic.

Adding the top display console

In this iteration, we will add a display console at the top of our player. This console will display the time counter for our music player. It will also display the currently played track.

We will also code a progress bar, which will show the progress of the current track being played.

At the end of this iteration, the top frame of our player will look like the following screenshot:

Prepare for Lift Off

We need to precisely place our timer clock text and the currently playing track text on the top of an image.

Recall that the Canvas widget allows for a deep nested placement of other widgets inside it with precise coordinate-based control. This is all that we want to display the console. We will, therefore, use the Canvas widget as the container for our console.

Engage Thrusters

Step 1 – creating the top console and progress bar

We accordingly define a new method named create_console_frame in our GUI class, which holds our image, clock text, and currently playing text for creating the top console and progress bar as follows(see *code 5.04 GUI.py*):

```
def create_console_frame(self):
    consoleframe = Frame(self.root)
    self.canvas = Canvas(consoleframe, width=370, height=90)
    self.canvas.grid(row=1)
    photo = PhotoImage(file='../icons/glassframe.gif')
    self.canvas.image = photo
    self.console = self.canvas.create_image(0, 10, anchor=NW,
                    image=photo)
    self.clock = self.canvas.create_text(32, 34, anchor=W,
                fill='#CBE4F6', font="DS-Digital 20", text="00:00")
    self.songname = self.canvas.create_text(115, 37, anchor=W,
                    fill='#9CEDAC', font="Verdana 10",
                    text='\"Currently playing: none [00.00] \"')
    self.progressBar = ttk.Progressbar(consoleframe, length =1,
                    mode="determinate")
    self.progressBar.grid(row=2, columnspan=10, sticky='ew',
                        padx=5)
    consoleframe.grid(row=1, pady=1, padx=0)
```

The description of the code is listed as follows:

▸ The code defines a new frame, consoleframe, and adds a Canvas widget of desired height and width to the frame.

▸ We use canvas.create_image to add the background image. The background image is provided in the icons folder.

- We use `canvas.create_text` to add one text for displaying the clock and another text to display the currently playing track. The desired location of each of these texts is specified using x, y coordinates.

- We also specify a special font for displaying our clock. If this font is installed on a computer, the text is displayed in the specified font. If the font is not installed, display occurs in the default font.

- Finally, we display a ttkProgressbar widget, which shall be used to display the progress of track as it plays. We use the determinate mode of the progress bar, because we want to display the completion of track relative to its overall length. For now, the overall length of track is initialized to 1. It will be updated as the song starts to play.

A ttkProgressbar widget displays the status of progress of an operation. The progress bar can run in two modes:

`Determinate`: This mode shows the amount of work completed relative to the total amount of work.

`Indeterminate`: This provides an animated show of the progress, but does not show the relative amount of work completed.

Step 2 – getting the total duration of a track

The contents of the display panel and the progress on the progress bar need to be updated every time a new song starts playing. In our current code, a new song starts playing when a user clicks on the Play button or double-clicks on a particular track, or when the Next or Previous button is clicked.

Before we update the clock or the progress bar, we need to know two things:

- Total length of current track
- Duration for which a current track has been played

Fortunately, pyglet provides API calls to determine both these things. As per its documentation, the total length of a song currently playing can be obtained from the code: `source.duration`.

Similarly, the current duration of play can be obtained using `myplayer.time`.

Let's, therefore, define two new methods in our `Player` class to get the value of these two variables, as follows (*code 5.04player.py*):

```
def song_len(self):
    try:
      self.song_length = self.source.duration
    except:
      self.song_length = 0
    return self.song_length
def current_time(self):
    try:
      current_time = self.myplayer.time
    except:
      current_time = 0
    return current_time
```

Now, we slightly modify our `start_play_thread` method to call our `song_len` method so that our `song_length` attribute is updated with the value of the song length.

```
def start_play_thread(self):
    player_thread = Thread(target=self.play_media)
    player_thread.start()
    time.sleep(1)
    self.song_len()
```

Notice that we made the method to sleep for one second, so as to enable to length metadata to populate. If we do not make it sleep for a second, the code would execute so fast that it would end even before the `song_length` variable is updated by pyglet.

Now, we have access to the total length and current duration of play. We now want to update the current track every time a new track is played.

Step 3 – updating console at launch of play

A new track is played when a user hits the Play button, or when he or she double-clicks a particular song, or when he or she clicks the Next or Previous button.

If you look at the code from previous iteration (*code 5.03 GUI.py*), all these methods call the `self.player.start_play_thread()` functionality to start the playback. However, now we need to update the console display every time a new player thread is started.

We, therefore, need to refactor our code. For one, we will route all calls to `player.start_play_thread()` through a single method, which will update the display as the player thread starts.

Step 4 – updating timer clock and progress bar at regular intervals

We, therefore, define a new method named `launch_play`, and replace all instances of `player.start_play_thread()` from previous code to now call our `launch_play` method, as follows (see *Code 5.04.py main-gui.py*):

```
def launch_play(self):
    try:
        self.player.pause()
    except:
        pass
    self.player.start_play_thread()
    song_lenminute = str(int(self.player.song_length/60))
    song_lenseconds = str (int(self.player.song_length%60))
    filename = self.currentTrack.split('/')[-1] + '\n
            ['+ song_lenminute+':'+song_lenseconds+']'
    self.canvas.itemconfig(self.songname, text=filename)
    self.progressBar["maximum"]=self.player.song_length
    self.update_clock_and_progressbar()
```

The description of the code is listed as follows:

▶ The code first tries to stop any other track that might be playing at that time, because we don't want multiple tracks playing at a given time.

▶ It then starts to play the next track in a separate thread. The thread method automatically updates the song length, and now we have access to the song length in the variable `self.player.song_len`.

▶ The next two lines break the song length into equivalent minutes and seconds.

▶ The next line breaks the file name and gets hold of the song name from the complete path. It then appends the time calculated in minutes and seconds to the file name.

▶ We set the `maximum` value for our progress bar, which is a floating point number specifying the maximum value of the progress bar. For viewing all configurable options for ttk Progressbar, enter the following into your Python interactive console:

```
>>> import ttk
>>> help(ttk.Progressbar)
```

▶ The next line uses `canvas.itemconfig` to update the song name and song length in the display console.

Just like we use `config` to change value of widget related options, the Canvas widget uses `itemconfig` to change the options for individual items within the canvas.

The format for `itemconfig` is as follows: `itemconfig(itemid, **options)`.

In this step, we will learn to update timer clock and progress bar at regular intervals. Although song name and song length are to be updated just once for a given song, the play duration and progress bar need to be updated at small intervals. We, therefore, handle it in a separate method named `update_clock_and_progressbar()`.

We want to display time in the format you normally find in a digital clock. We accordingly define a string format named `timepattern`, as follows:

`timepattern = '{0:02d}:{1:02d}'`.

Now, let us turn our attention to updating the display clock and the progress bar. We have already made a call to `update_clock_and_progressbar()` which is supposed to take care of this work. Let's now code this method, as follows(see *Code 5.04.py main-gui.py*):

```
def update_clock_and_progressbar(self):
    current_time = self.player.current_time()
    song_len = (self.player.song_len())
    currtimeminutes = int(current_time/60)
    currtimeseconds = int(current_time%60)
    currtimestrng = self.timepattern.format(currtimeminutes,
                    currtimeseconds)
    self.canvas.itemconfig(self.clock, text= currtimestrng)
    self.progressBar["value"] = current_time
    self.root.update()
    if current_time == song_len: #track is over
      self.canvas.itemconfig(self.clock, text= '00:00')
      self.timer=[0,0]
      self.progressBar["value"] = 0
    else:
      self.canvas.after(1000, self.update_clock_and_progressbar)
```

This code runs itself every 1000 ms, forces a root update, and changes the time and progress bar value. To keep running regularly, it calls back itself after every 1000 ms.

When a track is over, it resets the values of clock and progress bar to zero, and exits out of the update loop.

 We used the `canvas.after` method to call the same method at intervals of one second. Thus, this method would get to be called at one second interval throughout playing of the current track. We also kept a condition to break out of the loop when the current track ended playing.

Objective Complete – Mini Debriefing

This completes this iteration. In this iteration, we built a functional display console and a progress bar to display time and information about the current track.

We started by creating a blank canvas in the top area of our root window. We then added an image that resembles a display console. We then used `canvas.create_text` to precisely position the timer clock, name of currently playing track, and the total track length in the console.

We also created a ttk progress bar.

We then calculated the track length using the pyglet API. Next, we made all calls to play the track to be routed through an intermediate method which updated the console with information about the currently playing track.

We also added a method to update the clock and progress bar at regular intervals.

Looping over tracks

So now we have a functional player. It though lacks a vital feature. There is no tracking over loop. That means every time a user listens to a track, the player stops after playing that track. It does not jump to the next track in our playlist.

Let's provide some radio buttons to let the user choose the looping structure. By the end of this iteration, we will add the following to our player:

In essence, our player should provide choice amongst:

- ▶ **No loop**: Playing a track and ending there
- ▶ **Loop Current**: Playing a single track repeatedly
- ▶ **Loop All**: Playing through the entire playlist, one after another

Let's code this feature.

Engage Thrusters

Step 1 – creating the radio buttons

The corresponding code for creating radio buttons in the GUI class is as follows (see *Code 5.05 main-gui.py*):

```
#radio buttons added to create_bottom_frame
self.loopv = IntVar()
self.loopv.set(3)
for txt, val in self.loopchoices:
    Radiobutton(bottomframe, text=txt, variable=self.loopv,
                value=val).grid(row=5, column=4+val, pady=3)
```

Step 2 – on end of song callback

Let's look at the player end logic first when a song ends. We need a way to call a method once a song has completed playing. Luckily, the pyglet player allows for an on_eos (on end of song) callback.

We first modify our existing play_media method in the player class to include this callback.(See *Code 5.05 player.py*)

```
self.myplayer.push_handlers(on_eos=self.what_next)
```

This callback is executed on end of a given song. We add the callback to a method named what_next.

Step 3 – what next?

This what_next method essentially looks for the selected choice on looping and accordingly takes some action. The code for what_next is as follows:

```
def what_next(self):
    if self.stopped:
        self.stopped = False
```

```
        return None
    if self.parent.loopv.get() == 1:
        # No Loop
        return None
    if self.parent.loopv.get() == 2:
        # Loop current
        self.parent.launch_play()
    if self.parent.loopv.get() == 3:
        # Loop All
        self.fetch_next_track()
```

The description of the code is listed as follows:

- ▶ The `on_eos` callback is also called just in case a track is stopped in the middle. That means that if a stop action occurs, we don't want to do anything next. We, therefore, break out of the method by calling a blank return.

- ▶ The code then checks the value of `self.parent.selectedloopchoice`.

- ▶ If the selected loop value is 1(**No Loop**), it does not play the next song, but breaks out of the method with a return statement.

- ▶ If the loop value is 2 (loop over the current song), it again calls the `launch_play` method without changing the current track.

- ▶ If the loop value is 3 (**Loop All**), it calls another method named `fetch_next_track`.

Step 4 – fetching the next track

The code of `fetch_next_track` to fetch the next track is as follows:

```
def fetch_next_track(self):
    try:
        next_trackindx = self.parent.alltracks.index(
                        self.parent.currentTrack) +1
        self.parent.currentTrack =
                        self.parent.alltracks[next_trackindx]
        self.parent.launch_play()
    except:pass
        # end of list - do nothing
```

The description of the code is listed as follows:

- ▶ This code simply increments index by one, sets the current track variable to the next item in the list of all songs, and calls `launch_play()` to play the next track.

Objective Complete – Mini Debriefing

This completes the coding of looping in our player.

This iteration relied on the fact that pyglet allows an `on_oes` (on end of song) callback. At the end of a track, we use this callback to check the looping choice specified by the user.

If the user does not want to loop through the playlist, we pass a blank return statement. If the user wants to loop over the current song, we call the `launch_play` method without incrementing the current track. If the user wants to loop through the entire list, we call a method named `fetch_next_track`, which increments the index of song by one, and then calls the `launch_play` method to play the next song.

In this iteration, we also saw a sample usage of radio buttons.

Our player is now equipped to loop over a playlist based on preferences provided by the user.

Adding the contextual menu

In this quick iteration, we add a contextual pop-up menu or the right-click menu with shortcuts to some common operations on the player.

For now, we will add just two functions to the right-click menu: **Play** and **Delete**.

After completion, the right-click menu will open, as shown in the following screenshot:

Engage Thrusters

Step 1 – creating the contextual menu

We have done similar contextual menus in our text editor, so we do a quick round up.

We add a new method, `context_menu`, and call it from the GUI `__init__` method, as follows (see *Code 5.06 main-gui.py*):

```
def create_context_menu(self):
    self.context_menu = Menu(self.root, tearoff=0)
    self.context_menu.add_command(label="Play",
                        command=self.identify_track_to_play)
    self.context_menu.add_command(label="Delete",
                        command=self.del_selected)
```

We also define a `show_context_menu` method and bind it to right-click of mouse`<<Button-3>>` from within our `create_list_frame`, immediately next to where the Listbox widget is defined, as follows:

```
def show_context_menuContext_menu(self,event):
    self.context_menu.tk_popup(event.x_root+45, event.y_root+10,0)
```

Step 2: overriding the close button

While we are at it, let us code a little overlooked function. Now that we have the capability to loop over entire playlists, we do not want the player to close without stopping the songs being played. Let us, therefore, override the `root.destroy()` method to stop tracks before exiting.

To override the destroy method, we first add a protocol override method to our GUI `__init__` method, as follows (see *Code 5.06 main-gui.py*):

```
self.root.protocol('WM_DELETE_WINDOW', self.close_player)
```

Finally let's define our `close_player` method, as follows:

```
def close_player(self):
    if tkMessageBox.askokcancel("Quit", "Really want to quit?"):
        try:
            self.player.pause()
        except:
            pass
        self.root.destroy()
```

Objective Complete – Mini Debriefing

The contextual menu is now added to our program. A user can now right-click on an item and select to play or delete it.

We have also overridden our close button to ensure that any playing track is stopped before we exit the player.

Adding a tooltip and finalizing our player

In this iteration, we add tooltip also named the Balloon widget to all the buttons in our player.

A tooltip is a small popup, which shows up when you hover your mouse over the Bound widget (buttons in our case). A typical tooltip on our application would look as shown in the following screenshot:

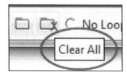

Prepare for Lift Off

Although core Tkinter has many useful widgets, it is far from complete. For us, the tooltip or Balloon widget is not provided as a core Tkinter widget. We, therefore, look for these widgets in what are named **Tkinter extensions**.

These extensions are nothing but modified Tkinter widgets to act and behave with new functionalities not offered by Tkinter.

There are literally hundreds of Tkinter extensions. In fact, we could write our own Tkinter extensions. However, some of the popular Tkinter extensions are as follows:

- **Python Mega Widgets (PMW)** available at `http://pmw.sourceforge.net`
- **Tix** available at `http://wiki.Python.org/moin/Tix`
- **TkZinc** available at `http://wiki.Python.org/moin/TkZinc`
- **Widget Construction Kit(WCK)** available at `http://effbot.org/zone/wck.htm`

PMW list of extensions

Talking about PMW, here is a quick list of widget extensions from the package:

Widgets

- ButtonBox
- ComboBox
- Counter

- ▸ EntryField
- ▸ Group
- ▸ HistoryText
- ▸ LabeledWidget
- ▸ MainMenuBar
- ▸ MenuBar
- ▸ MessageBar
- ▸ NoteBook
- ▸ OptionMenu
- ▸ PanedWidget
- ▸ RadioSelect
- ▸ ScrolledCanvas
- ▸ ScrolledField
- ▸ ScrolledFrame
- ▸ ScrolledListBox
- ▸ ScrolledText
- ▸ TimeCounter

Dialogs

- ▸ AboutDialog
- ▸ ComboBoxDialog
- ▸ CounterDialog
- ▸ Dialog
- ▸ MessageDialog
- ▸ PromptDialog
- ▸ SelectionDialog
- ▸ TextDialog

Miscellaneous

- ▸ Balloon
- ▸ Blt(used for graph generation)
- ▸ Color Module functions

PMW offers a large list of extended widgets. For a demonstration of all these widgets, browse into the PMW package that you installed earlier, and look for a directory named `demo`. Within `demo`, look for a file, `all.py`, which demonstrates all PMW extensions with sample working code.

Engage Thrusters

Step 1 – importing PMW

PMW provides the Balloon widget implementation, but it is not part of standard Tkinter library. We need to add it. To add PMW, refer to our discussion under the *Mission Checklist* section. Once added, you need to import PMW into your namespace, as follows (see *Code 5.07 main-gui.py*):

```
import Pmw
```

Step 2 – instantiating the Balloon widget

We then instantiate the Balloon widget within the mainloop from our __init__ method as follows:

```
self.balloon = Pmw.Balloon(self.root)
```

Step 3 – adding Balloon tooltips to all buttons in our player

Finally, we bind the Balloon widget to each of the button widgets in our player. We will not reproduce the code for each button. However, the format is as follows:

```
balloon.bind(name of widget, 'Description for the balloon')
```

So our Add File button would have a balloon binding as follows:

```
self.balloon.bind(add_filebtn, 'Add New File')
```

We add similar code for each button in *5.07 main-gui.py*.

Before we end this iteration, let us add a title to our player and add a title bar icon as well, as follows:

```
self.root.title('Media Player')
self.root.iconbitmap('../icons/mp.ico')
```

Objective Complete – Mini Debriefing

This completes the iteration. We added Balloon tooltips to our player buttons using PMW Tkinter extension.

Most importantly, we got to know about Tkinter extensions and when to use them.

 When you come across a widget implementation need that is not available as a core widget, try looking for implementations of it in PMW or Tix. If you don't find one that suits your need, search the Internet for some other Tkinter extension.

If you still don't find your desired implementation, try out WCK, which lets you implement all types of custom widgets. However, note that WCK is not under active development for long.

Mission Accomplished

This brings us to the end of this project. Our audio media player is ready!

Let us recap the things that we touched upon in this project.

Some of the topics we covered in this project could be summarized as follows:

- We reinforced a lot of GUI programming techniques that we discussed during previous projects
- We learned how to work with more widgets, such as Listbox, ttk Scale, Progressbar, and Radiobutton
- We got further insight into the power of the Canvas widget
- We saw how to work with external APIs to ease program development
- We got to know about some common Tkinter extensions, such as PMW, WCK, Tix, and others
- We also saw how to refactor code at each stage of development

A Hotshot Challenge

Here are some hotshot challenges on which you can work:

▸ Currently, our code adds each button separately. This makes the program long and adds unnecessary boilerplates. Refactor this code to add all buttons using loops. This should considerably shorten the length of our GUI class, while streamlining the buttons to be handled from a small loop.

▸ Currently, the program keeps record of songs only during a single program run. The songs need to be loaded in subsequent runs. Try to incorporate auto-playlist load based on last run playlist history using object persistence.

▸ Find a Python package that lets you extract useful metadata from your audio files: things such as its author, genre or frequencies, and number of channels. Use these metadata to display more information about the current track in the display console.

▸ Add skinning ability to the player, letting the user select a different skin for the player.

▸ Look out for some network related packages to support streaming of online audio. Incorporate the feature of being able to tune in to online radio stations.

Project 6

Drawing an Application

We are now on to developing our last major Tkinter application. In this project, we will develop a drawing application, making extensive use of the Tkinter Canvas widget while applying everything else that we have learned so far.

Mission Briefing

Our drawing program will enable the user to draw basic shapes such as lines, circles, rectangles, and polygons. It will also let the user draw with the brush tool using different colors that can be chosen from the color palette.

In its final form, our drawing program will look like the following screenshot:

Why Is It Awesome?

While the application itself is rudimentary, it is sufficient to demonstrate some important aspects related to GUI programming.

This project aims to drive home two important lessons. First, we will experience the power of the Canvas widget. Second, we will learn how to develop higher-level custom GUI frameworks for our applications.

As we shall see, custom GUI frameworks enable us to develop programs rapidly with minimal amount of code repetition.

By the end of this project, you should not only be in a position to extend this application to add many more features, but you should also be able to take up and implement GUI projects of increasing complexity.

Your Hotshot Objectives

The key learning objectives for this project can be outlined as follows:

- ▸ Learning to build custom GUI frameworks for rapid application development
- ▸ Writing small unit tests for our code
- ▸ Understanding how to use inheritance in our projects
- ▸ Getting to know of other Tkinter modules, such as `tkColorChooser`
- ▸ Creating and manipulating items on the Canvas widget
- ▸ Working with the tk ComboBox widget
- ▸ Getting to know the available `winfo` methods
- ▸ Working with mouse events on the Canvas widget
- ▸ Reinforcing things that we have learned in previous projects

Mission Checklist

If you have developed the game of chess, you might have installed the **Python Imaging Library** (**PIL**) to render PNG files. This is the only external dependency for our program. If you haven't already done so, download and install PIL from:

`http://www.pythonware.com/products/pil/`

If you are working on windows x64 (64 bit) or MacOSX machine, you may instead need to install and work with Pillow, which is a replacement for PIL available at:

`http://www.lfd.uci.edu/~gohlke/pythonlibs/#pillow`

After you have installed the package, go to your Python interactive prompt and type:

```
>>from PIL import ImageTk
```

If this executes without any error messages, you are ready to make our drawing application.

Developing a bare bone GUI framework

One of the most important lessons aimed in this project is to learn to develop custom GUI frameworks. Tkinter in itself is a GUI framework. However, the kind of framework we intend to build here is a higher-level framework, built on top of Tkinter to suit our custom programming needs.

We will not develop a full-blown framework. Rather, we will develop only a small segment of it to give you a flavor of building a custom framework.

Prepare for Lift Off

So why do we need another framework on top of Tkinter?

Consider a large program which has say 10 different menus, each menu having say 10 menu items. We will have to then write 100 lines of code simply to display these 100 menu items.

You not only need to make each widget by hand, but also have to link each of them manually to other commands besides having to set tons of options for each of them.

If we keep doing this for all our widgets, our GUI programming becomes an exercise in typing. Every extra line of code that you write adds to the program complexity, in a sense that it becomes more difficult for someone else to read, maintain, modify, and/or debug the code.

This is where developing a custom framework comes to our aid. Let's see what it means.

Assume that we anticipate that our drawing program will have a large number of menu items. Now we know how to add menu and menu items. Each new menu item would take at least one line of code to display.

To avoid writing so many lines of code, let's first make a framework to address this.

To ease the process of menu creation, we will write a piece of code that takes menu items listed as a tuple, and converts it to an equivalent menu code.

So given a tuple as follows:

```
menuitems = ('File- &New/Ctrl+N/self.new_file,
                    &Open/Ctrl+O/self.open_file',
             'Edit- Undo/Ctrl+Z/self.undo, Sep',
             'About- About//self.about')
```

should produce the corresponding menu items, where the first item of the string (before dash (-)) represents the menu button, and each subsequent part of string separated by commas represents one menu item, its accelerator key, and the attached command callback. The position of ampersand symbol (&) represents the position of the shortcut key to be underlined.

We also need to take care of adding separators between our menu items. To add a separator, we would add the string Sep at positions where it is required. More precisely, the string Sep must be capitalized.

In short, passing this tuple through our method should produce a GUI, as shown in the following screenshot:

To extend our menu items, all we would need to do is to extend the preceding tuple and simultaneously adding the corresponding command callback method.

Engage Thrusters

Step 1 – creating the GUI framework class

We build our framework in a file named framework.py, where we define a new class named GUIFramework as follows:

```
import Tkinter as tk
class GUIFramework(object):
    menuitems = None
    def __init__(self, root):
        self.root = root
        if self.menuitems is not None:
            self.build_menu()
```

Step 2 – creating menu builder

The two methods of GUIFramework that are used to create menu builder are as follows:

```
def build_menu(self):
        self.menubar = tk.Menu(self.root)
        for v in self.menuitems:
            menu = tk.Menu(self.menubar, tearoff=0)
            label, items = v.split('-')
            items = map(str.strip, items.split(','))
            for item in items:
                self.__add_menu_command(menu, item)
            self.menubar.add_cascade(label=label, menu=menu)
        self.root.config(menu=self.menubar)


    def __add_menu_command(self, menu, item):
        if item == 'Sep':
            menu.add_separator()
        else:
            name, acc, cmd = item.split('/')
            try:
                underline = name.index('&')
                name = name.replace('&', '', 1)
            except ValueError:
                underline = None
            menu.add_command(label=name, underline=underline,

                    accelerator=acc, command=eval(cmd))
```

The description of the code is listed as follows:

- ▶ The method, build_menu, operates on a tuple by the name self.menubar, which must specify all desired menu and menu items in the exact format, as previously discussed.

- ▶ It iterates through each item in the tuple, splitting the item based on - delimiter, building the top-menu button for each item left to the - delimiter.

- ▶ It then splits the second part of the string based on , (comma) delimiter.

- ▶ It then iterates through this second part, creating menu items for each of the parts, adding the accelerator key, command callback, and underline key using another method, __add_menu_command.

▸ The __add_menu_command method iterates through the string and adds a separator if it finds the string Sep. If not, it next searches for ampersand (&) in the string. If it finds one, it calculates its index position and assigns it to the underline variable. It then replaces ampersand value with an empty string, because we do not want to display the ampersand in our menu item.

▸ If ampersand is not found in a string, the code assigns None to the underline variable.

▸ Finally, the code adds command callback, accelerator key, and underline value to the menu item.

 The logic that we used to define the menu builder is a completely arbitrary representation. We could have as well used a dictionary or a list. We could also have a separate logic altogether to represent our menu items, as long as it served the purpose of generating the menu items for us.

Step 3 – testing our new framework

Finally, we add a TestThisFramework class to our file to test if our framework in general and our build_menu method in particular, works as expected.

The code for the TestThisFramework class is as follows(*framework.py*):

```
class TestThisFramework(GUIFramework):
    menuitems = (
        'File- &New/Ctrl+N/self.new_file,
                &Open/Ctrl+O/self.openFile',
        'Edit- Undo/Ctrl+Z/self.undo, Sep',
        'About- About//self.about'
    )
    def new_file(self):
        print 'newfile tested OK'
    def openFile(self):
        print 'openfile tested OK'
    def undo(self):
        print 'undo tested OK'
    def about(self):
        print 'about tested OK'

if __name__ == '__main__':
    root= tk.Tk()
    app = TestThisFramework(root)
    root.mainloop()
```

The description of the code is listed as follows:

- Our `TestThisFramework` class inherits from the `GUIFramework` class, thus being in a position to use the `build_menu` method defined in the parent class.

- It then adds a list of menu items, `menuitems`, and calls the method, `build_menu()`. It is important that the tuple be defined by the name, `menuitems`, because our `build_menu()` method is structured in the parent `GUIFramework` class to build menu only on the tuples named `menuitems`.

- The test class also adds dummy commands to handle command callbacks for each of the menu items.

- Running this test builds menu items as specified in the tuple. Try extending the tuple to add more menu items, and the framework will successfully include those items in the menu.

Like we added code to generate menus for us, we could have added similar code for other widgets that we foresee to be repeatedly used in our program. But we will leave the framework development there itself and proceed to developing our drawing application.

Developing a framework for smaller programs may be overkill, but they are invaluable assets for longer programs. Hopefully, you should now be able to appreciate the benefits of writing your own custom frameworks for larger programs.

Objective Complete – Mini Debriefing

Now that we have our `build_menu` ready, we can extend it to add as many menu items as required without having to write repetitive and similar code for each of them.

This ends our first iteration, where we laid the foundations for our custom GUI framework. We will not extend the framework further, but hopefully, you should now be in a position to extend it for other widgets, if required.

Classified Intel

In this section, you also saw how our `TestThisFramework` class inherited features from our `GUIFramework` class. This is the first time we have used inheritance in our program.

So far, we have always passed objects created as classes as arguments to other classes, and then used them using the . (dot) notation. This is named **composition**.

With inheritance, we do not need to access methods of another class using the dot notation. We can use the methods of a superclass in the subclass as though they belong to the subclass.

Inheritance brings in the advantage of dynamic binding and polymorphism.

Dynamic binding means the method to be invoked is decided at runtime, thus providing greater flexibility to design of our code. Polymorphism implies that variables of a superclass hold a reference to an object created from itself or from any of its subclasses.

Inheritance is fit for situations where the object of the subclass is of the same type as the superclass. In our example, menu items will remain the same whether you define them from the superclass or from the subclass. We, therefore, defined it in our superclass and inherited it in our subclass.

If, however, the object needs to appear or behave differently depending on an object's condition or state, composition is preferable.

Structuring our drawing program

Let's now get down to setting the basic structure for our drawing program. We want to achieve a structure, as shown in the following screenshot:

The structure here primarily consists of a top menu, which inherits from the GUI framework `build_menu` method that we created in the last iteration.

In addition, we create a top-bar frame towards the top(marked in yellow) with a method, `create_top_bar()`, and a toolbar frame to the left (marked with dark grey background) with `create_tool_bar()`. We also create a Canvas widget on the right side using the `create_drawing_canvas()` method, which is to serve as our drawing area.

We will not be reproducing the code for making the frames and canvas area, because we have done similar things in our previous projects and you should be comfortable making them by now. However, you can check the actual code in the file, *6.01.py*.

Engage Thrusters

Step 1 – importing framework

The first thing to note here is that we import our previously created framework module here and inherit its property in our main class, as follows:

```
import framework
class GUI(framework.GUIFramework):
```

This enables us to use the `build_menu` method that we had defined in the framework as though it belongs to the child class.

Step 2: building the top menu

Next, we define the actual menu items to build the top menu in a method defined `create_menu`, as follows:

```
def create_menu(self):
    self.menubar = Menu(self.root)
    self.menuitems = (
                    'File- &New/Ctrl+N/self.new_file,
                        &Open/Ctrl+O/self.open_file,
                    Save/Ctrl+S/self.save,
                    SaveAs//self.save_as,
                    Sep,
                    Exit/Alt+F4/self.close',
                    'Edit- Undo/Ctrl+Z/self.undo, Sep',
                    'About- About//self.about')
    self.build_menu()
    self.root.config(menu=self.menubar)
```

The description of the code is listed as follows:

- ▸ This actually creates three menu buttons: **File**, **Edit**, and **About**, adding menu items to each of them as per preceding provided tuple.

- ▸ Creating the menu also necessitates the creation of their associated command callbacks again, as defined in the preceding tuple. Accordingly, we create the methods associated with these command callbacks.

- ▸ We will not reproduce the code for functionalities, such as `new_file`, `open_file`, `close`, `undo`, and `about`, because we have done similar coding in our previous projects. However, let's take a look at the undo and save operations.

Step 3 – undo operation on the Canvas widget

Recall that the Tkinter text widget has built-in support for unlimited undo/redo functionality. The Canvas widget, however, does not have this built-in feature.

Here, we implement a very basic undo operation, which lets us delete the last drawn item on the canvas as follows:

```
def undo(self, event=None):
    self.canvas.delete(self.currentobject)
```

The description of the code is listed as follows:

- ▸ The Canvas widget provides a `widget.delete(items)` method that deletes a given item from the canvas.

However, once you delete a canvas item, it is gone forever. You cannot restore it unless you have implemented a method which stores all the configurable options for that item before deleting.

While it is possible to implement fully-featured undo/redo operation by storing all configurations for an item being deleted in an undo stack, we will not implement it here, because it would be a deviation from our core topic.

Step 4 – saving canvas objects

Tkinter lets you save canvas objects as a postscript file using the command `postscript()`, as follows (see *code 6.01.py*):

```
def actual_save(self):
    self.canvas.postscript(file=self.filename, colormode='color')
    self.root.title(self.filename)
```

Note, however, that this command does not include the images and embedded widgets on the canvas.

Step 5 – creating buttons in the left tool bar

Having coded command callbacks for all our menu items, let's now create buttons on the left toolbar. As per our original plan, we will need eight buttons on the toolbar. For now, let's show the button text as 0 through 7 as follows:

```
def create_tool_bar_buttons(self):
    for i in range(8):
        self.button = Button(self.toolbar, text=i,
        command=lambda i=i:self.selected_tool_bar_item(i))
        self.button.grid(row=i/2, column=1+i%2, sticky='nsew')
```

This creates eight buttons, arranging them in two columns depending on whether the button number is odd or even.

Step 6 – adding command callback to buttons

All buttons are attached to the same command callback, `selected_tool_bar_item`, which takes the button number as its argument. The callback method will be taken forward in the next iteration. However, for now, let's simply define the callback to print the number of the button that is clicked on, as follows:

```
def selected_tool_bar_item(self, i):
    print'You selected button {}'.format(i)
```

Step 7 – creating color palettes and color selection dialog

Lastly, let's create two color palettes to keep track of two colors named background and foreground color.

Tkinter provides a `tkColorChooser` module that pops up a color chooser dialog. When a user selects a color and clicks the **OK** button, the module returns a tuple of the form:

```
((r,g,b), 'hex color code')
```

The first element of the returned tuple is itself a tuple specifying the RGB coordinates for the given color, while the second element is the hexadecimal color code for the selected color.

The idea here is that clicking on a palette should open a color chooser. When a user selects a given color, it should update the foreground and background color attributes of the object, as shown in the following screenshot:

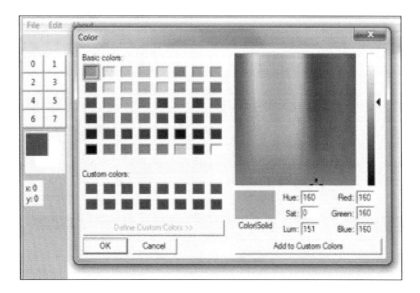

The code to achieve this functionality is as follows(see *code 6.01.py*):

```
from tkColorChooser import askcolor
    def create_color_pallete(self):
            self.colorpallete= Canvas(self.toolbar, height=55,
            width =55)
            self.colorpallete.grid(row=10, column=1, columnspan=2,
                            pady=5, padx=3)
            self.backgroundpallete =
            self.colorpallete.create_rectangle        (15,
            15,48,48,tags="backgroundpallete",
            outline=self.background, fill=self.background)
            self.foregroundpallete =
            self.colorpallete.create_rectangle
            (1,1,33,33,tags="foregroundpallete",
            outline=self.foreground, fill=self.foreground)
            self.colorpallete.tag_bind(self.backgroundpallete,
                        "<Button-1>", self.set_background_color)
            self.colorpallete.tag_bind(self.foregroundpallete,
            "<Button-1>", self.set_foreground_color)
```

The description of the code is listed as follows:

▸ We add two different tags to each of the square pieces, and then use the `tag_bind` command to bind them to the click of mouse button over them. Take a note of the difference between widget-level binding(`widget.bind`) and the item-specific binding using the `tag_bind` method

▸ To create the color palettes, we first create a Canvas widget within the toolbar frame. Within this canvas, we create two square areas using `canvas.create_rectangle` and bind them to a single mouse click event to call `set_background_color` and `set_foreground_color` respectively.

Step 8 – setting color of background and foreground palette

Color of the background and foreground palette can be set as follows:

```
def set_background_color(self, event=None):
    self.background = askcolor()[-1]
    self.colorpallete.itemconfig(self.backgroundpallete,
    outline=self.background, fill=self.background)

def set_foreground_color(self, event=None):
    self.foreground = askcolor()[-1]
    self.colorpallete.itemconfig(self.foregroundpallete,
    outline=self.foreground, fill=self.foreground)
```

Step 9 – displaying x and y coordinates of mouse movement

Finally, we add a static label to our toolbar frame to track the x and y coordinates of mouse movement. The actual tracking function will be created later but let's reserve the space by putting a static label for now, as follows:

```
self.curcoordlabel = Label(self.toolbar, text='x: 0\ny:0')
self.curcoordlabel.grid(row=13, column=1, columnspan=2, pady=5,
                        padx=1, sticky='w')
```

Objective Complete – Mini Debriefing

This completes our second iteration. In this iteration, we set the basic structure for our drawing program.

Importantly, we saw how to inherit features from our previously created framework to create menu items with minimal coding.

We also added the color selection dialog using the `tkColorChooser` module, which sets in two attributes, `self.background` and `self.foreground`, to be used application-wide.

Handling mouse events

Before we let the user draw on the canvas, we need to bind the canvas event to mouse movements and mouse click.

Drawing or adding any item on to the Canvas widget first requires that we know the coordinates of the location where the item is to be placed.

The Canvas widget uses two coordinate systems to track positions:

Window coordinate system: Coordinate as expressed in relation to root window

Canvas coordinate system: Coordinate as expressed as position of item within the canvas

You can convert from window coordinates to canvas coordinates using the `canvasx` and `canvasy` methods as follows:

```
canx = canvas.canvasx(event.x)
cany = canvas.canvasy(event.y)
```

Engage Thrusters

Step 1 – binding mouse down, mouse motion, and mouse release over the canvas

Drawing any item on the canvas would begin when the user clicks the mouse button. The drawing needs to continue till the mouse is moved with the button pressed and up to the time the mouse button is released.

Thus, we need to track the position of initial mouse down event. This is to be followed by tracking the mouse movement while the button is clicked on, up to the final button release event.

Accordingly, we add the following widget binding to our canvas (see *code 6.02.py*):

```
self.canvas.bind("<Button-1>", self.mouse_down)
self.canvas.bind("<Button1-Motion>",
self.mouse_down_motion)
self.canvas.bind("<Button1-ButtonRelease>", self.mouse_up)
```

Step 2 – calculating coordinates of mouse movement

Having bound the mouse click, mouse movement, and mouse release events, it's now time to define their corresponding callback methods.

In particular, we want the mouse_down method to give us the x and y coordinates for the first mouse click event, as follows:

```
def mouse_down(self, event):
    self.currentobject = None
    self.lastx = self.startx =
    self.canvas.canvasx(event.x)
    self.lasty = self.starty =
    self.canvas.canvasy(event.y)
```

We want to keep updating the lastx and lasty coordinates up till the mouse stops moving, as follows:

```
def mouse_down_motion(self, event):
    self.lastx = self.canvas.canvasx(event.x)
    self.lasty = self.canvas.canvasy(event.y)
```

Our mouse_up method should make the final update to our lastx and lasty coordinates, as follows:

```
def mouse_up(self, event):
    self.lastx = self.canvas.canvasx(event.x)
    self.lasty = self.canvas.canvasy(event.y)
```

The description of the code is listed as follows:

- ▸ The mouse_down method simply initializes the values of startx, starty, lastx, and lasty to the coordinates of the mouse click position.

- ▸ The mouse_down_motion method changes the value of lastx and lasty as the mouse motion keeps happening.

- ▸ Finally, the mouse_up method sets the value of lastx and lasty as coordinates of the point where the mouse button is released.

- ▸ Thus, using the three events: mouse_down, mouse_down_motion, and mouse_up, we manage to get the coordinates for starting point, coordinates for points through which the mouse pointer traverses, and the coordinates for the end point.

- ▸ Now we can use these values to place any item on the canvas at the given coordinates.

Step 3 – updating the current mouse position label in the left tool bar

In addition, we would also like to track the motion of the mouse over the canvas, even when the mouse button is not clicked down. We need to track this to update the current mouse position in the left toolbar. This is simple, as shown in the following code snippet:

```
self.canvas.bind("<Motion>", self.show_current_coordinates)

def show_current_coordinates(self, event = None):
    lx = self.canvas.canvasx(event.x)
    ly = self.canvas.canvasy(event.y)
    cord = 'x: %d \ny: %d '%(lx, ly)
    self.curcoordlabel.config(text = cord)
```

This code will ensure that any mouse movement over the canvas updates the label in the left toolbar with the current position of mouse.

Objective Complete – Mini Debriefing

Now our Canvas widget has become responsive to mouse movements and mouse clicks. Every time we click the mouse button over the canvas and drag the mouse pointer to a new place, the values of startx, starty, lastx and lasty get updated to reflect the coordinates for the mouse movement.

Together, these coordinates constitute what is called the bounding box for an item. In fact, if there are items on a canvas, you can retrieve the coordinates for any given item using the API:

```
canvas.bbox(item=itemName)
```

This returns the coordinates as a four-item tuple.

If the item name is not specified, this method returns the bounding box for all elements on the canvas.

Now that we have the coordinates available, we can think of drawing items on the canvas. We do some drawing in the next iteration.

Drawing items on the canvas

Let's now draw some items on the canvas. The Canvas widget natively supports drawing the following items:

Item	Code for adding the item
Arc	`w.create_arc( bbox, **options)`
Bitmap	`w.create_bitmap( bbox, **options)`
Image	`w.create_image( bbox, **options)`
Line	`w.create_line( bbox, **options)`
Oval	`w.create_oval( bbox, **options)`
Polygon	`w.create_ploygon( bbox, **options)`
Rectangle	`w.create_rectangle( bbox, **options)`
Text	`w.create_text( bbox, **options)`
Window	`w.create_window( bbox, **options)`

Let us add the ability to draw lines, rectangles, and ovals to our drawing program. We will also add a brush stroke feature to our program, as shown in the following screenshot:

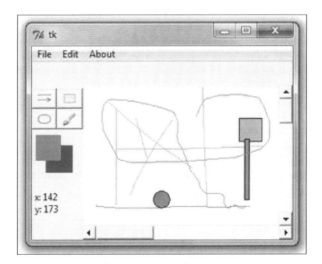

Engage Thrusters

Step 1 – creating a tuple of methods

We first create a tuple of methods that we intend to define here as follows:

```
all_toolbar_functions = ('draw_line', 'draw_rectangle',
'draw_oval', 'draw_brush')
```

Doing so ensures that we do not have to call each method explicitly from our code. We can instead use the index of the tuple to retrieve the method name and call it dynamically using:

```
getattr(self, self.all_toolbar_functions[index])
```

This makes sense here, because we would eventually add more features to our drawing program by simply extending our `all_toolbar_functions`.

Step 2 – add icons to our toolbar buttons

Our next task here is to add icons on the left toolbar for drawing these items.

We add the icons to our `icons` folder. We also ensure to rename each icon file to the name of the method called by it. This naming again helps in calling the methods dynamically, and this style of programming is what you could call programming using **conventions over configuration**.

Our current `create_tool_bar_buttons()` method creates eight buttons using a for loop. However, we will now modify our `create_tool_bar_buttons()` method to use the `enumerate()` method to loop overall items in our `all_toolbar_functions` tuple to add icons for each of the methods, as follows (see *code 6.03.py*):

```
def create_tool_bar_buttons(self):
    for i, item in enumerate(self.all_toolbar_functions):
        tbicon = PhotoImage(file='icons/'+item+'.gif')
        self.button = Button(self.toolbar, image=tbicon,
        command=lambda i=i:self.selected_tool_bar_item(i))
        self.button.grid(row=i/2, column=1+i%2, sticky='nsew')
        self.button.image = tbicon
```

Step 3 – keeping a tab on currently selected button

Next, we modify the method, `selected_tool_bar_item(i)`; the only purpose of which is to keep a tab on the currently selected button. Having this information, we can later call the associated method from `all_toolbar_functions` by using this index, as follows (see *code 6.03.py*):

```
def selected_tool_bar_item(self, i):
    self.selected_toolbar_func_index = i
```

Step 4 – code for drawing line, rectangle, and oval shapes

Now is the time to code the methods to draw these basic shapes. Note that this will not automatically create the drawings. Eventually, these methods will have to be called from somewhere to actually make the drawings. We will do that in step 6.

```
def draw_line(self, x, y, x2, y2):
    self.currentobject = self.canvas.create_line(x, y, x2, y2, fill=
            self.foreground )

def draw_rectangle(self, x, y, x2, y2):
    self.currentobject = self.canvas.create_rectangle(x, y, x2,
            y2, fill= self.foreground)
def draw_oval(self, x, y, x2, y2):
    self.currentobject=  self.canvas.create_oval(x, y, x2,
            y2, fill= self.foreground)
```

Step 5 – code for drawing in continuous stroke

Drawing in a continuous stroke is similar to drawing lines, but the fresh lines are redrawn after every small change in coordinates. In the current state of things, the value of `lastx` and `lasty` are only updated when the mouse button is released. But here we need to update the value of `lastx` and `lasty`, not on mouse release, but on mouse motion. To achieve this, we bind the mouse motion to a newly defined method `draw_brush_update_xy`, which updates the x and y coordinate in every subsequent loop turn.

Earlier, we had bound mouse down motion to another method named `mouse_down_motion`. For drawing continuous stroke, we will now bind it to a method named `draw_brush_update_xy`.

> Adding an event binding to more than one method wipes away the previous binding, whereby the new binding replaces any existing binding. Thus, when you exit out of the `draw_brush` loop, you need to rebind the event back to the `mouse_down_motion` method.
>
> Alternatively, you can use `add="+"` as an additional argument to keep more than one binding to the same event as follows:
> ```
> mywidget.bind("<SomeEvent>", method1, add="+")
> mywidget.bind("<SameEvent>", method2, add="+")
> ```

Thus, we create a loop where the `draw_brush` method calls another method, `draw_brush_update_xy`, on successive mouse motions to update the x and y coordinates as follows (see *code 6.03.py*):

```
def draw_brush(self, x, y, x2, y2):
    if not self.all_toolbar_functions[
    self.selected_toolbar_func_index] == 'draw_brush':
```

```
                  self.canvas.bind("<Button1-Motion>",
                       self.mouse_down_motion)
                  return# if condition to break out of draw_brush loop
              self.currentobject =
              self.canvas.create_line(x,y,x2,y2,fill=self.foreground)

        self.canvas.bind("<B1-Motion>", self.draw_brush_update_xy)

        def draw_brush_update_xy(self, event):
            self.startx, self.starty = self.lastx, self.lasty
            self.lastx, self.lasty = event.x, event.y
            self.draw_brush(self.startx, self.starty,self.lastx,
            self.lasty)
```

If the Draw Brush button is unselected, we break out of the loop and rebind the mouse motion back to the canvas `mouse_down_motion`.

Step 6 – executing code dynamically

We have planned to execute methods dynamically, based on index from the names of methods given in a tuple named `all_toolbar_functions`. However, the names are stored as strings, and we just cannot take a piece of string and expect Python to evaluate it. In order to that, we will use Python's built-in `getattr()` method.

We now define a method that takes a string and makes it suitable for execution as a method, as follows:

```
        def execute_method():
            fnc = getattr(self, self.all_toolbar_functions
            [self.selected_toolbar_func_index])
            fnc(self.startx, self.starty,self.lastx, self.lasty)
```

Step 7 – doing the actual drawing

Having defined methods to draw line, rectangle, oval, and brush strokes, we need to call them from somewhere for the drawing to happen. Intuitively, the drawings must begin on the first mouse down movement and the drawing must be deleted and redrawn up till the mouse button release.

Accordingly, these methods must be called from our `mouse_down_motion` method. We, therefore, modify our `mouse_down_motion` and `mouse_up` methods to do this, as follows:

```
        def mouse_down_motion(self, event):
            self.lastx = self.canvas.canvasx(event.x)
            self.lasty = self.canvas.canvasy(event.y)
            if self.selected_toolbar_func_index:
                    self.canvas.delete(self.currentobject)
                    self.execute_method()
```

```
def mouse_up(self, event):
    self.lastx = self.canvas.canvasx(event.x)
    self.lasty = self.canvas.canvasy(event.y)
    self.canvas.delete(self.currentobject)
    self.currentobject = None
    self.execute_method()
```

Objective Complete – Mini Debriefing

This completes our objective for the iteration.

We began by creating a tuple of method names so as to be able to call a method dynamically by specifying its index in the tuple.

We then added icons for our toolbar buttons. We then associated a button click to a method that keeps tab on currently selected button by assigning its index to the variable, `self.selected_toolbar_func_index`. We then defined methods to draw line, rectangle, and oval shapes on our canvas. We also showed how to utilize the ability to draw lines to draw in continuous strokes.

Finally, we called all the draw methods from `mouse_down_motion` and `mouse_release` method to do the actual drawing.

A user can now draw basic shapes, such as lines, rectangles, ovals, and brush strokes on to the canvas. The shapes are drawn in the currently set foreground color.

Setting the options toolbar at the top

Although our program can draw basic shapes, these shapes are currently filled with the foreground color and the outline of the shape is done in black.

The Canvas widget lets you specify the fill color, outline color, and border width for most of the shapes as its configurable options.

In addition to these, the Canvas widget also has several other configurable options for many of these basic shapes. For instance, for a line, you can specify if it will have an arrow head shape at the end or if it will be dashed.

Let's accordingly modify our program to allow the user to select configurable options for each of the four basic shapes, as shown in the following screenshot:

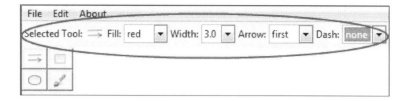

Engage Thrusters

Step 1 – showing the selected button icon at the top

Let's start with a simple thing first. When a user clicks on a button in the left toolbar, the top frame should display the text **Selected Tool:** followed by the icon representation for the selected button.

Because this event must occur on click of any button, we modify our `selected_tool_bar_item` method to include a call to two methods, as highlighted in the following code (see *code 6.04.py*):

```
def selected_tool_bar_item(self, i):
    self.selected_toolbar_func_index = i
    self.remove_options_from_topbar()
    self.show_selected_tool_icon_in_topbar()

def remove_options_from_topbar(self):
    for child in self.topbar.winfo_children():
        child.destroy()

def show_selected_tool_icon_in_topbar(self):
    Label(self.topbar,text='Selected Tool:').pack(side=LEFT)
    photo = PhotoImage(file='icons/'+
    'self.all_toolbar_functions[self.selected_toolbar_func_index]+
    '.gif')
    label = Label(self.topbar, image=photo)
    label.image = photo
    label.pack(side=LEFT)
```

The description of the code is listed as follows:

> ▸ The `remove_options_from_topbar` method ensures that when a new button is clicked, options for the previous button are deleted. The `show_selected_tool_icon_in_topbar` method actually displays the icon for the currently selected button.

`widget.winfo_children()` returns a list of all children for a given widget, in their stacking order from bottom to top.

You can extract a lot of window-related information using one of the many `winfo` methods. For a complete list of the `winfo` methods, refer to the *The basic widget methods* section in *Appendix B, Quick Reference Sheets*.

Alternatively, each widget has also its own children attribute, which is a dictionary where the keys are the IDs and the values are the widgets. So if the order is not relevant, this is the same as `widget.children.values()`.

Step 2 – adding the Combobox widget to let user select different fill options

Next, we need to define the selection combobox for a user to select options for fill, outline, width, arrow, and dash. We will use ttk Combobox to allow the user to make a selection, and as such, we import it into our current file, as follows:

```
import ttk
```

We will not reproduce the entire code here. However, for each of the preceding options, we define two methods: one that displays the combobox and the other sets the value of the current selection made by the user.

Thus, we set the following two definitions for fill option, as follows (see *code 6.04.py*):

```
def fill_options_combobox(self):
    Label(self.topbar,text='Fill:').pack(side=LEFT)
    self.fillcmbobx = ttk.Combobox(self.topbar,
            state='readonly', width=5)
    self.fillcmbobx.pack(side=LEFT)
    self.fillcmbobx['values'] = ('none', 'fg', 'bg', 'black',
    'white' )
    self.fillcmbobx.bind('<<ComboboxSelected>>',  self.set_fill)
    self.fillcmbobx.set(self.fill)

def set_fill(self, event=None):
    fl = self.fillcmbobx.get()
    if fl == 'none': self.fill = '' #transparent
    elif fl == 'fg': self.fill = self.foreground
    elif fl == 'bg': self.fill = self.background
    else: self.fill = fl
```

We similarly define other pair of methods for each of the sets, namely (see *code 6.04.py*):

- ❑ outline_options_combobox:set_outline
- ❑ width_options_combobox:set_width
- ❑ arrow_options_combobox:set_arrow
- ❑ dash_options_combobox:set_dash

Step 3 – modifying draw methods to add configurable options

Now that we have ways to set different values for fill, outline, arrow, and dash configurable options, let's modify our drawing code to include these in the actual drawing, as follows (see *code 6.04.py*):

```
def draw_line(self, x, y, x2, y2):
    self.currentobject = self.canvas.create_line(x, y, x2, y2,
          fill= self.fill, arrow=self.arrow, width=self.width,
    dash=self.dash )

def draw_rectangle(self, x, y, x2, y2):
    self.currentobject = self.canvas.create_rectangle(x, y,x2,
    y2, outline=self.outline, fill=self.fill,
    width=self.width)

def draw_oval(self, x, y, x2, y2):
    self.currentobject=  self.canvas.create_oval(x, y, x2,
    y2, outline=self.outline, fill=self.fill,
    width=self.width)

def draw_brush(self, x, y, x2, y2):
    if not self.all_toolbar_functions[
    self.selected_toolbar_func_index]=='draw_brush':
          self.canvas.bind("<Button1-Motion>",
    self.mouse_down_motion)
          return
    self.currentobject = self.canvas.create_line(x,y,x2,y2,
    fill=self.fill, width=self.width)

self.canvas.bind("<B1-Motion>", self.draw_brush_update_xy)
```

Having defined all these methods, it is now time to call them from somewhere.

While the fill combobox would be applicable to all the four basic shapes, the arrow option would only be applicable to drawing lines. Because there will be a different set of comboboxes for different selections, we define the following methods (see *code 6.04.py*):

```python
def draw_line_options(self):
    self.fill_options_combobox()
    self.width_options_combobox()
    self.arrow_options_combobox()
    self.dash_options_combobox()

def draw_rectangle_options(self):
    self.fill_options_combobox()
    self.outline_options_combobox()
    self.width_options_combobox()

def draw_oval_options(self):
    self.fill_options_combobox()
    self.outline_options_combobox()
    self.width_options_combobox()

def draw_brush_options(self):
    self.fill_options_combobox()
    self.width_options_combobox()
```

Finally, these methods have to be called from somewhere, depending on the selection made. So we modify our `selected_tool_bar_item` method to call a method dynamically, named by appending the string `_options` to the name of selected method as follows (see *code 6.04.py*):

```python
def selected_tool_bar_item(self, i):
    self.selected_toolbar_func_index = i
    self.remove_options_from_topbar()
    self.show_selected_tool_icon_in_topbar()
    opt = self.all_toolbar_functions[ self.selected_toolbar_func_
    index] +'_options'
    fnc = getattr(self, opt)
    fnc()
```

Objective Complete – Mini Debriefing

The program user can now select from the various options provided for each of the toolbar buttons (see *code 6.04.py*).

More importantly, we saw some of the configuration options available for items drawn on the Tkinter Canvas widget. We were also introduced to the `winfo` methods. These methods can be used to extract a lot of data about a widget and are a useful tool to have when programming a GUI application in Tkinter.

Adding some more features

Next in line, let's add a few more features to our drawing program. In particular, we will add the ability to delete objects from the canvas, add a paint bucket, the ability to move items up and down the stack, and the ability to drag items on the canvas, as shown in the following screenshot:

Engage Thrusters

Step 1 – extending our methods tuple

As a first thing, let us extend our `all_toolbar_functions` method to make provisions for the new methods that we will define here, as follows (see *code 6.05.py*):

```
all_toolbar_functions = ('draw_line', 'draw_rectangle',
'draw_oval', 'draw_brush',
'delete_object', 'fill_object',
'move_to_top', 'drag_item')
```

As usual, we have added icons to the `icon` folder by the same name as the method that would handle it. The buttons are automatically displayed in our left toolbar merely by adding new methods to this tuple and by adding corresponding icons to our `icon` folder because of the way we have designed the `create_tool_bar_buttons` method.

Step 2 – targeting a given item on the canvas

Before define the methods for handling the new features, let's pause and think about the kind of work we need to do here.

The operations that we want to do now are slightly different from their predecessors. Earlier, we were creating items on the canvas. Now we have to target items already present on the canvas.

The items that need to be targeted are the ones on which the user clicks on with his or her mouse.

We, therefore, need to identify the item on which mouse has been clicked before we can do any modification to the item itself. To do that, we modify our mouse_down method as follows (see *code 6.05.py*):

```
def mouse_down(self, event):
    self.currentobject = None
    self.lastx = self.startx = self.canvas.canvasx(event.x)
    self.lasty = self.starty = self.canvas.canvasy(event.y)
    if self.all_toolbar_functions[
                self.selected_toolbar_func_index]
    in ['fill_object', 'delete_object', 'move_to_top',
    drag_item']:
            try:
                self.selected_object =
                self.canvas.find_closest(self.startx,
                self.starty)[0]
            except:
                self.selected_object = self.canvas
```

The description of the code is listed as follows:

  ▸ This small modification to the mouse_down method means that if any of the last four buttons are clicked, the code locates the item located closest to the click position and assigns it to our newly defined attribute, selected_object, which stands for the current selected object.

  ▸ If there are no items on the canvas, the entire canvas is set to the selected_object attribute.

> The canvas method has a method named: `find_closest(x, y, halo=None, start=None)`.
>
> It returns the identifier for item closest to the given position on the canvas. This means that if there is only one item on the canvas, it will be selected regardless of how near or how far you click from it.
>
> If on the other hand, you want that objects only within a certain distance are selected, the Canvas widget provides an alternate implementation named `find_overlapping`.
>
> You will, however, have to place a small rectangle centered on the position to use this.

Now that we have a hold on the item to be manipulated, we can proceed to do whatever we want to do with the item.

Step 3 – deleting items from the canvas

The first method to delete items from canvas is `delete_object`, which simply deletes the selected item. So our `delete_object` method is defined as follows (see *code 6.05.py*):

```
def delete_object(self, x0, y0, x1, y1):
    self.canvas.delete(self.selected_object)
```

And, because our earlier code needed that for every method for which we define an options method, we define the method, `delete_object_options`, here. However, because we do not want to display anything in the option bar at the top, we simply ignore it with a pass statement, as follows:

```
def delete_object_options(self):
    pass
```

Step 4 – paint bucket feature

Next, we code our `fill_object` method, which acts somewhat like a paint bucket in common drawing programs.

This again is simple. You simply need to fill the color on the background of the selected item. If there is no item on the canvas, it simply fills the color on to the entire canvas, as follows:

```
def fill_object(self,x0,y0,x1,y1):
    if self.selected_object == self.canvas:
            self.canvas.config(bg=self.fill)
    else:
            self.canvas.itemconfig(self.selected_object,
            fill=self.fill)
```

And here, we want to let the user choose the fill color for the paint bucket. Hence, we call our previously defined method, `fill_options_combobox`, from within our `fill_object_options` method.

```
def fill_object_options(self):
    self.fill_options_combobox()
```

Step 5 – moving items on top of each other

Let's now define the methods for the next button. The button marked with a small hand icon can be used to raise items on top of others.

When you draw multiple items on the canvas, the items are placed in a stack. By default, new items get added on top of items previously drawn on the canvas. You can, however, change the stacking order using: `canvas.tag_raise(item)`.

If multiple items match, they are all moved, with their relative order preserved.

However, this method will not change the stacking order for any new window item that you draw within the canvas.

Then there are `find_above` and `find_below` methods that you can use to find items above or below an item in the canvas stacking order.

In addition, there is a `find_all` method that returns a tuple containing identifiers for all items on the canvas.

Accordingly, the code for moving items to the top of stack is as follows (see *code 6.05.py*):

```
def move_to_top(self,x0,y0,x1,y1):
    self.canvas.tag_raise(self.selected_object)
def move_to_top_options(self):
    pass # no items to display on the top bar
```

Step 6 – dragging items on the canvas

Finally, let's add drag-and-drop feature for items on the canvas. The ability to drag an item on the canvas requires that after selection of the object to be dragged, we recalculate the x and y coordinates for mouse movement, and move the object to the new coordinates provided by the mouse movement at small intervals.

In many ways the concept here is similar to one that we used for defining our paint brush.

The idea is to call our `drag_items` method after every small mouse movement using another method, `drag_item_update_xy`, which recalculates x and y coordinates after small mouse motion, moving the item to the newly calculated coordinates every time.

Then, we have a condition check, which breaks out of this loop if any other button is selected from the toolbar, as follows (see *code 6.05.py*):

```
def drag_item(self,x0,y0,x1,y1):
    if not self.all_toolbar_functions[
    self.selected_toolbar_func_index] == 'drag_item':
            self.canvas.bind("<Button1-Motion>",
                        self.mouse_down_motion)
            return # break out of loop
    self.currentobject = self.canvas.move(
                self.selected_object, x1-x0, y1- y0)
    self.canvas.bind("<B1-Motion>", self.drag_item_update_xy)

def drag_item_update_xy(self, event):
    self.startx, self.starty = self.lastx, self.lasty
    self.lastx, self.lasty = event.x, event.y
    self.drag_item(self.startx, self.starty,self.lastx,
    self.lasty)

def drag_item_options(self):
    pass # we want no options to be displayed at the top
```

 The Canvas widget provides a method: `canvas.move(item, dx, dy)`. The preceding method moves any matching item by a horizontal and vertical offset (`dx` and `dy`).

Objective Complete – Mini Debriefing

This brings us to the end of this iteration. We have now successfully added four new features to our drawing program, namely: `delete_object`, `fill_object`, `move_to_top`, and `drag_item`.

In the process, we saw some of the methods provided by the Canvas widget for item manipulation. We also saw the strategy that one might adopt when working on existing items on the Canvas widget.

Classified Intel

In this program, we extensively used the item identifier ID to target a particular item on the canvas. Recall that item identifier is the unique integer ID returned by the canvas method that creates the object.

So, for instance, when you create an oval item on your canvas, it returns an integer ID after creating the object. This is referred to its item identifier or the item handle, as follows:

```
my_item_identifier = self.canvas.create_oval(x, y, x2, y2)
```

Now you can act upon this oval using the handle, my_item_identifier.

However, this is not the only method by which you can identify an item on the canvas. Additionally, you can add tags to items, and then use these tags to identify the object for manipulation.

Working with item tags

Let's now look at some of the common operations involved in working with Canvas tags.

Adding a tag

To add a tag to an item, you specify the tag (which is a string) as its configurable option either at the time of creating the object or later using the itemconfig method, or add them using the addtag_withtag method, as follows:

```
rectid = canvas.create_rectangle(10, 10, 50, 50, tags="myshiny")
canvas.itemconfig(rectid, tags="shiv")
canvas.addtag_withtag("shiv", "takeonemore")
```

The same tag can be applied to more than one item on the canvas.

You can add multiple tags to an item together by passing in the tags as a tuple of strings, as follows:

```
canvas.itemconfig(rectid, tags=("tagA", "tagB"))
```

 Using tags to identify items to be manipulated is especially useful when you need to manipulate more than one item at one time, or if you want to manipulate items based on certain conditionals.

Retrieving tags

To get all tags associated with a specific item handle, use gettags as follows:

```
printcanvas.gettags(rectid)
```

This returns a tuple of all tags associated with that item handle, as follows:

```
("myshiny", "shiv", "takeonemore", "tagA", "tagB")
```

Getting items with a given tag

To get the item handles for all items having a given tag, use `find_withtag` as follows:

```
print canvas.find_withtag("shiv")
```

This returns the item handles for all items as a tuple.

Built-in tags

The canvas widget provides two built-in tags:

 ▸ ALL or all: It matches all items on the canvas
 ▸ CURRENT or current: It returns the item under the mouse pointer, if any

Mission Accomplished

There you have your own drawing program! You can easily extend it to add many more features.

Here's a quick summary of things we have seen in this project:

 ▸ Building custom GUI frameworks for rapid application development
 ▸ Understanding how to use inheritance in our projects
 ▸ Getting to know the `tkColoChooser` module
 ▸ Learning to create and manipulate items on the Canvas widget
 ▸ Working with the tk ComboBox widget
 ▸ Getting to know the available `winfo` methods
 ▸ Working with mouse events on the Canvas widget
 ▸ Reinforcing things that we have learned in previous projects

A Hotshot Challenge

Add the following features to your drawing program:

- ▸ The accelerator keys don't work for our menu items because we have not bound them to key events. Bind the menu-item accelerator keys to their associated command callback.

- ▸ Create an Eraser button and add its associated features.

- ▸ We have not implemented drawing of some other basic shapes, such as arc and polygons, even though the Canvas widget provides for methods to draw them. Add the ability to draw arcs and polygons to the drawing program.

- ▸ Create a new toolbar on the right side. Utilizing the stacking order for canvas items, display each item as a separate layer in the toolbar.

- ▸ Go through all the available Canvas widget options in your IDE by using Python's interactive help feature. Try adding more features to the program utilizing one or more of the options.

- ▸ We have already included the ability to add images to our program by navigating to **File | Open**. Add a few menu items to manipulate those images. Using some imaging library, add image manipulation features, such as color adjustment, brightness, contrast, grayscale, and other facilities for image manipulation provided by the imaging library that you choose to use.

- ▸ The Canvas widget is often used to draw custom widgets. Make a Progress Meter widget using the Canvas widget. Attach it to some function and run it to see that the oval should get filled with some color as the function progresses. You can use the fill option of the Canvas widget to show increase in progress.

Project 7

Some Fun Project Ideas

In the previous projects, we have explored most of the important features of Tkinter. Developing new projects is now about extending what we have learned so far. In this project, we will build several partly-functional applications that you can take forward.

Mission Briefing

In this project, we will develop "bare bone structures" for several applications from different domains. The applications we will build here include:

- ▶ Screen saver
- ▶ Snake game
- ▶ Weather Reporter
- ▶ Phonebook application
- ▶ Graphing with Tkinter

Why Is It Awesome?

You will find this project useful as we will delve further in to learning about the power of Tkinter **Canvas** widget, and develop some basic animations for our screen saver program.

When developing the Snake game, we will learn to develop a multithreaded Python application efficiently using the **Queue implementation**. As you will see, this is a handy tool to have when working on multithreaded applications.

The Weather Reporter application will introduce you to the basics of network programming. You will learn how to mine into the seemingly infinite resource that is available to us over the Internet.

The phonebook application will show you how to work with databases. This is vital for developing any large-scale application where persistence is required.

Finally, we look at basic graphing abilities of Tkinter. We also look at ways of embedding matplotlib graphs in Tkinter.

Your Hotshot Objectives

The key objectives outlined for this project include developing and understanding the followings:

▸ Basic animations with Tkinter canvas

▸ Queue implementation for a multithreaded Tkinter application

▸ Network programming and tapping into resources over the Internet

▸ Working with data interchange formats like JSON and XML

▸ Database programming and basic CRUD operations on a database

▸ Graphing with Tkinter

Building a screen saver

We will start by building a screen saver for our desktop. The screen saver will consist of several random-colored and random-sized balls bouncing all over the screen at random velocity, as shown in the following screenshot:

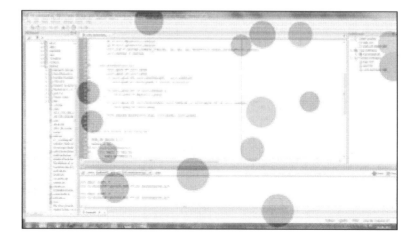

Engage Thrusters

Carry out the following steps to create the screen saver:

1. Let's create a class to generate balls with random attributes. Accordingly, we define a new class named `RandomBall` to achieve this (refer to the `7.01 screensaver.py` Python file, available in the code bundle):

```python
from random import randint
class RandomBall:
    def __init__(self, canvas, scrnwidth, scrnheight):
        self.canvas = canvas
        self.xpos = randint(10, int(scrnwidth))
        self.ypos = randint(10, int(scrnheight))
        self.xvelocity = randint(6,12)
        self.yvelocity = randint(6,12)
        self.scrnwidth = scrnwidth
        self.scrnheight = scrnheight
        self.radius = randint(40,70)
        r = lambda: randint(0,255)
        self.color = '#%02x%02x%02x' % (r(),r(),r())
```

The description of the code is as follows:

- The `__init__` method takes three arguments, an instance of the Canvas widget, the screen width and the screen height. It then initializes the initial *x* and *y* positions for a ball as random numbers, starting from 0 up to the maximum screen coordinates.

- It also initializes the velocity of the ball in *x* and *y* directions, the radius and color of the ball changes in a random fashion.

- Because the hexadecimal color coding system uses two hexadecimal digits for each of red, green and blue colors, there are 16^2 (256) possibilities for each color. We therefore create a lambda function that generates a random number from 0-255, and use this function to generate three random numbers. We convert this decimal number to its two-digit equivalent hexadecimal notation using the format %02x to generate a random color for the balls.

2. The second method creates the actual ball using the canvas `create_oval` method (refer to the `7.01 screensaver.py` Python file available in the code bundle):

```python
def create_ball(self):
    x1 = self.xpos-self.radius
    y1 = self.ypos-self.radius
```

```
        x2 = self.xpos+self.radius
        y2 = self.ypos+self.radius
        self.itm = canvas.create_oval(x1, y1, x2, y2,
        fill=self.color, outline=self.color)
```

3. Let's now code the method to handle ball movement on the screen.

    The method also checks if the ball has reached the end of the screen on any of the sides. If the ball has actually reached the end of the screen, it simply changes the direction by appending a negative sign to the velocity of the ball.

    The method finally moves the ball using the `canvas.move` method (refer to `7.01 screensaver.py`):

```
def move_ball(self):
    self.xpos += self.xvelocity
    self.ypos += self.yvelocity
    #Check if the Direction of ball movement is to be
    changed
    if self.ypos>= self.scrnheight - self.radius:
        self.yvelocity = - self.yvelocity # change
        direction
    if self.ypos<= self.radius :
        self.yvelocity = abs(self.yvelocity)
    if self.xpos>= self.scrnwidth- self.radius or
    self.xpos<= self.radius:
        self.xvelocity = -self.xvelocity # change
        direction
    self.canvas.move(self.itm, self.xvelocity,
    self.yvelocity)
```

    That is all to our `RandomBall` class. We can use this class to create as many ball objects as we want to display in our screen saver.

4. Now, that we have coded methods to generate balls and to move them, let's create our screen saver. We now create a class named `ScreenSaver` that will show the actual screen saver:

```
class ScreenSaver:
balls = []

def __init__(self, num_balls):
    self.root = Tk()
    w, h = self.root.winfo_screenwidth(),
    self.root.winfo_screenheight()
```

```
self.root.overrideredirect(1)
self.root.geometry("%dx%d+0+0" % (w, h))
self.root.attributes('-alpha', 0.3)
self.root.bind('<Any-KeyPress>', quit)
self.root.bind('<Any-Button>', quit)
self.root.bind('<Motion>', quit)
self.canvas = Canvas(self.root, width=w, height=h)
self.canvas.pack()
for i in range(num_balls):
    ball = RandomBall(self.canvas, scrnwidth=w,
      scrnheight=h)
    ball.create_ball()
    self.balls.append(ball)
self.run_screen_saver()
self.root.mainloop()
```

The description of the code is as follows:

- ❏ The __init__ method of the `ScreenSaver` class takes the number of balls (`num_balls`) as its argument.

- ❏ We then create a root window and calculate the height and width of the screen using the `winfo` method.

- ❏ We use `root.overrideredirect(1)` to remove the enclosing frame from the parent window.

- ❏ We then specify the geometry of the parent window to fill the entire screen.

- ❏ We make the parent window transparent using `root.attributes('-alpha', 0.3)`. We add a transparency of `0.3` to make the window translucent.

- ❏ We then bind the root to call our `quit` command on the event of clicking the mouse button, pressing any keyboard button, or mouse motion. This is to ensure that our program behaves like a screen saver, exiting on any interactions from the user's end.

- ❏ We then create a canvas to cover the entire screen with `Canvas(self.root, width=w, height=h)`.

- ❏ We create several random ball objects outs of the `RandomBall` class, passing along the Canvas widget instance, the width, and the height of the screen as its arguments.

- ❏ We finally make a call to run the screen saver with the `run_screen_saver()` method within the `ScreenSaver` class, which is discussed in the following.

5. In this step, we will run the `ScreenSaver` class:

```
def run_screensaver():
    for ball in balls:
        ball.move_ball()
    canvas.after(20, runScreenSaver)
```

The description of the code is as follows:

- The `run_screensaver()` method simply moves each ball by calling itself at a regular interval of 20 milliseconds

- We also define the `quit` method in our `ScreenSaver` class to quit from the main loop and exit the program:

```
def quit(event):
    root.destroy()
```

- To run the screen saver, we instantiate an object from our `ScreenSaver` class, passing the number of balls as its argument:

```
if __name__ == "__main__":
    ScreenSaver(18)   ##18 is the number of balls
```

We have used two Toplevel window methods `root.overrideredirect` and `root.attributes`, in the previous code.

For a complete list of methods that can be applied to the Toplevel window, refer to the *The Toplevel window methods* section in *Appendix B, Quick Reference Sheets*.

Objective Complete – Mini Debriefing

Our screen saver is ready!

In fact, if you are working on a Windows platform, and when you learn to create an executable program from Python programs (discussed in *Appendix A, Miscellaneous Tips*), you can create an executable file with `.exe` extension for this screen saver. So then, you can change its extension from `.exe` to `.scr` and right-click, and select **Install** to add it to your list of screensavers!

Building a Snake game

Let's now build a simple Snake game. As usual, we will be making use of the Canvas widget to provide the platform for our Snake program.

We will use `canvas.create_line` to draw our snake, and `canvas.create_rectangle` to draw the snake-food.

Prepare for Lift Off

One of the primary objectives for this project is to introduce the Queue implementation in Python as we used it in conjunction with the **threading** module.

So far, we have built single-threaded applications. However, threading can be difficult to handle when there is more than one thread in an application, and these threads need to share attributes or resources among them. In this case, you cannot predict the thread execution order at all. OS does it very randomly and swiftly each time.

To handle this complexity, threading module provides some synchronization tools, such as locks, join, semaphores, events, and condition variables. However, it is—in most cases—safer and simpler to use queues. Simply put, a **queue** is a compound memory structure that is thread-safe; queues effectively channel access to a resource to multiple threads in a sequential order, and are a recommended design pattern that uses threads for most of the scenarios that require concurrency.

The **Queue** module provides a way to implement different kinds of queuing, such as **FIFO** (default implementation), **LIFO** queue, and **Priority** queue, and this module comes with a built-in implementation of all locking semantics required for running multithreaded programs.

 More information about the Queue module can be found in the following link:
`http://docs.Python.org/2/library/queue.html`

Here's a quick roundup of the basic usage of the Queue module:

```
myqueue = Queue() #create empty queue
myqueue.put(data)# put items into queue
task = myqueue.get () #get the next item in the queue
myqueue.task_done() # called when a queued task has completed
myqueue.join() # called when all tasks in queue get completed
```

Let's see a simple demonstration of using queue to implement a multithreaded application (refer to `7.02 threading with queue.py` available in the code bundle):

```
import Queue
import threading
class Worker(threading.Thread):
    def __init__(self, queue):
        threading.Thread.__init__(self)
        self.queue = queue

    def run(self):
        while True:
            task = self.queue.get()
            self.taskHandler(task)

    def taskHandler(self, job):
        print'doing task %s'%job
        self.queue.task_done()
    def main(tasks):
        queue = Queue.Queue()
        for task in tasks:
            queue.put(task)
    # create some threads and assign them queue
        for i in range(6):
            mythread = Worker(queue)
            mythread.setDaemon(True)
            mythread.start()
        queue.join()
        print'all tasks completed'

    if __name__ == "__main__":
            tasks = 'A B C D E F'.split()
            main(tasks)
```

The description of the code is as follows:

▶ We first create a `Worker` class, which inherits from the `threading` module of Python. The `__init__` method takes in a queue as its argument.

▶ We then override the `run` method of the `threading` module to get each item from the queue using `queue.get()`, which is then passed on to the `taskHandler` method, which actually executes the task specified in the current queue item. In our example, it does nothing useful but printing the name of the task.

▸ After the work is done on a particular thread by our `taskHandler` method, it sends a signal to the queue telling that the task has been completed using the `queue.task_done()` method.

▸ Outside our `Worker` class, we create an empty queue in our `main()` method. This queue is populated with a list of tasks using `queue.put(task)`.

▸ We then create six different threads and pass this populated queue as its argument. Now that the tasks are handled by the queue, all threads automatically ensure that the tasks are completed in a sequence in which they are encountered by the threads, without causing any deadlocks or two different threads trying to work on the same queued task.

▸ At the time of creating each thread, we also create a pool of daemon threads using the `mythread.setDaemon(True)` method. Doing this passes control to our main program once all threads have completed execution. If you comment out the line, the program would still run, but would fail to exit after all threads have completed executing the tasks in the queue. Without the daemon threads, you'd have to keep track of all the threads and tell them to exit before your program could completely quit.

▸ Finally, the `queue.join()` method ensures that the program flow waits there until the queue is empty.

Now that we know how to use queues to handle multithreaded applications effectively, let's build our Snake game. In its final form, the game would be like the one shown in the following screenshot (refer to the `7.03 game of snake.py` Python file available in the code bundle):

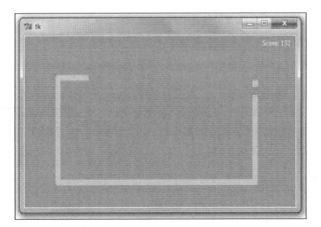

Engage Thrusters

1. Let's start coding our game, by first creating a basic GUI class.

```
class GUI(Tk):
    def __init__(self, queue):
        Tk.__init__(self)
        self.queue = queue
        self.is_game_over = False
        self.canvas = Canvas(self, width=495, height=305,
          bg='#FF75A0')
        self.canvas.pack()
        self.snake = self.canvas.create_line((0, 0),
          (0,0), fill='#FFCC4C', width=10)
        self.food = self.canvas.create_rectangle(0, 0, 0,
          0, fill='#FFCC4C', outline='#FFCC4C')
        self.points_earned = self.canvas.create_text(455,
          15, fill='white', text='Score: 0')
        self.queue_handler()
```

The description of the code is as follows:

- This code should be mostly familiar to you by now, because we have created similar GUI classes several times in the past.

- However, rather than passing the root instance as an argument to its __init__ method, our GUI class now inherits from the Tk class. The line `Tk.__init__(self)` ensures that the root window is available to all methods of this class. This way we can avoid writing `root` attribute on every line by referencing `self.root` simply as `self`.

- We then initialize the canvas, line (snake), rectangle (food) and text (to display score).

- We then call the function `queueHandler()`. This yet to be defined method would be similar to `main` method defined in the previous queue example. This would be the central method which will process all tasks in the queue. We will come back to define this method once we have added some tasks to the queue.

2. Now, we will create the Food class, as shown in the following code snippet:

```
class Food():
    def __init__(self, queue):
        self.queue = queue
        self.generate_food()

    def generate_food(self):
```

```
        x = random.randrange(5, 480, 10)
         y = random.randrange(5, 295, 10)
    self.position = x, y
    self.exppos = x - 5, y - 5, x + 5, y + 5
    self.queue.put({'food': self.exppos})
```

The description of the code is as follows:

❑   Because we want to process all data centrally from within a queue, we pass
    the queue as an argument to the __init__ method of the Food class.
    We choose to run this from the main program thread to demonstrate how
    a code which is being executed in the main thread can communicate with
    attributes and methods from other threads.

❑   The __init__ method calls another method called generate_food(),
    which is responsible for generating the snake-food at random positions
    on the canvas.

❑   The generate_food method generates a random *(x, y)* position on the
    canvas. However, because the place where the coordinates coincide is just a
    small point on the canvas, it would be barely visible. We therefore generate
    an expanded coordinate (self.exppos) ranging from five values less than
    the *(x,y)* coordinate up to five values higher than the same coordinate.
    Using this range, we can create a small rectangle on the canvas which
    would be easily visible and would represent our food.

> However, we do not create the rectangle here. Instead, we pass the
> coordinates for the food (rectangle) into our queue using queue.
> put. Because this queue is to be made available to all our classes, we
> will have a centralized worker named queue_handler(), which
> will process this queue to generate the rectangle from our GUI class
> later. This is the central idea behind a Queue implementation.

3.   Let's now create the Snake class. We have already passed a task to generate our
     food to the central queue. However, no thread was involved in the task. We could
     also generate our Snake class without using threads. However, because we are talking
     about ways to implement multithreaded applications, let's implement our Snake class
     to work from a separate thread (refer to 7.03 game of snake.py):

```
class Snake(threading.Thread):
    def __init__(self, gui, queue):
        threading.Thread.__init__(self)
        self.gui = gui
```

```
                self.queue = queue
                self.daemon = True
                self.points_earned = 0
                self.snake_points = [(495, 55), (485, 55), (475, 55),
                (465, 55), (455, 55)]
                self.food = Food(queue)
                self.direction = 'Left'
                self.start()

        def run(self):
            while not self.gui.is_game_over:
                self.queue.put({'move':self.snake_points})
                time.sleep(0.1)
                self.move()
```

The description of the code is as follows:

❏ First, we create a class named `Snake` to run from a separate thread. This class takes the GUI and queue as its input arguments.

❏ We initialize the points earned by the player from zero and set the initial location of the snake using the attribute `self.snake_points`.

❏ Finally, we start the thread and create an infinite loop to call the `move()` method at small intervals. During every run of the loop, the method populates the queue with a dictionary having the key as `'move'` and the value equal to the updated position of the snake through the `self.snake_points` attribute.

4. In this step, we will be making the snake move.

   The thread initialized above calls the `Snake` class `move()` method to move the snake around on the canvas. However, before we can move the snake, we need to know the direction in which the snake should move. This obviously depends on the particular key pressed by the user (Left/Right/Top/Down key).

   Accordingly, we need to bind these four events to the Canvas widget. We will do the actual binding later. However, we can now create a method named called `key_pressed`, which takes the `key_press` event itself as its argument and sets the direction value according to the key that is pressed.

```
def key_pressed(self, e):
        self.direction = e.keysym
```

Now that we have the directions, let's code the `move` method:

```python
def move(self):
    new_snake_point = self.calculate_new_coordinates()
    if self.food.position == new_snake_point:
        self.points_earned += 1
        self.queue.put({'points_earned':self.points_earned })
        self.food.generate_food()
    else:
        self.snake_points.pop(0)
        self.check_game_over(new_snake_point)
        self.snake_points.append(new_snake_point)

def calculate_new_coordinates(self):
    last_x, last_y = self.snake_points[-1]
    if self.direction == 'Up':
        new_snake_point = last_x, (last_y - 10)
    elif self.direction == 'Down':
        new_snake_point = last_x, (last_y + 10)
    elif self.direction == 'Left':
        new_snake_point = (last_x - 10), last_y
    elif self.direction == 'Right':
        new_snake_point = (last_x + 10), last_y
    return new_snake_point

def check_game_over(self, snake_point):
    x,y = snake_point[0], snake_point[1]
    if not -5 < x < 505 or not -5 < y < 315 or \
      snake_point in self.snake_points:
            self.queue.put({'game_over':True})
```

The description for the code is as follows:

❑ First, the `move` method obtains the latest coordinates for the snake depending on the keyboard event. It uses a separate method called `calculate_new_coordinates` to get the latest coordinates.

❑ It then checks if the location of the new coordinates coincide with the location of the food. If they match, it increases the score of the player by one and calls the `Food` class `generate_food` method to generate a new food at a new location.

❑ If the current point does not coincide with the food coordinates, it deletes the last item from the snake coordinates using `self.snake_points.pop(0)`.

❑ Then, it calls another method named `check_game_over` to check if the snake collides against the wall or against itself. If the snake does collide, it appends a new dictionary item in the queue with the value `'game_over':True`.

❑ Finally, if the game is not over, it appends the new position of the snake to the list `self.snake_points`. This is automatically added to the queue, because we have defined `self.queue.put({'move':self.snake_points})` in the `Snake` class's `run()` method to update every 0.1 seconds as long as the game is not over.

5. Now, let's create the Queue handler.

We now have a `Food` class feeding the centralized queue from the main program thread. We also have the `Snake` class adding data to the queue from one thread and a `GUI` class running the `queue_handler` method from another thread. So, the queue is the central point of interaction between these three threads.

Now, it is time to handle these data to update the content on the canvas. We accordingly define the `queue_handler()` method in our `GUI` class to work on items in the queue.

```
def queue_handler(self):
    try:
        while True:
            task = self.queue.get(block=False)
            if task.has_key('game_over'):
                self.game_over()
            elif task.has_key('move'):
                points = [x for point in task['move'] for
                x in point]
                self.canvas.coords(self.snake, *points)
            elif task.has_key('food'):
                self.canvas.coords(self.food,
                    *task['food'])
            elif task.has_key('points_earned'):
              self.canvas.itemconfigure(self.points_earned
                , text='Score:{}'.format(task
                    ['points_earned']))
            self.queue.task_done()
    except Queue.Empty:
        if not self.is_game_over:
            self.canvas.after(100, self.queue_handler)
```

The description for the code is as follows:

- ❑ The `queue_handler` method gets into an infinite loop looking for tasks in the queue using `task = self.queue.get(block=False)`. If the queue becomes empty, the loop is restarted using `canvas.after`.

- ❑ Once a task is fetched from the queue, the method checks its key.

- ❑ If the key is `'game_over'`, it calls another method named `game_over()` that we defined next.

- ❑ If the key of task is `'move'`, it uses `canvas.coords` to move the line to its new position.

- ❑ If the key is `'points_earned'`, it updates the score on the canvas.

- ❑ When execution of a task completes, it signals the thread with the `task_done()` method.

> `queue.get` can take both `block=True` (default) and `block=False` as its argument.
>
> When the block is set to `False`, it removes and returns an item from the queue, if available. If the queue is empty, it raises `Queue.Empty`. When the block is set to `True`, `queue.get` fetches an item from the queue by suspending the calling thread, if required, until an item is available.

6. In this step, we will code the method to handle the `game_over` feature for the game.

The `queue_handler` method calls the `game_over` method in case of a matching queue key:

```
def game_over(self):
    self.is_game_over = True
    self.canvas.create_text(200, 150, fill='white',
    text='Game Over')
    quitbtn = Button(self, text='Quit', command =
        self.destroy)
    self.canvas.create_window(200, 180, anchor='nw',
        window=quitbtn)
```

The description for the code is as follows:

- ❑ We first set the `game_over` attribute to `True`. This helps us exit out of the infinite loop of `queue_handler`. Then, we add a text on the canvas displaying the content **Game Over**.

- ❑ We also add a **Quit** button inside the canvas, which has a command callback attached to quit the root window.

> Take a note of how to attach other widgets inside the canvas widget.

7. Let's Run the game. The game is now ready. To run the game, we create a function outside all other classes named `main()`:

```
def main():
    queue = Queue.Queue()
    gui   = GUI(queue)
    snake = Snake(gui, queue)
    gui.bind('<Key-Left>', snake.key_pressed)
    gui.bind('<Key-Right>', snake.key_pressed)
    gui.bind('<Key-Up>', snake.key_pressed)
    gui.bind('<Key-Down>', snake.key_pressed)
    gui.mainloop()

if __name__ == '__main__':
    main()
```

We create an empty queue, and pass it as an argument to all three of our classes so that they can feed tasks into the queue. We also bind the four directional keys to the `key_pressed` method, which is defined earlier within our `Snake` class.

Objective Complete – Mini Debriefing

Our game is now functional. Go try your hands at controlling the snake, while keeping its stomach filled.

To summarize, we created three classes such as `Food`, `Snake`, and `GUI`. These three classes feed information about the task related to their class to a centralized queue which is passed as an argument to all the classes.

Then, we create a centralized method named `queue_handler`, which handle tasks from the queue by polling tasks one at a time and completing it in a non-blocking manner.

The game could have been implemented without threads and queues, but it would have been slower, longer, and more complex. By using queues to manage data from multiple threads effectively, we have been able to contain the program to less than 150 lines of code.

Hopefully, you should now be able to implement queues for managing other programs that you design at your work.

Creating a Weather Reporter

Let's now build a simple Weather Reporter application. The goal of this project is to introduce you to the basics of network programming, as used in conjunction with Tkinter.

Prepare for Lift Off

Python has great support for network programming. At the lowest level, Python provides a socket module that lets you connect and interact with the network using a simple-to-use object-oriented interface.

For those unaware of network programming, sockets are the fundamental concept behind any kind of network communications done by your computer. This is the lowest level at which a programmer can access the network. Underneath the socket layer lie raw UDP and TCP connections, which are handled by your computer's operating system with no direct access points for the programmers. For instance, when you type `www.packtpub.com` in your browser, the operating system on your computer opens a socket and connects to `packtpub.com` to fetch the web page and show it to you. Same happens with any application that needs to connect to the network.

Let's take a brief look at some of the APIs available in the socket module:

```
s = socket.socket(socket.AF_INET, socket.SOCK_STREAM) # create a
#socket
socket.gethostbyname( host ) # resolving host IP from host name
s.connect((ip , port)) #Connect to remote server
s.sendall(message)
s.recv(message_size)
```

If you look at the `7.04 socket demo.py` Python file in the code bundle of this project, you'll find that it sends a very obscure looking GET request to fetch the contents from the URL in the following line of code:

```
message = "GET / HTTP/1.1\r\n\r\n"
```

The data received from the server is also sent in packets, and it is our task to collect all the data and assemble them at our end. All these make direct socket programming a tedious approach. We do not want to be writing code for all that to fetch data from the network.

We will therefore use a higher-level module named `urllib`, which is built on top of sockets module but is easier to use. The `urllib` module forms a part of Python standard library. With this protocol, fetching contents of a web page turns into a four-line code (see the code in `7.05 urllib demo.py`):

```
import urllib
data = urllib.urlopen('http://www.packtpub.com')
print data.read()
data.close()
```

This prints the entire HTML source code or whatever is the response from the web page `http://www.packtpub.com`. This is, in essence, the core of mining the Web for data and information.

Now that we know how to get data from a URL, let's apply it to build a small Weather Reporter application.

This application should take the location as an input from the user, and fetch relevant weather-related data.

Engage Thrusters

1. First, we will create the GUI of the application. This should now be easy for you. We create a class `WeatherReporter`, and call it from outside the class within the main loop. See the code of `7.06 weather reporter.py`:

```
def main():
    root=Tk()
    WeatherReporter(root)
    root.mainloop()


if __name__ == '__main__':
    main()
```

The GUI component of the `WeatherReporter` class consists of two methods: `top_frame()` and `display_frame()`. The `top_frame()` method creates an entry widget and a button that says **Show Weather Info**.

The `display_frame()` method creates a canvas where the actual weather data would be displayed:

```
class WeatherReporter:
    def __init__(self, root):
        self.root = root
        self.top_frame()
        self.display_frame()


    def top_frame(self):
        topfrm = Frame(self.root)
        topfrm.grid(row=1, sticky='w')
        Label(topfrm, text='Enter Location').grid(row=1,
            column=2, sticky='w')
        self.enteredlocation = StringVar()
        Entry(topfrm, textvariable=self.enteredlocation)
            .grid(row=1, column=2, sticky='w')
        ttk.Button(topfrm, text='Show Weather Info', command=
            self.show_weather_button_clicked).grid(row=1,
            column=3, sticky='w')
```

```
def display_frame(self):
    displayfrm = Frame(self.root)
    displayfrm.grid(row=2, sticky='ew', columnspan=5)
    self.canvas = Canvas(displayfrm, height='410',
                width='300', background='black',
                borderwidth=5)
    self.canvas.create_rectangle(5, 5, 305, 415,
                                    fill='#F6AF06')
    self.canvas.grid(row=2, sticky='w', columnspan=5)
```

2. In the second step, we are going to fetch the weather data from a website.

    There are two ways to fetch data from a website. The first method involves getting an HTML response from a website, and then parsing the received HTML response for data that is relevant to us. This type of data extraction is called **site scraping**.

    Site scraping is a rather crude method which is employed only when a given website does not provide a structured way to retrieve data. On the other hand, some websites are willing to share data through a set of APIs, provided you query it for data using the specified URL structure. This is clearly more elegant than site scraping, because data is interchanged in a reliable and "mutually agreed" format.

    For our Weather Reporter application, we want to query some weather channel for a given location, and in turn retrieve and display the data in our canvas. Fortunately, there are several weather APIs which lets us do that.

 In our example, we will use the weather data provided by a the following website:
`http://openweathermap.org/`

    The OpenWeatherMap service provides free weather data and forecast APIs. This site collates weather data from more than 40,000 weather stations across the globe, and the data can be assessed by city name and geographic coordinates or their internal city ID.

    The website provides weather data in two data formats:

    ❏   JSON (JavaScript Object Notation)

    ❏   XML

XML and JSON are two popular interchangeable data serialization formats widely used for data-interchanging among different applications, which may be running on different platforms and using different programming languages, thus providing the benefit of interoperability.

JSON is simpler than XML, because its grammar is simpler and it maps more directly onto the data structures used in modern programming languages. JSON is better suited for data exchanging, but XML is good for document exchanging.

The API documentation for the website tells us that a query, such as `api.openweathermap.org/data/2.5/weather?q=London,uk` returns us weather data for London in a JSON format as follows:

```
{"coord":{"lon":-0.12574,"lat":51.50853},"sys":{"country":"GB","s
unrise":1377147503,"sunset":1377198481},"weather":[{"id":500,"mai
n":"Rain","description":"light rain","icon":"10d"}],"base":"gdps
stations","main":{"temp":294.2,"pressure":1020,"humidity":88,"te
mp_min":292.04,"temp_max":296.48},"wind":{"speed":1,"deg":0},"rain
":{"1h":0.25},"clouds":{"all":40},"dt":1377178327,"id":2643743,"na
me":"London","cod":200}
```

The syntax of JSON is simple. Any JSON data is a name/value pair where each data is separated from the others by commas. JSON uses curly braces { } to hold objects and square brackets [ ] to hold arrays. We accordingly define a method to get the weather data in JSON format in our application (refer to `7.06 weather reporter.py` available in the code bundle of this project):

```
def get_weather_data(self):
    try:
        apiurl = 'http://api.openweathermap.org/data
        /2.5/weather?q=%s'%self.enteredlocation.get()
        data =  urllib.urlopen(apiurl)
        jdata= data.read()
        returnjdata
    except IOError as e:
        tkMessageBox.showerror('Unable to connect', 'Unable to
                connect %s'%e)
```

This method uses `urllib` to retrieve responses from the website. It returns the response in JSON format.

3. Now, we'll start processing the JSON data. The weather data returned using API is encoded in JSON format. We need to convert this data into Python data type. Python provides a built-in `json` module that eases the process of "encoding-decoding" JSON data. We therefore import the `json` module into our current namespace.

Then, we'll use this module to convert the retrieved JSON data into Python dictionary format (refer to `7.06 weather reporter.py`):

```python
def json_to_dict(self, jdata):
    mydecoder = json.JSONDecoder()
    decodedjdata = mydecoder.decode(jdata)
    flatteneddict = {}
    for key, value in decodedjdata.items():
        if key == 'weather':
            forke,va in value[0].items():
                flatteneddict[str(ke)] = str(va).upper()
                continue
        try:
            fork,v in value.items():
            flatteneddict[str(k)] = str(v).upper()
        except:
            flatteneddict[str(key)] = str(value).upper()
    returnflatteneddict
```

4. Finally, we'll display the retrieved weather data. Now that we have a dictionary of all weather-related information provided by the API, let's add a command callback to the button:

```python
def show_weather_button_clicked(self):
    if not self.enteredlocation.get():
        return
    self.canvas.delete(ALL)
    self.canvas.create_rectangle( 5, 5,305,415,
                                    fill='#F6AF06')
    data = self.get_weather_data()
    data =self.json_to_dict(data)
    self.display_final(data)
```

The `display_final` method simply takes each item from the dictionary and displays it on the canvas using `create_text`. We do not include the code for `display_final` because it merely displays the data on the canvas, and this idea should be self-explanatory by now. The API also provides an icon-related data. The icons are stored in a folder named `weatherimages` (refer to the folder with the same name provided in the code bundle) and an appropriate icon is displayed using `canvas.create_image`.

Objective Complete – Mini Debriefing

Our Weather Reporter application is now functional. In essence, the application uses the `urllib` module to query the weather API provided by our data provider. The data is fetched in JSON format. The JSON data is then decoded into a Python-readable format (dictionary).

The converted data is then displayed on the canvas using `create_text` and `create_image` methods.

Classified Intel

When you access a server from your Python program, it is very important to send requests after small time gaps.

A typical Python program is capable of running several million instructions per second. However, the server that sends you the data at the other end is never equipped to work at that speed.

If you knowingly or unknowingly send large number of requests to a server within a short time-span, you may hamper it from servicing its routine requests from normal web users. This constitutes what is called the **denial of service** (**DOS**) attack on the server. You may be banned or, in worse case, sued for disrupting a server, if your program does not make a limited number of well-behaved requests.

Creating a phonebook application

Let's now build a simple phonebook application that allows the user to store names and phone numbers. The user should be able to create new records, read existing records, update existing records, and delete records from the database using this application. Together, these activities constitute what is known as **CRUD** (Create, Read, Update and Delete) operations on a database.

The main learning objective for this project relates to being able to use a relational database with Tkinter to store and manipulate records.

We have already seen some basic examples of object persistence with serialization. Relational databases extend this persistence using rules of relational algebra to store data into tables.

Python provides database interfaces for a wide range of database engines. In addition, Python provides a generic interface standard that can be used to access database engines, but it is not natively available as a Python module.

Some of the commonly-used database engines include MySQL, SQLite, PostgreSQL, Oracle, Ingres, SAP DB, Informix, Sybase, Firebird, IBM DB2, Microsoft SQL Server, Microsoft Access, and so on.

We will use SQLite to store data for our phonebook application.

Prepare for Lift Off

SQLite is a server-less, zero-configuration, self-contained SQL database engine suitable for developing embedded applications. The source code for SQLite is in the public domain, which makes it freely available for use in all sorts of commercial and non-commercial projects.

Unlike many other SQL databases, SQLite does not require running a separate server process. Instead, SQLite stores all the data directly onto flat files which get stored on a computer disk. These files are easily portable across different platforms, making it a very popular choice for smaller and simpler database implementation requirements.

Python 2.7 comes with a built-in standard library for sqlite3 support. However, we need to download the sqlite3 command-line tool that lets us create, modify, and access the database using a command-line tool. The command-line shell for Windows, Linux, and Mac OS X can be downloaded from `http://sqlite.org/download.html`.

Following the instruction on the website, install the SQLite command shell into any location of your choice.

Let us now implement our phonebook application. The application will look like the screenshot shown in the following. The application will demonstrate some of the common operations involved in database programming, as follows:

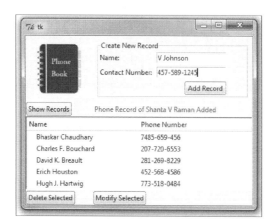

Engage Thrusters

1. In order to create the database, we open the command-line tool of our operating system. On Windows, we generally invoke the command line by typing `cmd` in the run console.

   Within the command line, we first navigate to the directory where we need to create the new database file. In order to create the database, we simply use this command:

   ```
   sqlite3 phonebook.db
   ```

   This creates a database file named `phonebook.db` in the folder from which we execute the command. It also displays a message similar to the one shown below:

   ```
   SQLite version 3.7.17 2013-05-20 00:56:22
   Enter ".help" for instructions
   Enter SQL statements terminated with a ";"
   sqlite>
   ```

   We have now created a database named `phonebook.db`. However, the database file is currently empty. It does not contain any tables or any data. So, we get no results if we run the command:

   ```
   sqlite> .tables
   ```

   Let's for now exit the command-line tool by typing:

   ```
   sqlite> .exit
   ```

2. We want to store contacts in our database, and that is why we need to create the `contacts` table. Intuitively, our database table should store a person's name and phone number. In addition, it is a good practice to keep a unique identification number for each person or each entry in the table. This is because multiple people might have the same name or same contact number.

   To create a table within our `phonebook.db` database, we again open the command-line tool and navigate to the directory where we had created the database. We again get into the sqlite3 terminal by typing:

   ```
   sqlite3 phonebook.db
   ```

   This time a new database is not created. Rather, the command now opens the existing `phonebook.db` database, because it is already present on the disk.

Next, we create a table named `contacts`, and add three columns to the table from the command line:

```
sqlite> CREATE TABLE contacts
(
contactid INTEGER PRIMARY KEY AUTOINCREMENT,
name STRINGNOT NULL,
contactnumber INTEGER NOT NULL
);
```

You can verify if the `contacts` table was created by typing the following command:

```
sqlite>.table
```

This prints the name of all the tables present in the currently open database. You will get the following output:

```
sqlite>.table
contacts
```

3. Let's first begin by creating a basic GUI that would let us add, view, delete, and modify the records. We create a class named `PhoneBook` and create all GUI widgets from within its `__init__` method (refer to `7.07 phonebook.py`):

```
class PhoneBook:
def __init__(self, master):
    # all widgets created here
```

We do not rewrite the code here, because we have created similar widgets in all our previous projects.

4. Let's start creating the records in the database file we created. A new record is to be created every time a user enters a new name and a phone number in the entry widgets provided, and clicks on the **Add Record** button.

```
def create_record(self):
    name = self.namefield.get()
    num = self.numfield.get()
    if name == "":
        self.msg["text"] = "Please Enter name"
        return
    if num == "":
```

```
            self.msg["text"] = "Please Enter Number"
            return
        conn = sqlite3.connect('phonebook.db')
        c = conn.cursor()
        c.execute("INSERT INTO contacts VALUES(NULL,?, ?)", (name,
                num))
        conn.commit()
        c.close()
        self.namefield.delete(0, END)
        self.numfield.delete(0, END)
        self.msg["text"] = "Phone Record of %s Added" %name
```

The description of the code is as follows:

- The `create_record` method, as defined above, is attached as a command callback to the **Add Record** button.

- When the `create_record` method is called, it retrieves the name and number values entered in the **Name** and **Contact Number** entry field.

- If the name or number field is empty, it prints an error message and exits.

- If name and number fields are valid, the method establishes connection to the `phonebook.db` database we had created earlier.

- The next line, `c = conn.cursor()`, creates a cursor object. The cursor is a control structure that is required as per SQL standards, and it enables us to traverse over the records in a database.

- The next line, `c.execute(query)` is the line that actually inserts the name and phone number into database. Note that it includes three insertion values: the first is the NULL value corresponding to autoincrement contact ID which is added through that we had created in our `contacts` table.

- The line `conn.commit()` actually commits these changes to the database and line `c.close()` closes the connection to the database.

5. After the above steps are carried out, we will view the records stored in the database. This method is responsible for fetching all the records from the database and displaying them in the tree widget.

```
def view_records(self):
    x = self.tree.get_children()
    for item in x:
        self.tree.delete(item)
```

```
conn = sqlite3.connect('phonebook.db')
c = conn.cursor()
list = c.execute("SELECT * FROM contacts ORDER BY name
                         desc")
for row in list:
    self.tree.insert("",0,text=row[1],values=row[2])
c.close()
```

The description of the code is as follows:

❑ The `view_records` method first deletes all existing items being displayed in the tree widget

❑ It then establishes a database connection and queries the database to fetch all the data sorted by name in descending order

❑ Finally, it iterates over the fetched record to update the tree widget with the content

6. Now, on the phonebook application we'll delete some records. The `delete_record` method is simply responsible for deleting a row from the database based on a given name criterion:

```
def delete_record(self):
    self.msg["text"] = ""
    conn = sqlite3.connect('phonebook.db')
      c = conn.cursor()
    name = self.tree.item(self.tree.selection())['text']
    query = "DELETE FROM contacts WHERE name = '%s';" %name
    c.execute(query)
    conn.commit()
    c.close()
    self.msg["text"] = "Phone Record for %s Deleted" %name
```

Although we have created this deletion query based on name, this method runs the risk of deleting multiple entries if two or more person have the same name. A better approach would be to delete the entries based on the primary key or contact id, which is unique for every entry in the table.

7. The final operation in the phonebook application is modifying the records. When a user selects a particular record and clicks on the **Modify Selected** button, it opens a new Toplevel window like the one shown here:

This window is created using the `open_modify_window` method, as defined in the
`7.07 phonebook.py` Python file. We will not reproduce the code for this method,
because you should be comfortable making such windows by now.

When a user specifies a new number and clicks the **Update Record** button,
it calls the `update_record` method, which is defined in the following:

```
def update_record(self, newphone,oldphone, name):
    conn = sqlite3.connect('phonebook.db')
    c = conn.cursor()
    c.execute("UPDATE contacts SET contactnumber=? WHERE
        contactnumber=? AND name=?", (newphone, oldphone, name))
    conn.commit()
    c.close()
    self.tl.destroy()
    self.msg["text"] = "Phone Number of %s modified" %name
```

Objective Complete – Mini Debriefing

We have completed coding a basic phonebook application.

More importantly, we have seen how to work with databases. Our phonebook application
has demonstrated how to execute basic create, read, update, and delete (CRUD) operations
on a database.

We have seen how to create database, add tables to the database, and query the database
to add, modify, delete, and view items in the database.

Furthermore, due to similarity of basic database operations, you can now consider working
with other database systems, such as MySQL, PostgreSQL, Oracle, Ingres, SAP DB, Informix,
Sybase, Firebird, IBM DB2, Microsoft SQL Server, and Microsoft Access.

Graphing with Tkinter

Let us wrap up this project by looking at the graphing abilities of the Tkinter canvas widget.

Engage Thrusters

In this recipe we will see how we can plot:

- Pie chart
- Scatter chart
- Bar graph
- Embedding matplotlib graphs

Let's look at the pie chart first:

1. You can easily create pie charts in Tkinter using the Canvas widget's `create_arc` method. A sample Pie Chart code is provided in `7.08 pie chart.py`:

```
import Tkinter
root = Tkinter.Tk()
def prop(n):
    return 360.0 * n / 1000

Tkinter.Label(root, text='Pie Chart').pack()
c = Tkinter.Canvas(width=154, height=154)
c.pack()
c.create_arc((2,2,152,152), fill="#FAF402", outline="#FAF402",
start=prop(0), extent = prop(200))
c.create_arc((2,2,152,152), fill="#00AC36", outline="#00AC36",
start=prop(200), extent = prop(400))
```

```
c.create_arc((2,2,152,152), fill="#7A0871", outline="#7A0871",
start=prop(600), extent = prop(50))
c.create_arc((2,2,152,152), fill="#E00022", outline="#E00022",
start=prop(650), extent = prop(200))
c.create_arc((2,2,152,152), fill="#294994", outline="#294994",
start=prop(850), extent = prop(150))
root.mainloop()
```

The description of the code is as follows:

▸ Each portion of the pie chart is drawn by changing the two following `create_arc` options:

> `start`: This option specifies the start angle. Default is `0.0`.
>
> `extent`: This option specifies the size of `arc` relative to the start angle. Default is `90.0`.

2. Next, we'll plot a sample scatter chart:

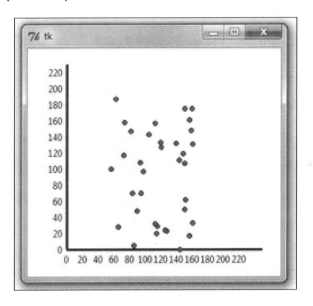

Similarly, we can use `create_line` to draw the *x* and *y* axes and `create_oval` to draw the scatter plots, as shown in the preceding screenshot here. A sample scatter plot code is provided in the `7.09 scatter plot.py` Python file:

```
import Tkinter
import random
root = Tkinter.Tk()
```

```
c = Tkinter.Canvas(root, width=350, height=280, bg='white')
c.grid()
#create x-axis
c.create_line(50, 250, 300, 250, width=3)
for i in range(12):
    x = 50 + (i * 20)
c.create_text(x, 255, anchor='n', text='%d'% (20*i))
# create y-axis
c.create_line(50, 250, 50, 20, width=3)
for i in range(12):
    y = 250 - (i * 20)
c.create_text(45, y, anchor='e', text='%d'% (20*i))
#create scatter plots from random x-y values
for i in range(35):
    x,y = random.randint(100,210), random.randint(50,250)
    c.create_oval(x-3, y-3, x+3, y+3, width=1, fill='red')
root.mainloop()
```

3. Now, let's plot a sample bar graph:

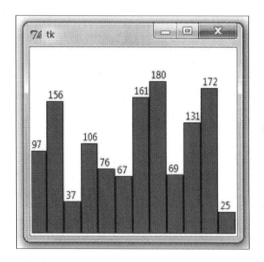

A bar graph can be easily generated using the Canvas widget's `create_rectangle` method. A sample bar graph code is provided in `7.10 bar graph.py`:

```
import Tkinter
import random
root = Tkinter.Tk()
cwidth = 250
cheight = 220
```

```
barWidth = 20
canv = Tkinter.Canvas(root, width=cwidth, height=cheight,
bg= 'white')
canv.pack()

plotdata= [random.randint(0,200) for r in xrange(12)]

for x, y in enumerate(plotdata):
    x1 = x  + x * barWidth
    y1 = cheight - y
    x2 = x  + x * barWidth + barWidth
    y2 = cheight
    canv.create_rectangle(x1, y1, x2, y2, fill="blue")
    canv.create_text(x1+3, y1, text=str(y), anchor='sw')

root.mainloop()
```

4. Finally, we're going to look at how to embed matplotlib graphs in Tkinter Toplevel window.

    Using Tkinter Canvas to draw graphs may work fine for trivial cases. However, Tkinter may not be the best library when it comes to drawing more sophisticated and interactive graphs.

    In fact, matplotlib is used in conjunction with the **NumPy** module is the preferred choice when it comes to producing professional-quality graphs with Python.

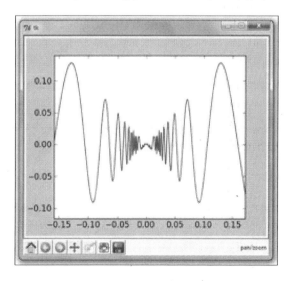

Although a detailed discussion on matplotlib is beyond the scope of this book, we will take a brief look at embedding matplotlib-generated graphs on a Tkinter canvas.

 If you are interested in exploring advanced graphing with Python, you can install matplotlib and NumPy (a dependency for matplotlib) with the help of the installation instructions available at
`http://matplotlib.org/users/installing.html`

```
import Tkinter as Tk
from numpy import arange, sin, pi
from matplotlib.backends.backend_tkagg import FigureCanvasTkAgg,
NavigationToolbar2TkAgg
from matplotlib.figure import Figure
root = Tk.Tk()
#creating the graph
f = Figure(figsize=(5,4), dpi=100)
a = f.add_subplot(111)
t = arange(-1.0,1.0,0.001)
s = t*sin(1/t)
a.plot(t,s)
# embedding matplotlib figure 'f' on a tk.DrawingArea
canvas = FigureCanvasTkAgg(f, master=root)
canvas.get_tk_widget().pack(side=Tk.TOP, fill=Tk.BOTH, expand=1)
#creating toolbar
toolbar = NavigationToolbar2TkAgg( canvas, root )
toolbar.update()
root.mainloop()
```

Objective Complete – Mini Debriefing

This completes our brief discussion on the graphing abilities of Tkinter.

In this iteration, we saw how to use Tkinter Canvas to draw basic graphs such as pie chart, scatter plots, and bar graphs.

We also saw how to embed more sophisticated matplotlib graphs, on the Tkinter drawing area.

Mission Accomplished

This brings us to the end of this project. In this project, we took a deeper look into some of the many things that can be done with Tkinter Canvas widget.

We also learned how to use the Queue implementation to program a multithreaded application.

The Weather Reporter application introduced us to the basics of network programming and how to tap into the Internet for our data needs.

The phonebook application showed us how to work with databases.

Finally, we looked at basic graphing abilities of Tkinter, and we also looked at ways of embedding matplotlib graphs in Tkinter.

A Hotshot Challenge

> ▸ **Screen saver challenge**: We have used the `create_oval` method of the Canvas widget to create multiple balls in our screen saver program. Try to experiment by replacing the oval with other canvas-supported shapes, such as lines, rectangles, and arcs.
>
> In fact, because you can use the `create_image` method on Canvas, how about creating an aquarium brimming with different varieties of fishes, snails, aquatic animals, and plants? You can even add sky divers bubbling their way through the marine life!
>
> ▸ **Snake game challenge**: Implement different levels of the Snake game by introducing mazes on the canvas.
>
> ▸ **Network programming challenge**: Implement any other program that leverages the data available on the Internet to provide some value to the end user.
>
> ▸ **Database challenge**: Revisit your media player program and implement a database to store playlists and automatically populate the media player when it is run.
>
> ▸ **Graphing challenge**: Explore advanced graphing capabilities of matplotlib.

Miscellaneous Tips

We are now into the final section of the book. Let's conclude by discussing concepts that do form a common theme in many GUI applications but did not appear in our applications.

Mission Briefing

The topics covered here include:

- Tracing Tkinter variables
- Widget traversal
- Validating user input
- Formatting widget data
- More on fonts
- Working with Unicode characters
- Tkinter class hierarchy
- Custom-made mixins
- Tips for code cleanup and program optimization
- Distributing the Tkinter application
- Limitations of Tkinter
- Tkinter alternatives
- Getting interactive help
- Tkinter in Python 3.*x*

Tracing Tkinter variables

When you specify a Tkinter variable as a `textvariable` for a widget (`textvariable = myvar`), the widget automatically gets updated whenever the value of the variable changes. However, there might be times when, in addition to updating the widget, you need to do some extra processing at the time of reading or writing (or modifying) the variable.

Tkinter provides a method to attach a callback method that would be triggered every time the value of a variable is accessed. Thus, the callback acts as a **variable observer**. The callback method is named `trace_variable(self, mode, callback)`, or simply `trace(self, mode, callback)`.

The mode argument can take any one of `'r'`, `'w'`, `'u'` values, which stand for read, write, or undefined. Depending upon the mode specifications, the callback method is triggered if the variable is read or written.

The callback method gets three arguments by default. The arguments in order of their position are:

▸ Name of the Tkinter variable

▸ The index of the variable, if the Tkinter variable is an array, else an empty string

▸ The access modes (`'w'`, `'r'`, or `'u'`)

Note that the triggered callback function may also modify the value of the variable. This modification does not, however, trigger any additional callbacks.

Let's see a small example of variable tracing in Tkinter, where writing into the Tkinter variable into an entry widget triggers a callback function (refer to the `8.01 trace variable.py` Python file available in the code bundle):

```
from Tkinter import *
root = Tk()
myvar = StringVar()
def trace_when_myvar_written(var,indx,mode):
    print"Traced variable %s"%myvar.get()

myvar.trace_variable("w", trace_when_myvar_written)
Label(root, textvariable=myvar).pack(padx=5, pady=5)
Entry(root, textvariable=myvar).pack(padx=5, pady=5)

root.mainloop()
```

The description of the preceding code is as follows:

- ▶ This code creates a trace variable on the Tkinter variable `myvar` in the write (`"w"`) mode

- ▶ The trace variable is attached to a callback method named `trace_when_myvar_written` (this means that every time the value of `myvar` is changed, the callback method will be triggered)

Now, every time you write into the entry widget, it modifies the value of `myvar`. Because we have set a trace on `myvar`, it triggers the callback method, which in our example, simply prints the new value into the console.

The code creates a GUI window similar to the one shown here:

It also produces a console output in IDLE, which shows like the following once you start typing in the GUI window:

```
Traced variable T
Traced variable Tr
Traced variable Tra
Traced variable Trac
Traced variable Traci
Traced variable Tracin
Traced variable Tracing
```

The trace on a variable is active until it is explicitly deleted. You can delete a trace using:

```
trace_vdelete(self, mode, callbacktobedeleted)
```

The trace method returns the name of the callback method. This can be used to get the name of the callback method that is to be deleted.

Widget traversal

When a GUI has more than one widget, a given widget can come under focus by an explicit mouse-click on the widget. Alternatively, the focus can be shifted to another given widget by pressing the *Tab* key on the keyboard in the order the widgets were created in the program.

It is therefore vital to create widgets in the order we want the user to traverse through them, or else the user will have a tough time navigating between the widgets using the keyboard.

Different widgets are designed to behave differently to different keyboard strokes. Let's therefore spend some time trying to understand the rules of traversing through widgets using the keyboard.

Let's look at the code of the `8.02 widget traversal.py` Python file to understand the keyboard traversal behavior for different widgets. Once you run the mentioned `.py` file, it shows a window something like the following:

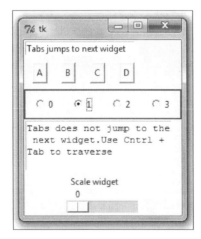

The code is simple. It adds an entry widget, a few buttons, a few radio buttons, a text widget, and a scale widget. However, it also demonstrates some of the most important keyboard traversal behaviors for these widgets.

Here are some important points to note (refer to `8.02 widget traversal.py`):

- The *Tab* key can be used to traverse forward, and *Shift + Tab* can be used to traverse backwards.
- The text widget cannot be traversed using the *Tab* key. This is because the text widget can contain tab characters as its content. Instead, the text widget can be traversed using *Ctrl + Tab*.

▸ Buttons on the widget can be pressed using the spacebar. Similarly, check buttons and radio buttons can also be toggled using the spacebar.

▸ You can go up and down the items in a Listbox widget using the up and down arrows.

▸ The Scale widget responds to both the left and right keys or up and down keys. Similarly, the Scrollbar widget responds to both the left/right or up/down keys, depending on their orientation.

▸ Most of the widgets (except Frame, Label, and Menus) get an outline by default when they have the focus set on them. This outline normally displays as a thin black border around the widget. You can even set the Frame and Label widgets to show this outline by specifying the `highlightthickness` option to a non-zero `Integer` value for these widgets.

▸ We change the color of the outline using `highlightcolor= 'red'` in our code.

▸ Frame, Label, and Menu are not included in the tab navigation path. However, they can be included in the navigation path by using the `takefocus = 1` option. You can explicitly exclude a widget from the tab navigation path by setting the `takefocus= 0` option.

▸ The *Tab* key traverses widgets in the order they were created. It visits a parent widget first (unless it is excluded using `takefocus = 0`) followed by all its children widgets.

▸ You can use `widget.focus_force()` to force the input focus to the widget.

Validating user input

Let's now discuss input data validation.

Most of the applications we have developed in our book are point and click-based (drum machine, chess, drawing application), where validation of user input is not required.

However, data validation is a *must* in programs like our phonebook application, where the user enters some data, and we store it in a database.

Ignoring the user input validation can be dangerous in such applications because input data can be misused for SQL injection. In general, any application where an user can enter textual data, is a good candidate for validating user input. In fact, it is almost considered a maxim not to trust user inputs.

A wrong user input may be intentional or accidental. In either case, if you fail to validate or sanitize the data, you may cause unexpected error in your program. In worst cases, user input can be used to inject harmful code that may be capable of crashing a program or wiping out an entire database.

Widgets such as Listbox, Combobox, and Radiobuttons allow limited input options, and hence, cannot normally be misused to input wrong data. On the other hand, widgets such as Entry widget, Spinbox widget, and Text widget allow a large possibility of user inputs, and hence, need to be validated for correctness.

To enable validation on a widget, you need to specify an additional option of the form `validate = 'validationmode'` to the widget.

For example, if you want to enable validation on an entry widget, you begin by specifying the validate option as follows:

```
Entry( root, validate="all", validatecommand=vcmd)
```

The validation can occur in one of the following **validation modes**:

Validation Mode	Explanation
none	This is the default mode. No validation occurs if `validate` is set to `"none"`
focus	When `validate` is set to `"focus"`, the `validate` command is called twice; once when the widget receives `focus` and once when the `focus` is lost
focusin	The `validate` command is called when the widget receives `focus`
focusout	The `validate` command is called when the widget loses `focus`
key	The `validate` command is called when the entry is `edited`
all	The `validate` command is called in all the above cases

The code of the `8.03 validation mode demo.py` file demonstrates all these validation modes by attaching them to a single validation method. Note the different ways different Entry widgets respond to different events. Some Entry widgets call the validation method on focus events while others call the validation method at the time of entering key strokes into the widget, while still others use a combination of focus and key events.

Although we did set the validation mode to trigger the `validate` method, we need some sort of data to validate against our rules. This is passed to the `validate` method using **percent substitution**. For instance, we passed the mode as an argument to our `validate` method by performing a percent substitution on the `validate` command, as shown in the following:

```
vcmd = (self.root.register(self.validate), '%V')
```

We followed by passing the value of `v` as an argument to our validate method:

```
def validate(self, v)
```

In addition to `%V`, Tkinter recognizes the following percent substitutions:

Percent substitutions	Explanation
`%d`	Type of action that occurred on the widget—`1` for insert, `0` for delete, and `-1` for focus, forced, or textvariable validation.
`%i`	Index of `char` string inserted or deleted, if any, else it will be `-1`.
`%P`	The value of the entry if the edit is allowed. If you are configuring the Entry widget to have a new textvariable, this will be the value of that textvariable.
`%s`	The current value of entry, prior to editing.
`%S`	The text string being inserted/deleted, if any, `{ }` otherwise.
`%v`	The type of validation currently set.
`%V`	The type of validation that triggered the callback method (key, focusin, focusout, and forced).
`%W`	The name of the Entry widget.

These validations provide us with the necessary data we can use to validate the input.

Let's now pass all these data and just print them through a dummy `validate` method just to see the kind of data we can expect to get for carrying out our validations (refer to the code of `8.04 percent substitutions demo.py`):

Take particular note of data returned by `%P` and `%s`, because they pertain to the actual data entered by the user in the Entry widget.

In most cases, you will be checking either of these two data against your validation rules.

Now that we have a background of rules of data validation, let's see two practical examples that demonstrate input validation.

Key Validation

Let's assume that we have a form that asks for a user's name. We want the user to input only alphabets or space characters in the name. Thus, any number or special character is not to be allowed, as shown in the following screenshot of the widget:

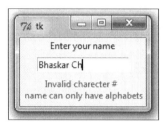

This is clearly a case of `'key'` validation mode, because we want to check if an entry is valid after every key press. The percent substitution that we need to check is `%S`, because it yields the text string being inserted or deleted in the Entry widget. Accordingly, the code that validates the entry widget is as follows (refer to `8.05 key validation.py`):

```python
import Tkinter as tk
class KeyValidationDemo():
    def __init__(self):
        root = tk.Tk()
        tk.Label(root, text='Enter your name').pack()
        vcmd = (root.register(self.validate_data), '%S')
        invcmd = (root.register(self.invalid_name), '%S')
        tk.Entry(root, validate="key", validatecommand=vcmd,
                invalidcommand=invcmd).pack(pady=5, padx=5)
        self.errmsg = tk.Label(root, text= '', fg='red')
        self.errmsg.pack()
        root.mainloop()

def validate_data(self, S):
    self.errmsg.config(text='')
    return (S.isalpha() or S =='') # always return True or False

def invalid_name(self, S):
    self.errmsg.config(text='Invalid characters \n name can
                        only have alphabets'%S)

app= KeyValidationDemo()
```

The description of the preceding code is as follows:

- We first register two options `validatecommand` (`vcmd`) and `invalidcommand` (`invcmd`).

- In our example, `validatecommand` is registered to call the `validate_data` method, and the `invalidcommand` option is registered to call another method named `invalid_name`.

- The `validatecommand` option specifies a method to be evaluated which would validate the input. The validation method must return a Boolean value, where a `True` signifies that the data entered is valid, and a `False` return value signifies that data is invalid.

- If the validate method returns `False` (invalid data), no data is added to the Entry widget and the script registered for `invalidcommand` is evaluated. In our case, a `False` validation would call the `invalid_name` method. The `invalidcommand` method is generally responsible for displaying error messages or setting back the focus to the Entry widget.

> Let's look at the code `register(self, func, subst=None, needcleanup=1)`.
>
> The `register` method returns a newly created `Tcl` function. If this function is called, the Python function `func` is executed. If an optional function `subst` is provided it is executed before `func`.

Focus Out Validation

The previous example demonstrated validation in `'key'` mode. This means that the validation method was called after every key press to check if the entry was valid.

However, there are situations when you might want to check the entire string entered into the widget, rather than checking individual key stroke entries.

For example, if an Entry widget accepts a valid e-mail address, we would ideally like to check the validity after the user has entered the entire e-mail address, and not after every key stroke entry. This would qualify as validation in `'focusout'` mode.

Check out the code of `8.06 focus out validation.py` for a demonstration on e-mail validation in the `focusout` mode:

```
import Tkinter as tk
import re
class FocusOutValidationDemo():
    def __init__(self):
        self.master = tk.Tk()
        self.errormsg = tk.Label(text='', fg='red')
        self.errormsg.pack()
        tk.Label(text='Enter Email Address').pack()
        vcmd = (self.master.register(self.validate_email), '%P')
        invcmd = (self.master.register(self.invalid_email), '%P')
        self.emailentry = tk.Entry(self.master, validate =
                "focusout",    validatecommand=vcmd,
                invalidcommand=invcmd)
        self.emailentry.pack()
        tk.Button(self.master, text="Login").pack()
        tk.mainloop()

    def validate_email(self, P):
        self.errormsg.config(text='')
        x = re.match(r"[^@]+@[^@]+\.[^@]+", P)
        return (x != None)# True(valid email)/False(invalid email)

    def invalid_email(self, P):
        self.errormsg.config(text='Invalid Email Address')
        self.emailentry.focus_set()

app = FocusOutValidationDemo()
```

The description of the preceding code is as follows:

The code has a lot of similarities to the previous validation example. However, note the following differences:

- The validate mode is set to `'focusout'` in contrast to the `'key'` mode in the previous example. This means that the validation would be done only when the Entry widget loses `focus`.

- This program uses data provided by the `%P` percentage substitution, in contrast to `%S`, as used in the previous example. This is understandable as `%P` provides the value entered in the Entry widget, but `%S` provides the value of the last key stroke.

> ▶ This program uses regular expressions to check if the entered value corresponds to a valid e-mail format. Validation usually relies on regular expressions and a whole lot of explanation to cover this topic, but it is out of the scope of this project and the book. For more information on regular expression modules, visit the following link:

```
http://docs.python.org/2/library/re.html
```

This concludes our discussion on input validation in Tkinter. Hopefully, you should now be able to implement input validation to suit your custom needs.

Formatting widget data

Several input data such as date, time, phone number, credit card number, website URL, IP number, and so on have an associated display format. For instance, date is better represented in a MM/DD/YYYY format.

Fortunately, it is easy to format the data in the required format as the user enters them in the widget (refer to `8.07 formatting entry widget to display date.py`). The mentioned Python file formats the user input automatically to insert forward slashes at the required places to display user-entered date in the MM/DD/YYYY format.

```python
from Tkinter import *
class FormatEntryWidgetDemo:
    def __init__(self, root):
        Label(root, text='Date(MM/DD/YYYY)').pack()
        self.entereddata = StringVar()
        self.dateentrywidget = \
                        Entry(textvariable=self.entereddata)
        self.dateentrywidget.pack(padx=5, pady=5)
        self.dateentrywidget.focus_set()
        self.slashpositions = [2, 5]
        root.bind('<Key>', self.format_date_entry_widget)

    def format_date_entry_widget(self, event):
```

```
            entrylist = [c for c in self.entereddata.get() if c != '/']
            for pos in self.slashpositions:
                if len(entrylist) > pos:
                    entrylist.insert(pos, '/')
            self.entereddata.set(''.join(entrylist))
            # Controlling cursor
            cursorpos = self.dateentrywidget.index(INSERT)
            for pos in self.slashpositions:
                if cursorpos == (pos + 1): # if cursor is on slash
                    cursorpos += 1
              if event.keysym not in ['BackSpace', 'Right', 'Left',
                                      'Up', 'Down']:
                    self.dateentrywidget.icursor(cursorpos)
root = Tk()
FormatEntryWidgetDemo(root)
root.mainloop()
```

The description of the preceding code is as follows:

> ▶ The Entry widget is bound to the key press event, where every new key press calls
> the related callback `format_date_entry_widget` method.

> ▶ First, the `format_date_entry_widget` method breaks down the entered text
> into an equivalent list by the name `entrylist`, also ignoring any slash `'/'` symbol
> if entered by the user.

> ▶ It then iterates through the `self.slashpositions` list and inserts the slash
> symbol at all required positions in the `entrylist` argument. The net result of this is
> a list that has slash inserted at all the right places.

> ▶ The next line converts this list into an equivalent string using `join()`, and then sets
> the value of our Entry widget to this string. This ensures that the Entry widget text is
> formatted into the aforementioned date format.

> ▶ The remaining pieces of code simply control the cursor to ensure that the cursor
> advances by one position whenever it encounters a slash symbol. It also ensures
> that key presses, such as `'BackSpace'`, `'Right'`, `'Left'`, `'Up'`, and `'Down'`
> are handled properly.

Note that this method does not validate the date value and the user may add any invalid
date. The method defined here will simply format it by adding forward slash at third and sixth
positions. Adding date validation to this example is left as an exercise for you to complete.

This concludes our brief discussion on formatting data within widgets. Hopefully, you
should now be able to create formatted widgets for a wide variety of input data that
can be displayed better in a given format.

More on fonts

Many Tkinter widgets let you specify custom font specifications either at the time of widget creation or later using the `configure()` option. For most cases, default fonts provide a standard look and feel. However, should you want to change font specifications, Tkinter lets you do so. There is one caveat though.

When you specify your own font, you need to make sure it looks good on all platforms where the program is intended to be deployed. This is because a font might look good and match well on a particular platform, but may look awful on another. Unless you know what you are doing, it is always advisable to stick to Tkinter's default fonts.

Most platforms have their own set of standard fonts that are used by the platform's native widgets. So, rather than trying to reinvent the wheel on what looks good on a given platform or what would be available for a given platform, Tkinter assigns these standard platform-specific fonts into its widget, thus providing a native look and feel on every platform.

> Tkinter assigns nine fonts to nine different names, which you can therefore use in your programs. The font names are as follows:
>
> ► `TkDefaultFont`
> ► `TkTextFont`
> ► `TkFixedFont`
> ► `TkMenuFont`
> ► `TkHeadingFont`
> ► `TkCaptionFont`
> ► `TkSmallCaptionFont`
> ► `TkIconFont`
> ► `TkTooltipFont`

Accordingly, you can use them in your programs in the following way:

```
Label(text="Sale Up to 50% Off !", font="TkHeadingFont 20")

Label(text="**Conditions Apply", font="TkSmallCaptionFont 8")
```

Using these kinds of fonts mark up, you can be assured that your font will look native across all platforms.

Finer Control over Font

In addition to the above method on handling fonts, Tkinter provides a separate `Font` class implementation. The source code of this class is located at the following link: `<Python27_installtion_dir>\Lib\lib-tk\tkfont.py`.

To use this module, you need to import `tkFont` into your namespace.(refer to `8.08 tkfont demo.py`):

```
from Tkinter import Tk, Label, Pack
import tkFont
root=Tk()
label = Label(root, text="Humpty Dumpty was pushed")
label.pack()
currentfont = tkFont.Font(font=label['font'])
print'Actual :' + str(currentfont.actual())
print'Family :' + currentfont.cget("family")
print'Weight :' + currentfont.cget("weight")
print'Text width of Dumpty : %d' %currentfont.measure("Dumpty")
print'Metrics:' + str(currentfont.metrics())
currentfont.config(size=14)
label.config (font=currentfont)
print'New Actual :' + str(currentfont.actual())
root.mainloop()
```

The console output of this program is as follows:

```
Actual :{'family': 'Segoe UI', 'weight': 'normal', 'slant': 'roman',
'overstrike': 0, 'underline': 0, 'size': 9}

Family : Segoe UI

Weight : normal

Text width of Dumpty : 43

Metrics:{'fixed': 0, 'ascent': 12, 'descent': 3, 'linespace': 15}
```

As you can see, the `tkfont` module provides a much better fine-grained control over various aspects of fonts, which are otherwise inaccessible.

Font Selector

Now that we have seen the basic features available in the `tkfont` module, let's use it to implement a font selector. The font selector would look like the one shown here:

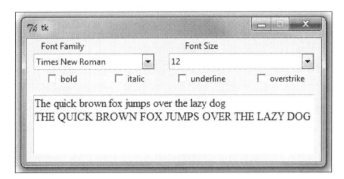

The code for the font selector is as follows (refer to `8.09 font selector.py`):

```
from Tkinter import *
import ttk
import tkFont
class FontSelectorDemo():
    def __init__(self):
        self.currentfont      = tkFont.Font(font=('Times New Roman',
                                                   12))
        self.family           = StringVar(value='Times New Roman')
        self.fontsize         = StringVar(value='12')
        self.fontweight       =StringVar(value=tkFont.NORMAL)
        self.slant            =  StringVar(value=tkFont.ROMAN)
        self.underlinevalue = BooleanVar(value=False)
        self.overstrikevalue= BooleanVar(value=False)
        self.gui_creator()
```

The description of the preceding code is as follows:

- ► We import `Tkinter` (for all widgets), `ttk` (for the Combobox widget), and `tkfont` for handling font-related aspects of the program

- ► We create a class named `FontSelectorDemo` and use its __init__ method to initialize al attributes that we intend to track in our program.

- ► Finally, the __init__ method calls another method named `gui_creator()`, which is be responsible for creating all the GUI elements of the program

Creating the GUI

The code represented here is a highly abridged version of the actual code (refer to `8.09 font selector.py`). Here, we removed all the code that creates basic widgets, such as Label and Checkbuttons, in order to show only the font-related code:

```
def gui_creator(self):
    # create the top labels - code removed
    fontList = ttk.Combobox(textvariable=self.family)
    fontList.bind('<<ComboboxSelected>>', self.on_value_change)
    allfonts = list(tkFont.families())
    allfonts.sort()
    fontList['values'] = allfonts
      # Font Sizes
    sizeList = ttk.Combobox(textvariable=self.fontsize)
    sizeList.bind('<<ComboboxSelected>>', self.on_value_change)
    allfontsizes = range(6,70)
    sizeList['values'] = allfontsizes
    # add four checkbuttons to provide choice for font style
    # all checkbuttons command attached to self.on_value_change
    #create text widget
    sampletext ='The quick brown fox jumps over the lazy dog'
    self.text.insert(INSERT, '%s\n%s'%
                        (sampletext,sampletext.upper()),'fontspecs')
    self.text.config(state=DISABLED)
```

The description of the preceding code is as follows:

▶ We have highlighted the code that creates two Combobox widgets; one for the **Font Family**, and the other for the **Font Size** selection.

▶ We use `tkfont.families()` to fetch the list of all the fonts installed on a computer. This is converted into a list format and sorted before it is inserted into the `fontList` Combobox widget.

▶ Similarly, we add a font size range of values from 6 to 70 in the **Font Size** combobox.

▶ We also add four Checkbutton widgets to keep track of font styles **bold**, **italics**, **underline**, and **overstrike**. The code for this has not been shown previously, because we have created similar check buttons in some of our previous programs.

▶ We then add a Text widget and insert a sample text into it. More importantly, we add a tag to the text named `fontspec`.

▶ Finally, all our widgets have a command callback method connecting back to a common method named `on_value_change`. This method will be responsible for updating the display of the sample text at the time of changes in the values of any of the widgets.

Updating Sample Text

```
def on_value_change(self, event=None):
    try:
        self.currentfont.config(family=self.family.get(),
          size=self.fontsize.get(), weight=self.fontweight.get(),
                          slant=self.slant.get(),
                underline=self.underlinevalue.get(),
                    overstrike=self.overstrikevalue.get())
        self.text.tag_config('fontspecs', font=self.currentfont)
    except ValueError:
        pass ### invalid entry - ignored for now. You can use a
          tkMessageBox dialog to show an error
```

The description of the preceding code is as follows:

▸ This method is called at the time of a state change for any of the widgets

▸ This method simply fetches all font data and configures our `currentfont` attribute with the updated font values

▸ Finally, it updates the text content tagged as `fontspec` with the values of the current font

Working with Unicode characters

Computers only understand binary numbers. Therefore, all that you see on your computer, for example, texts, images, audio, video, and so on need to be expressed in terms of binary numbers.

This is where encoding comes into play. An **encoding** is a set of standard rules that assign unique numeral values to each text character.

Python 2.*x* default encoding is ASCII (American Standard Code for Information Interchange). The ASCII character encoding is a 7-bit encoding that can encode 2^7 (128) characters.

Because ASCII encoding was developed in America, it encodes characters from the English alphabet, namely, the numbers 0-9, the letters a-z and A-Z, some common punctuation symbols, some teletype machine control codes, and a blank space.

It is here that Unicode encoding comes to our rescue. The following are the key features of Unicode encoding:

▸ It is a way to represent text without bytes

▸ It provides unique code point for each character of every language

- It defines more than a million code points, representing characters of all major scripts on the earth

- Within Unicode, there are several **Unicode Transformation Formats (UTF)**

- UTF-8 is one of the most commonly used encodings, where **8** means that 8-bit numbers are used in the encoding

- Python also supports UTF-16 encoding, but it's less frequently used, and UTF-32 is not supported by Python 2.*x*

Say you want to display a Hindi character on a Tkinter Label widget. You would intuitively try to run a code like the following:

```
from Tkinter import *
root = Tk()
Label(root, text = "भारतमेंआपकासुवागतहै").pack()
root.mainloop()
```

If you try to run the previous code, you will get an error message as follows:

```
SyntaxError: Non-ASCII character '\xe0' in file 8.07.py on line 4, but
no encoding declared; see http://www.Python.org/peps/pep-0263.html for
details.
```

This means that Python 2.*x*, by default, cannot handle non-ASCII characters. Python standard library supports over 100 encodings, but if you are trying to use anything other than ASCII encoding you have to explicitly declare the encoding.

Fortunately, handling other encodings is very simple in Python. There are two ways in which you can deal with non-ASCII characters. They are described in the following sections:

Declaring line encoding

The first way is to mark a string containing Unicode characters with the prefix u explicitly, as shown in the following code snippet (refer to `8.10 line encoding.py`):

```
from Tkinter import *
root = Tk()
Label(root, text = u"भारतमेंआपकासुवागतहै").pack()
root.mainloop()
```

When you try to run this program from IDLE, you get a warning message similar to the following one:

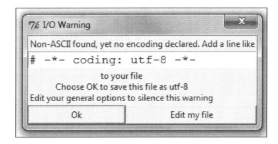

Simply click on **Ok** to save this file as UTF-8 and run this program to display the Unicode label.

Declaring file encoding

Alternatively, you can explicitly declare the entire file to have UTF-8 encoding by including a header declaration in your source file in the following format:

```
# -*- coding: <encoding-name> -*-
```

More precisely, the header declaration must match the regular expression:

```
coding[:=]\s*([-\w.]+)
```

 This declaration must be included in either the first or second line of your program. If you add some other declaration or comments in the first two lines, Python won't recognize this as a header declaration.

So, if you are dealing with UTF-8 characters, you will add the following header declaration in the first or second line of your Python program:

```
# -*- coding: utf-8 -*-
```

Simply by adding this header declaration, your Python program can now recognize Unicode characters. So, our code can be rewritten as (refer to 8.11 file encoding.py):

```
# -*- coding: utf-8 -*-
from Tkinter import *
root = Tk()
Label(root, text = "भारतमेंआपकासुवागतहै").pack()
root.mainloop()
```

Both of the above code examples generate an interface similar to the one shown here:

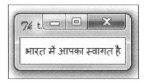

 The default encoding in Python 3.*x* is Unicode (UTF-8). This means that you don't need an explicit Unicode declaration in Python 3.*x* to display non-ASCII characters.

Tkinter class's hierarchy

As programmers, we hardly need to understand the class hierarchy of Tkinter. After all, we have been able to code all the applications so far without bothering about the overall class hierarchy.

However, knowing about class hierarchy enables us to trace the origin of a method within the source code or source documentation of a method. A brief review of the class hierarchy will also help us prevent accidental overriding of methods in our programs.

In order to understand the class hierarchy of Tkinter, let us take a look at the source code of Tkinter. On Windows installation, the source code of Tkinter is located at `C:\Python27\ Lib\lib-tk\Tkinter.py`.

When we open this file in a code editor and look at its list of class definitions, we can see the following structure:

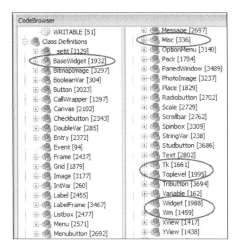

So, what do we notice here? We have class definitions for each of the core Tkinter widgets. In addition, we have class definitions for different geometry managers and different variable types defined within Tkinter. These class definitions are what you would normally expect to be there.

However, in addition to these, we notice some strange-looking class names, such as `BaseWidget`, `Misc`, `Tk`, `Toplevel`, `Widget`, and `Wm`. All these classes are circled in the above screenshot. So what services do these classes provide, and where do they fit in the larger scheme of things?

Let's use the `inspect` module to look at the class hierarchy of Tkinter. We will first inspect the class hierarchy of the Frame widget as a representation of class hierarchies for all other widgets. We will also look at the class hierarchy of the `Tk` and `Toplevel` classes to estimate their role in the overall class hierarchy of Tkinter (refer to `8.12 tkinter class hierarchy.py`):

```
import Tkinter
import inspect
print 'Class Hierarchy for Frame Widget'
for i, classname in enumerate(inspect.getmro(Tkinter.Frame)):
    print'%s: %s'%(i, classname)

print 'Class Hierarchy for Toplevel'
for i, classname in enumerate(inspect.getmro(Tkinter.Toplevel)):
    print '%s: %s'%(i, classname)

print 'Class Hierarchy for Tk'
for i, classname in enumerate(inspect.getmro(Tkinter.Tk)):
    print'%s: %s'%(i, classname)
```

The output of the preceding program is as follows:

```
Class Hierarchy for Frame Widget
0: Tkinter.Frame
1: Tkinter.Widget
2: Tkinter.BaseWidget
3: Tkinter.Misc
4: Tkinter.Pack
5: Tkinter.Place
6: Tkinter.Grid
Class Hierarchy for Toplevel
0: Tkinter.Toplevel
1: Tkinter.BaseWidget
2: Tkinter.Misc
3: Tkinter.Wm
```

```
Class Hierarchy for Tk
0:  Tkinter.Tk
1:  Tkinter.Misc
2:  Tkinter.Wm
```

The description of the preceding code is as follows:

▶ The `getmro(classname)` function from the inspect module returns a tuple, consisting of all the ancestors of `classname` in the order specified by the **Method Resolution Order (MRO)**. Method Resolution Order refers to the order in which base classes are searched when looking for a given method.

▶ By inspecting the MRO and the source code, we come to know that the `Frame` class inherits from the `Widget` class, which in turn inherits from the `BaseWidget` class.

▶ In addition, the `Frame` class also inherits from the `Misc` class, which is a generic **mixin** that provides a lot of functionality that we have used in our applications.

▶ For a list of functionalities provided by the `Misc` class, run the following commands into your Python interactive shell:

```
>>> import Tkinter
>>> help(Tkinter.Misc)
```

▶ Finally, all our widgets get properties from the geometry mixins—Pack, Grid, and Place.

▶ Next, let us take a look at the `Tk` and `Toplevel` classes.

▶ The `Tk` class represents the Toplevel widget of Tkinter, which represents the main window of an application. The `Toplevel` class provides several methods for constructing and managing a Toplevel widget with a given parent.

▶ For a list of methods provided by the `Toplevel` and `Tk` classes, run the following commands into your Python interactive shell:

```
>>>help(Tkinter.Toplevel)
>>>help(Tkinter.Tk)
```

▶ In addition to inheriting from the `Misc` mixin class, the `Toplevel` and `Tk` classes also inherit methods from the `Wm` mixin class.

▶ The `Wm` (window manager) mixin class provides a lot of functions to communicate with the window manager. For a list of functions provided by the `Wm` class, run the following command into your Python interactive shell:

```
>>>help(Tkinter.Wm)
```

After translating the class hierarchy—as obtained from the previous program—into an image, we get a hierarchy image similar to the one shown in the following:

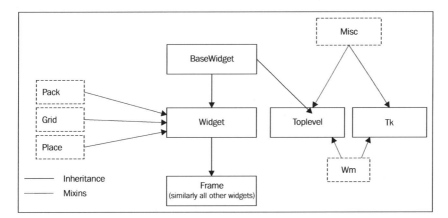

In addition to the normal inheritance relation (shown in the preceding diagram by unspotted lines), Tkinter provides a list of mixins (or helper classes). A **mixin** is a class that is designed not to be used directly, but to be combined with other classes using multiple inheritances.

Tkinter mixins can be broadly classified into two categories:

- ▶ Geometry mixins, which includes the Grid, Pack, and Place classes
- ▶ Implementation mixins, which includes:
    - ❑ The `Misc` class, which is used by the root window and widget classes, provides several Tk and window-related services
    - ❑ The `Wm` class, which is used by the root window and the Toplevel widget, provides several window manager services.

Custom-made mixins

We created a "bare bone" GUI framework in order to avoid repetition of the code that creates widgets. Similar to this concept, there is another way to avoid writing boilerplate code by using what are named **custom GUI mixins**. Take for example, the code of `8.13 creating custom mixins.py`. This program creates an interface similar to the one shown here:

Let's look at the code of 8.13 creating custom mixins.py:

```
from Tkinter import *

def frame(parent,  row, col):
    widget = Frame(parent)
    widget.grid(row= row, column=col)
    return widget

def label(parent,  row, col, text):
    widget = Label(parent, text=text)
    widget.grid(row=row, column=col,  sticky='w', padx=2)
    return widget

def button(parent, row, col, text, command):
    widget = Button(parent, text=text, command=command)
    widget.grid(row= row, column=col, sticky='e', padx=5, pady=3)
    return widget

def entry(parent,  row, col, var):
    widget = Entry(parent,textvariable= var)
    widget.grid(row= row, column=col, sticky='w', padx=5)
    return widget

def button_pressed(uname, pwd):
    print'Username: %s' %uname
    print'Password: %s'%pwd

if __name__ == '__main__':
    root = Tk()
    frm = frame(root, 0, 0)
    label(frm, 1, 0, 'Username:')
    uname= StringVar()
    entry(frm, 1, 1, uname)
    label(frm, 2, 0, 'Password:')
    pwd= StringVar()
    entry(frm, 2, 1, pwd)
    button(frm, 3, 1, 'login', lambda:
                        button_pressed(uname.get(), pwd.get()) )
    root.mainloop()
```

The description of the preceding code is as follows:

▸ This program first creates functions for different widgets, such as Frame, Label, Button, and Entry. Each method can be named a mixin, because it takes care of both widget creation and its geometry management using the grid method. These are essentially convenience functions to help us avoid writing similar code for a similar set of widgets.

▸ Now, in the main section of the program, we can create a widget in a single line of code without having to add a separate line for handling its geometry. The end result of this is fewer lines of code in our actual program. This strategy can reduce the size of your program by many lines if there are a large number of widgets in your program.

However, mixins are highly case specific. A mixin defined for one particular case scenario or application may not be applicable to another application. For instance, while defining the earlier mentioned mixins, we made a few assumptions, such as all our widgets will use the grid geometry manager, and similarly, buttons would stick to east and entries would stick to the west side. These assumptions may not hold for a different application.

Tips for code cleanup and program optimization

Let's now spend some time discussing the tips and tricks that will help improve the performance of our Python program. In a normal case scenario of GUI programming, this generally involves speeding up sections of program that contribute to improving the overall user experience.

Program optimization is often obsessively taken as an exercise in reducing code execution time. For programs where timing is a crucial factor, this obsession is genuine. However, if you are developing a simple GUI application, a correct and consistent user experience is generally more important than mere fast user experience.

Trying to optimize a code even before it is functional is premature optimization and should be avoided. However, a GUI program with correct but considerably long response time probably needs to be optimized, and this is the subject of discussion of the following sections.

Choose the right data structure

Selecting the right data structure can have a profound impact on the performance of a program. If your program is to spend considerable time on lookups, use a dictionary, if feasible. When all you need is to traverse over a collection, prefer to choose a list over dictionaries, because dictionaries take more space.

When your data is immutable, prefer to choose tuples over lists, because tuples can be traversed faster than lists.

Working with Variables

The way you select variables in your program can considerably affect the speed of the execution of your program. For instance, if you do not need to change the content or attributes of a widget after its instantiation, do not create a class-wide instance of the widget.

For example, if a Label widget is to remain static, use `Label(root, text='Name').pack(side=LEFT)`, instead of using the following snippet:

```
self.mylabel = Label(root, text='Name')
self.mylabel.pack(side=LEFT)
```

Similarly, do not create local variables if you are not going to use them more than once. For example, use `mylabel.config (text= event.keysym)` instead of first creating a local variable `key` and then using it only once:

```
key = event.keysym
mylabel.config (text=key)
```

If the local variable is to be used more than once, it may make sense to create a local variable.

Using Exceptions

Now here is a small caveat. In order to concentrate on illustrating core Tkinter concepts, we have deliberately ignored the clean exception handling in all our examples in this book.

We have implemented a "catch all errors" exception using simple try-except blocks in most of our projects. However, when programming your applications, you would ideally want to be as specific as possible about the exception you want to handle.

Python follows the EAFP (easier to ask for forgiveness than permission) style of coding, as opposed to the LBYL (look before you leap) style followed by most other programming languages.

Thus, using exception handling similar to the following one is normally cleaner in Python than checking conditions using the if-then block:

```
try:
    doSomethingNormal()
except SomethingWrong:
    doSomethingElse()
```

An example of an if-then block is shown in the following code snippet:

```
if SomethingWrong:
    doSomethingElse()
else:
    doSomethingNormal()
```

Filter and map

Python provides two built-in functions named `filter` and `map` to manipulate lists directly, rather than having to directly iterate over each item in the list. The `filter`, `map`, and `reduce` functions are faster than using loops, because a lot of the work is done by the underlying code written in C.

▸ Filter: The `filter(function, list)` function returns a list (iterators in Python 3.*x*) that contains all the items for which the function returns a true value. For example:

```
print filter(lambda num: num>6, range(1,10))# prints [7, 8, 9]
```

This is faster than running a conditional if-then check against the list.

▸ Map: The `map(func, list)` function applies `func` to each item in the list and returns the values in a new list (returns iterators instead of lists in Python 3.*x*). For example:

```
print map(lambda num: num+5, range(1,5)) #prints [6, 7, 8, 9]
```

This again is faster than running the list through a loop, adding 5 to each element.

Profiling

Profiling involves generating detailed statistics to show how often and for how long various routines of a program execute. This helps is isolating offending parts of a program, and those parts probably need redesigning.

Python 2.7.*x* provides a built-in module named cProfile, which enables generation of detailed statistics about a program. The module gives details such as the total program-running time, time taken to run each function, and the number of times each function is called. These statistics make it easy to determine the parts of code that need optimization.

In particular, **cProfile** provides the following data for a function or script:

▶ **ncalls**: The number of times a function is called

▶ **tottime**: The time spent on a function, excluding time spent on calling other functions

▶ **percall**: tottime divided by ncalls

▶ **cumtime**: The time spent on a function, including calls to other functions

▶ **percall**: cumtime divided by tottime

You can profile an individual function with the help of this:

```
import cProfile
cProfile.run('spam()','spam.profile')
```

You can then view the results of profiling using another module called pstats:

```
import pstats
stats = pstats.Stats('spam.profile')
stats.strip_dirs().sort_stats('time').print_stats()
```

More importantly, you can profile an entire script. Let's say you want to profile a script named myscript.py. You simply navigate to the directory of the script using a command-line tool, and then type and run:

Python -m cProfilemyscript.py

This produces an output similar to the following:

```
1014 function calls in 0.093 CPU seconds

Ordered by: standard name

ncallstottimepercallcumtimepercallfilename:lineno(function)
1      0.000    0.000    0.000    0.000 Tkinter.py:3686(Studbutton)
1      0.000    0.000    0.000    0.000 Tkinter.py:3694(Tributton)
416    0.001    0.000    0.002    0.000 Tkinter.py:74(_cnfmerge)
1      0.011    0.011    0.028    0.028 myscript.py:19(<module>)
2      0.058    0.029    0.086    0.043 myscript.py:20(setAge)
```

```
7520.105    0.0000.257    0.129 myscript.py:23(findAudio)
10.001     0.001     0.013     0.013 myscript.py:25(createGUI)
1     40.004    0.000     0.005     0.005 myscript.py:4(saveAudio)
1     0.000     0.000     0.000     0.000 myscript.py:49(<module>)
```

After this, you can analyze the code to see the functions that take more time to execute. In our hypothetical example in the preceding output, we notice that the functions `findAudio` and `saveAudio` take the maximum time to execute. We can then analyze these two functions to see if they can be optimized.

In addition to the cProfile module, there are other modules, such as **PyCallGraph** and **objgraph**, and they provide visual graphs for profile data.

Other Optimization Tips

Optimization is a vast topic and there is a lot that you can do. If you are interested in knowing more about code optimization, you might start with the official Python optimization tips at the following link:

```
http://wiki.python.org/moin/PythonSpeed/PerformanceTips
```

Distributing the Tkinter application

So, you have your new application ready and now you want to share it with the rest of the world. How do you do that?

Of course, you need Python installation for your program to run. Windows does not come with preinstalled Python. Most modern Linux distributions and Mac OS X come preinstalled with Python, but you don't just need any version of Python. You need a version of Python that is compatible with the version on which the program was originally written.

And then, if your program uses third-party modules, you need the appropriate module installed for the required Python version. Sure this is too much diversity to handle.

Fortunately, we have tools, such as **Freeze** tools, which allows us to distribute Python programs as standalone applications.

Given the diversity of platforms to be handled, there is a large number of Freeze tool options from which to choose. Therefore, a detailed discussion on any one of the tools is beyond the scope of this book.

We will list some of the most evolved freezing tools in the following sections. If you find a tool fitting into your distribution requirement, you can look at its documentation for more information.

py2exe

If you only need to distribute your Python application on Windows, **py2exe** is perhaps the most hardened tool. It converts Python programs into executable Windows programs that can run without requiring a Python installation. More information, a download link, and tutorials are available at `http://www.py2exe.org/`.

py2app

py2app performs the same tasks in Mac OS X that py2exe does for Windows. If you just need to distribute your Python application on Mac OS X, py2app is a time-tested tool. More information is available at `http://svn.pythonmac.org/py2app/py2app/trunk/doc/index.html`.

PyInstaller

PyInstaller has gained popularity as a freezing tool in the last few years partly because it supports a wide variety of platforms, such as Windows, Linux, Mac OS X, Solaris, and AIX.

In addition, executables created using PyInstaller are claimed to take less space than other freezing tools because it uses transparent compression. Another important feature of PyInstaller is its out of the box compatibility with a large number of third-party packages.

The full list of features, downloads, and documentation can be assessed at `http://www.pyinstaller.org/`.

Other Freezing Tools

Other freezing tool include:

> ▸ Freeze: This tool ships with standard Python distribution. Freeze can be used to compile executables only on Unix systems. However, the program is overly simplistic, as it fails to handle even the common third-party libraries. More information is available at this link:
>
> `http://wiki.python.org/moin/Freeze`

> ▸ cx_Freeze: This tool is similar to py2exe and py2app, but claims to be portable across all platforms on which that Python itself works. More information is available at this link:
>
> `http://cx-freeze.sourceforge.net/index.html`

If you're distributing a small program, a freeze tool might be just what you need. However, if you have a large program, say, with lots of external third-party library dependencies or dependencies not supported by any existing freezing tool, your application might be the right candidate for bundling the Python interpreter with your application.

Limitations of Tkinter

We have already explored the power of Tkinter. Perhaps the greatest power of Tkinter lies in its ease of use and a lightweight footprint.

However, ease of use and lightweightiness of Tkinter also result in some limitations.

Limited number of core widgets

Tkinter provides only a small number of basic widgets, and lacks a collection of more modern widgets. It needs `ttk`, `Pmw`, `Tix`, and other extensions to provide some really useful widgets. Even with these extensions, Tkinter fails to match the range of widgets provided by other GUI tools, such as **wxPython** advanced widget set and **PyQt**.

For instance, wxPython's HtmlWindow widget lets the user display HTML content with ease. There have been attempts to provide similar extensions in Tkinter, but they are far from satisfactory. Similarly, there are other widgets from Advanced User Interface Library and mixins in wxPython, such as floating/docking frames, perspective loading and saving, and others, which Tkinter users can only hope to be included in future releases.

Tkinter supporters often tend to refute this criticism by citing how easily you can construct new widgets from a collection of basic widgets.

No Support for printing

Tkinter is rightfully criticized for providing no support for printing features. Compare this to wxPython, which provides a complete printing solution in the form of a printing framework.

No support for newer image formats

Tkinter natively does not support image formats such as JPEG and PNG. The `PhotoImage` class of Tkinter can read images only in GIF and PGM/PPM formats.

Although there are workarounds, such as using ImageTk and Image submodules from the PIL module, it would have been better if Tkinter natively supported the popular image formats.

Inactive development community

Tkinter is often criticized as having a relatively inactive development community. This is true to a large extent. The documentation of Tkinter has remained a work-in-progress for many years now.

A large number of Tkinter extensions appeared over the years, but most of them have not been under active development for a long time.

Tkinter supporters refute this with the logic that Tkinter is a stable and mature technology that does not need frequent revisions like some other GUI modules that are being newly developed.

Alternatives to Tkinter

In addition to Tkinter, there are several other popular Python GUI toolkits. Most popular ones include wxPython, PyQt, **PySide**, and **PyGTK**. Here's a brief discussion on these toolkits.

wxPython

wxPython is aPython interface to **wxWidgets**, a popular open source GUI library. Code written in wxPython is portable across most major platforms such as Windows, Linux, and Mac OS X.

The wxPython interface is generally considered better than Tkinter at building more complex GUIs primarily because it has a large base of natively supported widgets. However, Tkinter supporters do contest this claim.

The wxWidgets interface is originally written in C++ programming language, and hence, wxPython inherits a large portion of the complexity that is typical of C++ programs. wxPython provides a very large base of classes, and it often takes more code to produce the same interface than it would take in Tkinter. However, in exchange for this complexity, wxPython provides a larger base of built-in widgets than Tkinter. Moreover, some people prefer the appearance of wxPython widgets over that rendered by Tkinter.

Owing to its inherent complexity, wxPython has seen the emergence of several GUI builder toolkits, such as **wxGlade**, **wxFormBuilder**, **wxDesigner**, and so on.

The wxPython installation comes with demo programs that can help you get started with the toolkit quickly. To download the toolkit or for more information on wxPython, visit the following link:

```
http://wxpython.org/
```

PyQt

PyQt is a Python interface of the cross-platform GUI toolkit Qt, a project currently developed and maintained by British firm Riverbank Computing.

PyQt, with several hundred classes and thousands of functions is perhaps the most fully-featured GUI library that is currently available for GUI programming in Python. However, this feature load brings in a lot of complexity and a steep learning curve.

Qt (and hence pyQt) has a very rich set of supported widgets. In addition, it includes built-in support for network programming, SQL databases, threads, multimedia framework, regular expressions, XML, SVG, and much more. The designer feature of Qtletsus generates GUI code from a WYSIWYG (What You See Is What You Get) interface.

PyQt is available under variety of licenses including **GNU**, **General Public License (GPL)**, and commercial license. However, its greatest disadvantage is that unlike Qt, it is unavailable under the LGPL.

PySide

If you are looking for a LGPL version of Qt bindings for Python, you may want to explore PySide. PySide was originally released under the LGPL in August 2009 by Nokia, the former owners of the **Qttoolkit**. It is now owned by Digia. More information on PySide can be obtained from the following link:

```
http://qt-project.org/wiki/PySide
```

PyGTK

PyGTK is a collection of Python bindings for the GTK + GUI library. PyGTK applications are cross-platform, and can run on Windows, Linux, MacOS X, and others. PyGTK is a free software and licensed under the LGPL. You can therefore use, modify, and distribute it with very little restrictions.

More information about PyGTK can be obtained at the following link:

```
http://www.pygtk.org/
```

Other Options

Besides these most popular toolkits, there is a range of toolkits available for GUI programming in Python.

Java programmers who are comfortable with Java GUI libraries, such as swing and AWT, can seamlessly access these libraries by using **Jython**. Similarly C# programmers can use **IronPython** to access GUI construction features from the .NET framework.

For a comprehensive list of other GUI tools available to a Python developer visit this link:

```
http://wiki.python.org/moin/GuiProgramming
```

Getting interactive help

This section is not just true about Tkinter, but for any Python object for which you need help.

Let's say you need a reference on Tkinter Pack geometry manager, you can get interactive help in your Python interactive shell using the help command, as shown in the following command lines:

```
>>> import Tkinter
>>> help(Tkinter.Pack)
```

This provides a detailed help documentation on all the methods defined under the `Pack` class in Tkinter.

You can similarly view help for all other individual widgets. For instance, you can check comprehensive and authoritative help documentation for Label widget in the interactive shell by typing:

```
>>>help(Tkinter.Label)
```

This provides a list of:

- All methods defined in class `Label`
- All standard and widget specific options for Label widget
- All methods inherited from other classes

Finally, when in doubt about a method, look into the source file located at `<location-of-python-installation>\lib\lib-tk\Tkinter.py`.

The `lib-tk` directory is the home to some great Tkinter code that you can study. In particular, you may also want to take a look at the source code of:

- turtle.py: A popular way to introduce programming to kids. It includes some cool animated effects
- Tkdnd.py: An experiment code that lets you drag and drop items on the Tkinter window.

You might also find it useful to look at the source code implementation of various other modules, such as the color chooser, file dialogs, ttk module, and others.

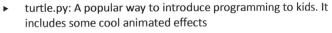

Tkinter in Python 3.*x*

In 2008, Guido van Rossum, the author of Python, forked the language into two branches— 2.*x*, and 3.*x*. This was done to clean up and make the language more consistent.

Python 3.*x* broke backward compatibility with the Python 2.*x*. For example, the print statement in Python 2.*x* was replaced by `print()` function that would now take arguments as parameters.

We coded all our Tkinter programs in Python Version 2.7, because it has a richer set of third-party libraries than Python 3.*x*, which is still considered a developing version.

The core functionality of Tkinter remains the same between 2.*x*, and 3.*x*. The only significant change to Tkinter when moving from Python 2.*x* to Python 3.*x* involves changing the way Tkinter modules are imported.

Tkinter has been renamed to **tkinter** in Python 3.*x* (capitalization has been removed). Note that in 3.*x*, the directory `lib-tk` was renamed to `tkinter`. Inside the directory, the file `Tkinter.py` was renamed to `__init__.py`, thus making tkinter an importable module.

Accordingly, the biggest major difference lies in the way you import the Tkinter module into your current namespace:

```
from Tkinter import *    # for Python2
from tkinter import *    # for Python3
```

Further, take a note of the following changes:

Python 2.x	Python 3.x
`import ttk`	`import tkinter.ttk    OR`
	`from tkinter import ttk`
`import tkMessageBox`	`import tkinter.messagebox`
`import tkColorChooser`	`import tkinter.colorchooser`
`import tkFileDialog`	`import tkinter.filedialog`
`import tkSimpleDialog`	`import tkinter.simpledialog`
`import tkCommonDialog`	`import tkinter.commondialog`
`import tkFont`	`import tkinter.font`
`import ScrolledText`	`import tkinter.scrolledtext`
`import Tix`	`import tkinter.tix`

Conclusion

To conclude, let's summarize some of the key steps involved in designing an application:

▶ Depending on what you want to design, choose a suitable data structure to represent your needs logically.

▶ If required, combine primitive data structures to form complex structures like, say, a list of dictionaries or a tuple of dictionaries.

▶ Create classes for objects that constitute your application. Add attributes that need to be manipulated and methods to manipulate those attributes.

▶ Manipulate attributes using different API provided by a rich set of Python standard and external libraries.

We tried to build several partly-functional applications in this book. And then we put up an explanation for the code. However, when you try to explain a software development process in a sequential text, you sometimes mislead your readers to imply that development of software programs is a linear process. This is hardly true.

Actual programming doesn't usually work this way. In fact, small-to-medium-sized programs are normally written in an incremental trial and error process where assumptions get changed and structures modified throughout the course of application development.

Here is how you would develop a small to medium application:

1. Start with a simple script.

2. Set a small achievable goal, implement it, and then think of adding the next feature to your program in an incremental fashion.

3. You may or may not introduce a class structure initially. If you are clear about the problem domain, you may introduce the class structure right from the very beginning.

4. If you are not sure about the class structure initially, start with simple procedural code. As your program starts to grow, you will probably start getting lot of global variables. It is here that you will start getting a glimpse of the structural dimensions of your program. It is now time to refactor and restructure your program to introduce a class structure.

> If you are writing a small program, the evolutionary **trial and error** strategy works well.
>
> If, however, you get into developing medium to large-scale applications, it is better to do some serious upfront planning before you sit down to write your code, because the cost of failure of a large program is way higher than what we can generally afford.
>
> An analogy would explain this better. You can build a small shed on a trial and error basis, but you would not attempt to build a skyscraper without some serious planning.

It is also important not to be unnecessarily bogged down by ever evolving jargons in the technical world. Programming is less about knowing a particular API or even a particular programming language. You can literally get to know the basic constructs of a programming language in a small sitting. Programming is rather a tool for finding solution to your immediate problems.

That brings us to the end of the book. I hope this book has taught you something about GUI programming with Python and Tkinter.

Beyond reading books, there is really no substitute for doing some original GUI programming. So, take up an original programming challenge and execute it for the fun of it.

How you implement it is a matter of individual experiences and taste. Do what feels comfortable to you, but keep yourself open to the idea of continuous refactoring at every stage of development.

Quick Reference Sheets

Options common to widgets

The following table consists options common to most of the widgets their functionalities and the list of widgets to which the options are not applicable:

Widget option	Function	Not applicable to widgets
`background` (bg)	Picks background color.	
`borderwidth` (bd)	Defines width of border in pixel.	
`cursor`	It is the mouse cursor to be used for the widget.	
`relief`	It specifies the border style for a widget.	
`takefocus`	If window accepts focus during keyboard traversal.	
`width`	An integer specifying the relative width of a widget.	Menu
`font`	It specifies font family and font size.	Toplevel, Canvas, Frame, and Scrollbar

Widget option	Function	Not applicable to widgets
`foreground (fg)`	It specifies foreground color.	Toplevel, Canvas, Frame, and Scrollbar
`highlightbackground`	color	Menu
`highlightcolor`	color	Menu
`highlightthickness`	It is measured in pixels.	Menu
`relief`	Specifies the 3D effect to be applied to a given widget. Valid values are RAISED, SUNKEN, FLAT, RIDGE, SOLID, and GROOVE.	
`takefocus`	Specified as 1 or 0 representing whether or not a widget takes focus during keyboard tab-based traversal.	
`width`	Integer specifying the width of a widget.	Menu

The following table consists options common to most of the widgets their functionalities and the list of widgets to which the options are applicable:

Widget Option	Function	Applicable to
`activebackground`	Color of background when widget is active.	Menu, Menubutton, Button, Checkbutton, Radiobutton, Scale, and Scrollbar
`activeforeground`	Color of foreground when widget is active.	Menu, Menubutton, Button, Checkbutton, and Radiobutton
`anchor`	Indicates where text or a bitmap would be displayed on a widget. Valid values are n, ne, e, se, s, sw, w, nw, or center.	Menubutton, Button, Checkbutton, Radiobutton, Label, and Message
`bitmap`	Indicates a bitmap to display in the widget.	Menubutton, Button, Checkbutton, Radiobutton, and Label
`command`	Indicates a command callback to associate with the widget, which would be normally invoked on mouse button 1 release over the widget.	Button, Checkbutton, Radiobutton, Scale, and Scrollbar

Widget Option	Function	Applicable to
`disabledforeground`	Indicates the foreground color to display when a widget is in disabled state.	Menu, Menubutton, Button, Checkbutton, and Radiobutton
`height`	Indicates height of widget, in units in which the font has been specified for the given widget.	Toplevel, Menubutton, Button, Checkbutton, Radiobutton, Label, Frame, Listbox, and Canvas
`image`	Indicates an image to display in the widget.	Menubutton, Button, Checkbutton, Radiobutton, and Label
`justify`	Applicable when multiple lines of text are displayed in a widget. This determines how the text lines line up with each other. Must be one of LEFT, CENTER, or RIGHT.	Menubutton, Button, Checkbutton, Radiobutton, Label, Entry, and Message
`selectbackground`	Indicates the background color to show when displaying selected items.	Text, Listbox, Entry, and Canvas
`selectborderwidth`	Indicates the border width to show when displaying selected items.	Text, Listbox, Entry, and Canvas
`selectforeground`	Indicates the foreground color to show when displaying selected items.	Text, Listbox, Entry, and Canvas
`state`	Indicates one of two or three states that a widget may be under. Valid values `normal`, `active`, or `disabled`.	Menubutton, Button, Checkbutton, Radiobutton, Text, Entry, and Scale
`text`	Indicates a string to be displayed inside the widget.	Menubutton, Button, Checkbutton, Radiobutton, Label, and Message
`textvariable`	Indicates the name of a variable. The value of the variable is changed to string in order to be displayed in the widget. The widget automatically updates as and when the variable value changes.	Menubutton, Button, Checkbutton, Radiobutton, Label, Entry, and Message
`underline`	Indicates the integer index of a character to underline in the widget.	Menubutton, Button, Checkbutton, Radiobutton, and Label
`wraplength`	Indicates the maximum line length for widgets that have word wrapping.	Menubutton, Button, Checkbutton, Radiobutton, and Label

Widget-specific options

We do not reproduce all widget-specific options. You can obtain all available options for a given widget in the Python interactive shell using the help command.

To obtain help on any `Tkinter` class, you first import Tkinter into the namespace like:

```
>>>import Tkinter
```

The following commands can then be used to get information on a particular widget:

Widget Name	Getting Help
Label	`help(Tkinter.Label)`
Button	`help(Tkinter.Button)`
Canvas	`help(Tkinter.Canvas)`
CheckButton	`help(Tkinter.Checkbutton)`
Entry	`help(Tkinter.Entry)`
Frame	`help(Tkinter.Frame)`
LabelFrame	`help(Tkinter.LabelFrame)`
Listbox	`help(Tkinter.Listbox)`
Menu	`help(Tkinter.Menu)`
Menubutton	`help(Tkinter.Menubutton)`
Message	`help(Tkinter.Message)`
OptionMenu	`help(Tkinter.OptionMenu)`
PanedWindow	`help(Tkinter.PanedWindow)`
RadioButton	`help(Tkinter.Radiobutton)`
Scale	`help(Tkinter.Scale)`
Scrollbar	`help(Tkinter.Scrollbar)`
Spinbox	`help(Tkinter.Spinbox)`
Text	`help(Tkinter.Text)`
Bitmap Class	`help(Tkinter.BitmapImage)`
Image Class	`help(Tkinter.Image)`

The pack manager

The pack geometry manager is the oldest geometry manager available with Tk and Tkinter. The pack geometry manager places slave widgets in a master widget, adding them one at a time in the order in which slaves are introduced. Following table shows the available `pack()` methods and options:

Methods	Description
`config = configure = pack_ configure(self, cnf={}, **kw)`	Pack a widget in the parent widget. Use as options: ▸ `after=widget`: pack it after you have packed widget ▸ `anchor=NSEW` (or subset): position widget according to given direction ▸ `before=widget`: pack it before you will pack widget ▸ `expand=bool`: expand widget if parent size grows ▸ `fill=NONE` (or `X` or `Y` or `BOTH`): fill widget if widget grows ▸ `in=master`: use master to contain this widget ▸ `in_=master`: see 'in' option description ▸ `ipadx=amount`: add internal padding in x direction ▸ `ipady=amount`: add internal padding in y direction ▸ `padx=amount`: add padding in x direction ▸ `pady=amount`: add padding in y direction ▸ `side=TOP` (or `BOTTOM` or `LEFT` or `RIGHT`): where to add this widget
`forget = pack_ forget(self)`	Unmap this widget and do not use it for the packing order.
`info = pack_ info(self)`	Return information about the packing options for this widget.
`propagate =pack_ propagate(self, flag=['_ noarg_']) from Tkinter.Misc`	Set or get the status for propagation of geometry information. A Boolean argument specifies whether the geometry information of the slaves will determine the size of this widget. If no argument is given, the current setting will be returned.
`slaves = pack_ slaves(self) from Tkinter. Misc`	Return a list of all slaves of this widget in its packing order.

The grid manager

The grid is easy to implement and equally easy to modify, making it the most popular choice for most use cases. Following is a list of methods and options available for layout management with the `grid()` geometry manager:

Methods defined here	Description
`bbox = grid_ bbox(self, column=None, row=None, col2=None, row2=None) from Tkinter.Misc`	Return a tuple of integer coordinates for the bounding box of this widget controlled by the geometry manager grid. If `column`, `row` is given, the bounding box applies from the cell with row and column 0 to the specified cell. If `col2` and `row2` are given, the bounding box starts at that cell. The returned integers specify the offset of the upper left corner in the master widget and the width and height.
`columnconfigure = grid_columnconfigure (self, index, cnf={}, **kw) from Tkinter.Misc`	Configures column `index` of a grid. Valid resources are minsize (minimum size of the column),weight (how much does additional space propagate to this column), and pad (how much space to let additionally).
`grid = config = configure = grid_ configure(self, cnf={}, **kw)`	Position a widget in the parent widget in a grid. Use as options: ▶ `column=number`: use cell identified with given column (starting with 0) ▶ `columnspan=number`: this widget will span several columns ▶ `in=master`: use master to contain this widget ▶ `in_=master`: see 'in' option description ▶ `ipadx=amount`: add internal padding in x direction ▶ `ipady=amount`: add internal padding in y direction ▶ `padx=amount`: add padding in x direction ▶ `pady=amount`: add padding in y direction ▶ `row=number`: use cell identified with given row (starting with 0) ▶ `rowspan=number`: this widget will span several rows ▶ `sticky=NSEW`: if cell is larger on which sides will this widget stick to the cell boundary
`forget = grid_ forget(self)`	Un-map this widget.

Methods defined here	Description
`info = grid_` `info(self)`	Return information about the options for positioning this widget in a grid.

`grid_location(self,`
`x, y) from Tkinter.`
`Misc`
	Return a tuple of column and row which identify the cell at which the pixel at position X and Y inside the master widget is located.

`grid_propagate(self,`
`flag=['_noarg_'])`
`from Tkinter.Misc`
	Set or get the status for propagation of geometry information.
	
	A Boolean argument specifies whether the geometry information of the slaves will determine the size of this widget. If no argument is given, the current setting will be returned.

`grid_remove(self)`	Un-map this widget, but remember the grid options.

`grid_`
`rowconfigure(self,`
`index, cnf={}, **kw)`
`from Tkinter.Misc`
	Configure row index of a grid.
	
	Valid resources are minsize (minimum size of the row),weight (how much does additional space propagate to this row), and pad (how much space to let additionally) .

`size = grid_`
`size(self) from`
`Tkinter.Misc`
	Return a tuple of the number of column and rows in the grid.

`slaves = grid_`
`slaves(self,`
`row=None,`
`column=None) from`
`Tkinter.Misc`
	Return a list of all slaves of this widget in its packing order.

`location = grid_`
`location(self, x, y)`
`from Tkinter.Misc`
	Return a tuple of column and row which identify the cell at which the pixel at position X and Y inside the master widget is located.

`propagate = grid_`
`propagate(self,`
`flag=['_noarg_'])`
`from Tkinter.Misc`
	Set or get the status for propagation of geometry information.
	
	A Boolean argument specifies whether the geometry information of the slaves will determine the size of this widget. If no argument is given, the current setting will be returned.

`rowconfigure = grid_`
`rowconfigure(self,`
`index, cnf={}, **kw)`
`from Tkinter.Misc`
	Configure row INDEX of a grid.
	
	Valid resources are minsize (minimum size of the row),weight (how much does additional space propagate to this row), and pad (how much space to let additionally).

The place manager

The `place()` geometry manager allows for precise positioning of widgets based on absolute or relative coordinates for a given window. The following table lists methods and options available under place geometry manager:

Methods defined here	Description

`config =`
`configure`
`= place_`
`configure(self,`
`cnf={}, **kw)`
	Place a widget in the parent widget. Use as options:
	
	▸ `in=master`: master relative to which the widget is placed
	
	▸ `in_=master`: see 'in' option description
	
	▸ `x=amount`: locate anchor of this widget at position x of master
	
	▸ `y=amount`: locate anchor of this widget at position y of master
	
	▸ `relx=amount`: locate anchor of this widget between 0.0 and 1.0 relative to width of master (1.0 is right edge)
	
	▸ rely=amount: locate anchor of this widget between 0.0 and 1.0 relative to height of master (1.0 is bottom edge)
	
	▸ `anchor=NSEW` (or subset): position anchor according to given direction
	
	▸ `width=amount`: width of this widget in pixel
	
	▸ `height=amount`: height of this widget in pixel
	
	▸ `relwidth=amount`: width of this widget between 0.0 and 1.0 relative to width of master (1.0 is the same width as the master)
	
	▸ `relheight=amount`: height of this widget between 0.0 and 1.0 relative to height of master (1.0 is the same height as the master)
	
	▸ `bordermode="inside"` (or `"outside"`): whether to take border width of master widget into account

`forget = place_` `forget(self)`	Un-map this widget.
`info = place_` `info(self)`	Return information about the placing options for this widget.

`slaves = place_`
`slaves(self)`
`from Tkinter.`
`Misc`
	Return a list of all slaves of this widget in its packing order.

The event types

The general format for representing an event is as follows:

```
<[event modifier-]...event type [-event detail]>
```

It is compulsory to specify the event types for any event binding. Also note that event types, event modifier, and event details vary across platforms. The following table represents event types with their description:

Event type	Description
Activate	Change in the state option of a widget from inactive (grayed out) to active.
Button	Press of a mouse button. The event detail part specifies which button.
ButtonRelease	Release of a pressed mouse button.
Configure	Change of size of a widget.
Deactivate	Change in the state option of a widget from active to inactive (grayed out).
Destroy	Destruction of a widget using the `widget.destroy` method.
Enter	Mouse pointer enters a visible part of a widget.
Expose	At least some part of widget becomes visible after remaining covered by another window.
FocusIn	Widget gets input focus either due to a user event (like using the *Tab* key or mouse click) or on call of `.focus_set()` on a widget
FocusOut	Focus moved out of a widget.
KeyPress/Key	Press of a key on the keyboard. The event-detail part specifies which key.
KeyRelease	Release of a pressed key.
Leave	Mouse pointer moves out of a widget.
Map	Widget is mapped (made visible). Occurs say when you call a geometry manager on a widget.
Motion	Mouse pointer moves entirely within a widget.
Un-map	Widget is unmapped (made invisible). For example, when you use the `remove()` method.
Visibility	At least a part of the window becomes visible.

The event modifiers

The event modifiers are an optional component for creating an event binding. A list of event modifiers is listed as follows. However, note that most of the event modifiers are platform-specific and may not work across all platforms.

Modifier	Description
Alt	True when *Alt* key is pressed.
Any	Generalizes an event type. For example `<Any-KeyPress>` is True when any key is pressed.
Control	True when *Ctrl* (Control) key is pressed.
Double	Specifies two events occurring in rapid succession. For example, `<Double-Button-1>`is double-click of mouse button 1.
Lock	True if *Caps Lock/Shift* lock is pressed
Shift	True if *Shift* key is pressed
Triple	Similar to Double (three events occurring in rapid succession)

The event details

Event details are optional components for creating an event binding. They generally denote the mouse button or details of a key stroke on the keyboard using a key symbol abbreviated as **keysym**.

List of all available event details is as follows:.keysym	.keycode	.keysym_num	Key
Alt_L	64	65513	Left *Alt* key
Alt_R	113	65514	Right *Alt* key
BackSpace	22	65288	*Backspace*
Cancel	110	65387	Break
Caps_Lock	66	65549	*CapsLock*
Control_L	37	65507	Left *Ctrl* key
Control_R	109	65508	Right *Ctrl* key
Delete	107	65535	*Delete*
Down	104	65364	Down arrow key

List of all available event details is as follows:.keysym	.keycode	.keysym_num	Key
End	103	65367	*End*
Escape	9	65307	*Esc*
Execute	111	65378	*SysRq*
F1 - F11	67 to 95	65470 to 65480	Function key *F1* to *F11*
F12	96	65481	Function key *F12*
Home	97	65360	*Home*
Insert	106	65379	*Insert*
Left	100	65361	Left side arrow key
Linefeed	54	106	Linefeed/*Ctrl + J*
KP_0	90	65438	*0* on keypad
KP_1	87	65436	*1* on keypad
KP_2	88	65433	*2* on keypad
KP_3	89	65435	*3* on keypad
KP_4	83	65430	*4* on keypad
KP_5	84	65437	*5* on keypad
KP_6	85	65432	*6* on keypad
KP_7	79	65429	*7* on keypad
KP_8	80	65431	*8* on keypad
KP_9	81	65434	*9* on keypad
KP_Add	86	65451	*+* on keypad
KP_Begin	84	65437	Center key on keypad (same as key *5*)
KP_Decimal	91	65439	Decimal (.) key on keypad
KP_Delete	91	65439	Delete (*Del*) key on keypad
KP_Divide	112	65455	*/* on keypad
KP_Down	88	65433	Down arrow key on keypad
KP_End	87	65436	*End* on keypad
KP_Enter	108	65421	*Enter* on keypad
KP_Home	79	65429	*Home* on keypad

List of all available event details is as follows:.keysym	.keycode	.keysym_num	Key
KP_Insert	90	65438	*Insert* on keypad
KP_Left	83	65430	Left arrow key on keypad
KP_Multiply	63	65450	* on keypad
KP_Next	89	65435	*Page Down* on keypad
KP_Prior	81	65434	*Page Up* on keypad
KP_Right	85	65432	Right arrow key on keypad
KP_Subtract	82	65453	- on keypad
KP_Up	80	65431	Up arrow key on keypad
Next	105	65366	*Page Down*
Num_Lock	77	65407	*Num Lock*
Pause	110	65299	*Pause*
Print	111	65377	*Prt Scr*
Prior	99	65365	*Page Up*
Return	36	65293	*Enter* key / *Ctrl + M*
Right	102	65363	Right arrow key
Scroll_Lock	78	65300	*Scroll Lock*
Shift_L	50	65505	Left *Shift* key
Shift_R	62	65506	Right *Shift* key
Tab	23	65289	*Tab* key
Up	98	65362	Up arrow key

Other event-related methods

Binding of a handler to an event can happen at various levels using `bind`, `bind_all`, `bind_class`, and `tag_bind`.

If an event binding is registered to a callback function, the callback function is called with an Event as its first argument. The event argument has the following attributes:

Attribute	Description	Valid for event types
event.serial	Serial number of event.	All
event.num	Mouse button pressed.	ButtonPress and ButtonRelease
event.focus	Whether the window has the focus.	Enter and Leave
event.height	Height of the exposed window.	Configure and Expose
event.width	Width of the exposed window.	Configure and Expose
event.keycode	Keycode of the pressed key.	KeyPress and KeyRelease
event.state	State of the event as a number.	ButtonPress, ButtonRelease, Enter, KeyPress, KeyRelease, Leave, and Motion
event.state	State as a string.	Visibility
event.time	When the event occurred.	All
event.x	It gives the x-position of the mouse.	All
event.y	It gives the y-position of the mouse.	All
event.x_root	It gives the x-position of the mouse on the screen.	ButtonPress, ButtonRelease, KeyPress, KeyRelease, and Motion
event.y_root	It gives the y-position of the mouse on the screen.	ButtonPress, ButtonRelease, KeyPress, KeyRelease, and Motion
event.char	It gives the pressed character.	KeyPress and KeyRelease
event.keysym	It gives the keysym of the event as a string.	KeyPress and KeyRelease
event.keysym_num	It gives the keysym of the event as a number.	KeyPress and KeyRelease
event.type	Type of the event as a number.	All
event.widget	Widget in which the event occurred.	All
event.delta	Delta of wheel movement.	MouseWheel

List of available cursor

The cursor widget option allows a Tk programmer to change the mouse cursor for a particular widget. The cursor names recognized by Tk on all platforms are:

X_cursor	arrow	based_ arrow_ down	based_ arrow_up	boat	bogosity
bottom_ left_ corner	bottom_ right_ corner	bottom_ side	box_ spiral	center_ ptr	circle
clock	coffee_ mug	cross	cross_ reverse	crosshair	diamond _cross
dot	dotbox	double_ arrow	draft_ large	draft_ small	draped_ box
exchange	fleur	gobbler	gumby	hand1	hand2
heart	icon	iron_ cross	left_ptr	left_side	left_tee
leftbutton	ll_angle	lr_angle	man	bottom_ tee	middle button
mouse	pencil	pirate	plus	question_ arrow	right_ptr
right_side	right_ tee	right button	rtl_logo	sailboat	sb_down_ arrow
sb_h_ double_ arrow	sb_left_ arrow	sb_right_ arrow	sb_up_ arrow	sb_v_ double_ arrow	shuttle
sizing	spider	spraycan	star	target	tcross
top_left_ arrow	top_ left_ corner	top_ right_ corner	top_side	top_tee	trek
ul_angle	umbrella	ur_angle	watch	xterm	

See *9.01 all cursor demo.py* for a demonstration of all cross platform cursors.

Potability issues

▸ Windows: The cursors that have native mapping on Windows are, arrow, center_ ptr, crosshair, fleur, ibeam, icon, sb_h_double_arrow, sb_v_double_ arrow, watch, **and** xterm.

And the following additional cursors available are, no, `starting`, `size`, `size_ne_sw`, `size_ns`, `size_nw_se`, `size_we`, `uparrow`, `wait`.

The `no` cursor can be specified to eliminate the cursor.

▶ Mac OS X: The cursors that have native mapping on Mac OS X systems are, `arrow`, `cross`, `crosshair`, `ibeam`, `plus`, `watch`, `xterm`.

And the following additional native cursors available are, `copyarrow`, `aliasarrow`, `contextualmenuarrow`, `text`, `cross-hair`, `closedhand`, `openhand`, `pointinghand`, `resizeleft`, `resizeright`, `resizeleftright`, `resizeup`, `resizedown`, `resizeupdown`, `none`, `notallowed`, `poof`, `countinguphand`, `countingdownhand`, `countingupanddownhand`, `spinning`.

The basic widget methods

These methods are provided under class Widget in module Tkinter. You can view the documentation for these methods in your interactive shell using the following commands:

```
>>> import Tkinter
>>>help(Tkinter.Widget)
```

A list of available methods under Widgets class is as follows:

Method	Description
after(self, ms, func=None, *args)	Calls function once after given time. MS specifies the time in milliseconds. FUNC gives the function, which shall be called. Additional parameters are given as parameters to the function call. Return: identifier to cancel scheduling with after_cancel.
after_cancel(self, id)	Cancel scheduling of function identified with ID. Identifier returned by after or after_idle must be given as first parameter.
after_idle(self, func, *args)	Call FUNC once if the Tcl main loop has no event to process. Return an identifier to cancel the scheduling with after_cancel.
bbox = grid_bbox(self, column=None, row=None, col2=None, row2=None)	Return a tuple of integer coordinates for the bounding box of this widget controlled by the geometry manager grid. If COLUMN, ROW are given, the bounding box applies from the cell with row and column 0 to the specified cell. If COL2 and ROW2 are given, the bounding box starts at that cell. The returned integers specify the offset of the upper left corner in the master widget and the width and height.

Method	Description

`bind(self,`
`sequence=None,`
`func=None, add=None)`
	Bind to this widget at event SEQUENCE a call to function FUNC. SEQUENCE is a string of concatenated event patterns. An event pattern is of the form `<MODIFIER-MODIFIER-TYPE-DETAIL>`. An event pattern can also be a virtual event of the form `<<AString>>` where AString can be arbitrary. This event can be generated by `event_generate`. If events are concatenated, they must appear shortly after each other.

	FUNC will be called if the event sequence occurs with an instance of Event as argument. If the return value of FUNC is "break", no further bound function is invoked.
	An additional Boolean parameter ADD specifies whether FUNC will be called additionally to the other bound function or whether it will replace the previous function. Bind will return an identifier to allow deletion of the bound function with unbind without memory leak.
	If FUNC or SEQUENCE is omitted, the bound function or list of bound events are returned.

`bind_all(self,`
`sequence=None,`
`func=None, add=None)`
	Bind to all widgets at an event SEQUENCE a call to function FUNC. An additional Boolean parameter ADD specifies whether FUNC will be called additionally to the other bound function, or whether it will replace the previous function. See bind for the return value.

`bind_class(self,`
`className,`
`sequence=None,`
`func=None, add=None)`
	Bind to widgets with bind tag CLASSNAME at event SEQUENCE a call of function FUNC. An additional Boolean parameter ADD specifies whether FUNC will be called additionally to the other bound function or whether it will replace the previous function. See bind for the return value.

`bindtags(self,` `tagList=None)`	Set or get the list of bindtags for this widget. With no argument, return the list of all bindtags associated with this widget. With a list of strings as argument the bindtags are set to this list. The bindtags determine in which order events are processed (see bind).
`cget(self, key)`	Return the resource value for a Key given as string.
`clipboard_append(self,` `string, **kw)`	Append String to the Tk clipboard. A widget specified at the optional display of keyword argument specifies the target display. The clipboard can be retrieved with `selection_get`.
`clipboard_clear(self,` `**kw)`	Clear the data in the Tk clipboard. A widget specified for the optional display of keyword argument specifies the target display.

Method	Description
`clipboard_get(self, **kw)`	Retrieve data from the clipboard on window's display. The window keyword defaults to the root window of the Tkinter application. The type keyword specifies the form in which the data is to be returned, and should be an atom name, such as STRING or FILE_NAME. Type defaults to `String`. This command is equivalent to: `selection_get(CLIPBOARD)`.
`columnconfigure = grid_columnconfigure (self, index, cnf={}, **kw)`	Configure column `Index` of a grid. Valid resources are minsize (minimum size of the column),weight (how much does additional space propagate to this column), and pad (how much space to let additionally).
`config = configure(self, cnf=None, **kw)`	Configure resources of a widget. The values for resources are specified as keyword arguments. To get an overview about the allowed keyword arguments, call the method keys.
`event_add(self, virtual, *sequences)`	Bind a virtual event `virtual` (of the form <<Name>>) to an event `sequence` such that the virtual event is triggered whenever SEQUENCE occurs.
`event_delete(self, virtual, *sequences)`	Unbind a virtual event `virtual` from `sequence`.
`event_generate(self, sequence, **kw)`	Generate an event `sequence`. Additional keyword arguments specify parameter of the event(for example, x, y, rootx, and rooty).
`event_info(self, virtual=None)`	Return a list of all virtual events or the information about the `sequence` bound to the virtual event `virtual`.
`focus = focus_set(self)`	Direct input focus to this widget. If the application currently does not have the focus, this widget will get the focus if the application gets the focus through the window manager.
`focus_displayof(self)`	Return the widget which has currently the focus on the display where this widget is located. Return None if the application does not have the focus.
`focus_force(self)`	Direct input focus to this widget even if the application does not have the focus. Use with caution!
`focus_get(self)`	Return the widget which has currently the focus in the application. Use `focus_displayof` to allow working with several displays. Return None if application does not have the focus.
`focus_lastfor(self)`	Return the widget which would have the focus if top level for this widget gets the focus from the window manager.

Method	Description
`focus_set(self)`	Direct input focus to this widget. If the application currently does not have the focus this widget will get the focus if the application gets the focus through the window manager.
`getboolean(self, s)`	Return a Boolean value for Tclboolean values true and false given as parameter.
`getvar(self, name='PY_VAR')`	Return value of Tcl variable `name`.
`grab_current(self)`	Return widget which has currently the grab in this application or None.
`grab_release(self))`	Release grab for this widget if currently set.
`grab_set(self)`	Set grab for this widget. A grab directs all events to this and descendant widgets in the application.
`grab_set_global(self)`	Set global grab for this widget. A global grab directs all events to this and descendant widgets on the display. Use with caution - other applications do not get events anymore.
`grab_status(self)`	Return None, "local" or "global" if this widget has no, a local or a global grab.
`grid_bbox(self, column=None, row=None, col2=None, row2=None)`	Return a tuple of integer coordinates for the bounding box of this widget controlled by the geometry manager grid. If `column`, `row` is given, the bounding box applies from the cell with row and column 0 to the specified cell. If `col2` and `row2` are given, the bounding box starts at that cell. The returned integers specify the offset of the upper left corner in the master widget and the width and height.
`grid_columnconfigure(self, index, cnf={}, **kw)`	Configure column `index` of a grid. Valid resources are minsize (minimum size of the column), weight (how much does additional space propagate to this column), and pad (how much space to let additionally).
`grid_location(self, x, y)`	Return a tuple of column and row which identify the cell at which the pixel at position `x` and `y` inside the master widget is located.
`grid_propagate(self, flag=['_noarg_'])`	Set or get the status for propagation of geometry information. A Boolean argument specifies whether the geometry information of the slaves will determine the size of this widget. If no argument is given, the current setting will be returned.

Method	Description
grid_rowconfigure(self, index, cnf={}, **kw)	Configure row index of a grid. Valid resources are minsize (minimum size of the row),weight (how much does additional space propagate to this row), and pad (how much space to let additionally).
grid_size(self)	Return a tuple of the number of column and rows in the grid.
grid_slaves(self, row=None, column=None)	Return a list of all slaves of this widget in its packing order.
image_names(self)	Return a list of all existing image names.
image_types(self)	Return a list of all available image types (e.g. photo bitmap).
keys(self)	Return a list of all resource names of this widget.
lift = tkraise(self, aboveThis=None)	Raise this widget in the stacking order.
lower(self, belowThis=None)	Lower this widget in the stacking order.
mainloop(self, n=0)	Call the mainloop of Tk.
nametowidget(self, name)	Return the Tkinter instance of a widget identified by its Tcl name NAME.
option_add(self, pattern, value, priority=None)	Set a value (second parameter) for an option PATTERN (first parameter). An optional third parameter gives the numeric priority (defaults to 80).
option_clear(self)	Clear the option database. It will be reloaded if option_add is called.
option_get(self, name, className)	Return the value for an option NAME for this widget with classname. Values with higher priority override lower values.
option_readfile(self, fileName, priority=None)	Read file filename into the option database. An optional second parameter gives the numeric priority.
propagate =pack_propagate(self, flag=['_noarg_'])	Set or get the status for propagation of geometry information. A Boolean argument specifies whether the geometry information of the slaves will determine the size of this widget. If no argument is given, the current setting will be returned.
pack_slaves(self)	Return a list of all slaves of this widget in its packing order.
quit(self)	Quit the Tcl interpreter. All widgets will be destroyed.

Method	Description
`register = _ register(self, func, subst=None, needcleanup=1)`	Return a newly created Tcl function. If this function is called, the Python function `func` will be executed. An optional function `subst` can be given, which will be executed before `func`.
`rowconfigure = grid_ rowconfigure(self, index, cnf={}, **kw)`	Configure row `index` of a grid. Valid resources are minsize (minimum size of the row), weight (how much does additional space propagate to this row), and pad (how much space to let additionally).
`selection_clear(self, **kw)'`	Clear the current X selection.
`selection_get(self, **kw)`	Return the contents of the current X selection. A keyword parameter selection specifies the name of the selection and defaults to PRIMARY. A keyword parameter display of specifies a widget on the display to use.
`selection_handle(self, command, **kw)`	Specify a function `command` to call if the X selection owned by this widget is queried by another application. This function must return the contents of the selection. The function will be called with the arguments OFFSET and LENGTH, which allows the chunking of very long selections. The following keyword parameters can be provided: selection - name of the selection (default PRIMARY), type - type of the selection (for example, `string`, FILE_NAME).
`selection_own(self, **kw)`	Become owner of X selection. A keyword parameter selection specifies the name of the selection (default PRIMARY).
`selection_own_get(self, **kw)`	Return owner of X selection. The following keyword parameter can be provided: selection - name of the selection (default PRIMARY), type - type of the selection (e.g. STRING, FILE_NAME).
`send(self, interp, cmd, *args)`	Send Tcl command CMD to different interpreter INTERP to be executed.
`setvar(self, name='PY_ VAR', value='1')`	Set Tcl variable NAME to VALUE.
`size = grid_size(self)`	Return a tuple of the number of column and rows in the grid.
`slaves = pack_ slaves(self)`	Return a list of all slaves of this widget in its packing order.
`tk_focusFollowsMouse (self)`	The widget under mouse will get automatically focus. Cannot be disabled easily.

Method	Description
`tk_focusNext(self)`	Return the next widget in the focus order which follows widget which has currently the focus. The focus order first goes to the next child, then to the children of the child recursively and then to the next sibling which is higher in the stacking order. A widget is omitted if it has the takefocus resource set to 0.
`tk_focusPrev(self)`	Return previous widget in the focus order. See `tk_focusNext` for details.
`tk_setPalette(self, *args, **kw)`	Set a new color scheme for all widget elements. A single color as argument will cause that all colors of Tk widget elements are derived from this. Alternatively, several keyword parameters and its associated colors can be given. The following keywords are valid: `activeBackground`, `foreground`, `selectColor`, `activeForeground`, `highlightBackground`, `selectBackground`, `background`, `highlightColor`, `selectForeground`, `disabledForeground`, `insertBackground`, and `troughColor`.
`tkraise(self, aboveThis=None)`	Raise this widget in the stacking order.
`unbind(self, sequence, funcid=None)`	Unbind for this widget for event SEQUENCE the function identified with FUNCID.
`unbind_all(self, sequence)'`	Unbind for all widgets for event SEQUENCE all functions.
`unbind_class(self, className, sequence)`	Unbind all widgets with bindtag `classname` for event `sequence` all functions.
`update(self)`	Enter event loop until all pending events have been processed by Tcl.
`update_idletasks(self)`	Enter event loop until all idle callbacks have been called. This will update the display of windows, but not process events caused by the user.
`wait_variable(self, name='PY_VAR')`	Wait until the variable is modified. A parameter of type `IntVar`, `StringVar`, `DoubleVar`, or `BooleanVar` must be given.
`wait_visibility(self, window=None)`	Wait until the visibility of a Widget changes(for example, it appears).If no parameter is given self is used.
`wait_window(self, window=None)`	Wait until a Widget is destroyed. If no parameter is given, self is used.

Method	Description
`waitvar = wait_variable(self, name='PY_VAR')`	Wait until the variable is modified. A parameter of type `IntVar`, `StringVar`, `DoubleVar`, or `BooleanVar` must be given.
`winfo_atom(self, name, displayof=0)`	Return integer which represents atom name.
`winfo_atomname(self, id, displayof=0)`	Return name of atom with identifier ID.
`winfo_cells(self)`	Return number of cells in the colormap for this widget.
`winfo_children(self)`	Return a list of all widgets which are children of this widget.
`winfo_class(self)`	Return window class name of this widget.
`winfo_colormapfull(self)`	Return true if at the last color request the `colormap` was full.
`winfo_containing(self, rootX, rootY, displayof=0)`	Return the widget which is at the root coordinates rootX, rootY.
`winfo_depth(self)`	Return the number of bits per pixel.
`winfo_exists(self)`	Return true if this widget exists.
`winfo_fpixels(self, number)`	Return the number of pixels for the given distance NUMBER (e.g. "3c") as float.
`winfo_geometry(self)`	Return geometry string for this widget in the form "widthxheight+X+Y".
`winfo_height(self)`	Return height of this widget.
`winfo_id(self)`	Return identifier ID for this widget.
`winfo_interps(self, displayof=0)`	Return the name of all Tcl interpreters for this display.
`winfo_ismapped(self)`	Return true if this widget is mapped.
`winfo_manager(self)`	Return the window manager name for this widget.
`winfo_name(self)`	Return the name of this widget.
`winfo_parent(self)`	Return the name of the parent of this widget.
`winfo_pathname(self, id, displayof=0)`	Return the pathname of the widget given by ID.
`winfo_pixels(self, num)`	Rounded integer value of winfo_fpixels.
`winfo_pointerx(self)`	Return the x coordinate of the pointer on the root window.
`winfo_pointerxy(self)`	Return a tuple of x and y coordinates of the pointer on the root window.
`winfo_pointery(self)`	Return the y coordinate of the pointer on the root window.

Method	Description
winfo_reqheight(self)	Return requested height of this widget.
winfo_reqwidth(self)	Return requested width of this widget.
winfo_rgb(self, color)	Return tuple of decimal values for red, green, blue for color in this widget.
winfo_rootx(self) / winfo_rooty(self)	Return x/y coordinate of upper left corner of this widget on the root window.
winfo_screen(self)	Return the screen name of this widget.
winfo_screencells(self)	Return the number of the cells in the colormap of the screen of this widget.
winfo_screendepth(self)	Return the number of bits per pixel of the root window of the screen of this widget.
winfo_screenheight(self)	Return the number of pixels of the height of the screen of this widget in pixel.
winfo_screenmmheight(self)	Return the number of pixels of the height of the screen of this widget in mm.
winfo_screenmmwidth(self)	Return the number of pixels of the width of the screen of this widget in mm.
winfo_screenwidth(self)	Return the number of pixels of the width of the screen of this widget in pixel.
winfo_toplevel(self)	Return the Toplevel widget of this widget.
winfo_viewable(self)	Return true if the widget and all its higher ancestors are mapped.
winfo_visual(self) = winfo_screenvisual(self)	Return one of the strings directcolor, grayscale, pseudocolor, staticcolor, staticgray, or truecolor for the colormodel of this widget.
winfo_visualid(self)	Return the X identifier for the visual for this widget.
winfo_visualsavailable(self, includeids=0)	Return a list of all visuals available for the screen of this widget.
winfo_vrootheight(self)	Return the height of the virtual root window associated with this widget in pixels. If there is no virtual root window, return the height of the screen.
winfo_vrootwidth(self)	Return the width of the virtual root window associated with this widget in pixel. If there is no virtual root window, return the width of the screen.
winfo_vrootx(self)	Return the x offset of the virtual root relative to the root window of the screen of this widget.

Method	Description
`winfo_vrooty(self)`	Return the y offset of the virtual root relative to the root window of the screen of this widget.
`winfo_width(self)`	Return the width of this widget.
`winfo_x(self)`	Return the x coordinate of the upper left corner of this widget in the parent.
`winfo_y(self)`	Return the y coordinate of the upper left corner of this widget in the parent.

ttk widgets

The ttk widget is based on a revised and enhanced version of TIP #48 (`http://tip.tcl.tk/48`) specified style engine.

FILE: `path\to\python27\\lib\lib-tk\ttk.py`

The basic idea is to separate, to the extent possible, the code implementing a widget's behavior from the code implementing its appearance. Widget class bindings are primarily responsible for maintaining the widget state and invoking callbacks, and all aspects of the widgets appearance lies under themes.

You can substitute some Tkinter widgets with their corresponding ttk widgets (Button, Checkbutton, Entry, Frame, Label, LabelFrame, Menubutton, PanedWindow, Radiobutton, Scale, and Scrollbar).

However, Tkinter and ttk widgets are not completely compatible. The main difference is that Tkinter widget styling options like `fg`, `bg`, `relief`, and others are not supported options for ttk widgets. These styling options are instead moved to `ttk.Style()`.

Here's a small Tkinter code sample:

```
Label(text="Who", fg="white", bg="black")
Label(text="Are You ?", fg="white", bg="black")
```

And here's its equivalent code in ttk:

```
style = ttk.Style()
style.configure("BW.TLabel", foreground="white",
background="black")
ttk.Label(text="Who", style="BW.TLabel")
ttk.Label(text="Are You ?", style="BW.TLabel")
```

ttk also provides six new widget classes which are not available in Tkinter. These are `Combobox`, `Notebook`, `Progressbar`, `Separator`, `Sizegrip`, and `Treeview`.

ttk style names are as follows:

Widget class	Style name
Button	TButton
Checkbutton	TCheckbutton
Combobox	TCombobox
Entry	TEntry
Frame	TFrame
Label	TLabel
LabelFrame	TLabelFrame
Menubutton	TMenubutton
Notebook	TNotebook
PanedWindow	TPanedwindow (note window is not capitalized!)
Progressbar	Horizontal.TProgressbar or Vertical.TProgressbar, based on the orient option.
Radiobutton	TRadiobutton
Scale	Horizontal.TScale or Vertical.TScale, based on the orient option.
Scrollbar	Horizontal.TScrollbar or Vertical.TScrollbar, based on the orient option.
Separator	TSeparator
Sizegrip	TSizegrip
Treeview	Treeview (note only single 'T' meaning notTTreview!)

Options available to all ttk widgets are as follows:

Option	Description
class	Specifies the window class. The class is used when querying the option database for the window's other options, to determine the default bindtags for the window, and to select the widget's default layout and style. This is a read-only option which may only be specified when the window is created.
cursor	specifies mouse cursor to be displayed for the widget

Option	Description
takefocus	Determines whether the window accepts the focus during keyboard traversal. 0, 1 or an empty string is returned. If 0, the window should be skipped entirely during keyboard traversal. If 1, the window should receive the input focus as long as it is viewable. An empty string means that the traversal scripts make the decision about whether or not to focus on the window.
style	May be used to specify a custom widget style.

Options accepted by all scrollable ttk widgets are as follows:

Option	Description
xscrollcommand	Used to communicate with horizontal scrollbars. When the view in the widget's window changes, the widget will generate a Tcl command based on the scrollcommand. Usually, this option consists of the Scrollbar.set() method of some scrollbar. This will cause the scrollbar to be updated whenever the view in the window changes.
yscrollcommand	Command for vertical scrollbars.

Methods from ttk.Widget class with their description are as follows:

Method	Description
identify(self, x, y)	Returns the name of the element at position x, y, or the empty string if the point does not lie within any element. x and y are pixel coordinates relative to the widget.
instate(self, statespec, callback=None, *args, **kw)	Test the widget's state. If callback is not specified, returns True if the widget state matches statespec and False otherwise. If callback is specified, then it will be invoked with *args, **kw if the widget state matches statespec. statespec is expected to be a sequence.
state(self, statespec=None)	Modify or inquire widget state. Widget state is returned if statespec is None, otherwise it is set according to the statespec flags, and then a new state spec is returned, indicating which flags were changed. statespec is expected to be a sequence.

We will not show all ttk widget specific options here. To obtain a list of available options for a ttk widget, use the help command.

To obtain help on any ttk widget/class, import ttk into the namespace using following command:

```
>>>import ttk
```

The following commands can then be used to get information on a particular widget:

Widget Name	Getting Help
Label	help(ttk.Label)
Button	help(ttk.Button)
CheckButton	help(ttk.Checkbutton)
Entry	help(ttk.Entry)
Frame	help(ttk.Frame)
LabelFrame	help(ttk.LabelFrame)
Menubutton	help(ttk.Menubutton)
OptionMenu	help(ttk.OptionMenu)
PanedWindow	help(ttk.PanedWindow)
RadioButton	help(ttk.Radiobutton)
Scale	help(ttk.Scale)
Scrollbar	help(ttk.Scrollbar)
Combobox	help(ttk.Combobox)
Notebook	help(ttk.Notebook)
Progressbar	help(ttk.Progressbar)
Separator	help(ttk.Separator)
Sizegrip	help(ttk.Sizegrip)
Treeview	help(ttk.Treeview)

The following given are some ttkVirtual events and situation when they are triggered:

Virtual Event	Triggered when
<<ComboboxSelected>>	The user selects an element from the list of values in the Combobox widget
<<NotebookTabChanged>>	A new tab is selected in the Notebook widget
<<TreeviewSelect>>	Selection changes in the Treeview widget.
<<TreeviewOpen>>	Just before settings the focus item to open = True.
<<TreeviewClose>>	Just after setting the focus item to open = False.

Each widget in ttk is assigned a style, which specifies the set of elements making up the widget and how they are arranged, along with dynamic and default settings for element options.

By default, the style name is the same as the widget's class name, but it may be overridden by the widget's style option. If the class name of a widget is unknown, use the method `Misc.winfo_class()` (`somewidget.winfo_class()`). Following given are few methods with their description of ttk styling:

Method	Description
`configure(self, style, query_opt=None, **kw)`	Query or sets the default value of the specified option(s) in style. Each key in `kw` is an option, and each value is either a string or a sequence identifying the value for that option.
`element_create(self, elementname, etype, *args, **kw)`	Create a new element in the current theme of given `etype`.
`element_names(self)`	Returns the list of elements defined in the current theme.
`element_options(self, elementname)`	Return the list of `elementname` options.
`layout(self, style, layoutspec=None)`	Define the widget layout for given style. If `layoutspec` is omitted, return the layout specification for given style.
	`layoutspec` is expected to be a list or an object different than None that evaluates to False if you want to "turn off" that style. If it is a list (or tuple, or something else), each item should be a tuple, where the first item is the layout name, and the second item should have the format described below

A layout can be just `None`, if it takes no options, or a dictionary of options specifying how to arrange the element. The layout mechanism uses a simplified version of the pack geometry manager: given an initial cavity, each element is allocated a parcel.

Valid options: Values	Description
`side: whichside`	Specifies which side of the cavity to place the element; one of top, right, bottom or left. If omitted, the element occupies the entire cavity.
`sticky: nswe`	Specifies where the element is placed inside its allocated parcel.
`children: [sublayout... ]`	Specifies a list of elements to place inside the element. Each element is a tuple (or other sequence) where the first item is the layout name, and the other is a layout.

Valid options: Values	Description
`lookup(self, style, option, state=None, default=None)`	Returns the value specified for option in style. If state is specified, it is expected to be a sequence of one or more states. If the default argument is set, it is used as a fallback value in case no specification for option is found.
`map(self, style, query_opt=None, **kw)`	Query or sets dynamic values of the specified option(s) in style. Each key in kw is an option, and each value should be a list or a tuple (usually) containing `statespecs` grouped in tuples, or list, or something else of your preference. A `statespec` is compound of one or more states, and then a value.
`theme_ create(self, themename, parent=None, settings=None)`	Creates a new theme. It is an error if themename already exists. If parent is specified, the new theme will inherit styles, elements and layouts from the specified parent theme. If settings are present, they are expected to have the same syntax used for `theme_settings`.
`theme_ names(self)`	Returns a list of all known themes.
`theme_ settings(self, themename, settings)`	Temporarily sets the current theme to `themename`, apply specified settings, and then restores the previous theme. Each key in settings is a style and each value may contain the keys `configure`, `map`, `layout`, and `element create` and they are expected to have the same format as specified by the methods `configure`, `map`, `layout`, and `element_ create` respectively.
`theme_use(self, themename=None)`	If `themename` is None, returns the theme in use; otherwise, set the current theme to `themename`, refreshes all widgets and emits a `<<ThemeChanged>>` event.

The Toplevel window methods

These methods enable communication with the window manager. They are available on the root window (Tk), and also on Toplevel instances.

Note that different window managers behave in different ways. For example, some window managers don't support icon windows; some don't support window groups, and so on.

`aspect = wm_ aspect(self, minNumer=None, minDenom=None, maxNumer=None, maxDenom=None)`	Instruct the window manager to set the aspect ratio (width/height) of this widget to be between `minNumer`/`minDenom` and `maxNumer`/`maxDenom`. Return a tuple of the actual values if no argument is given.

`attributes = wm_`
`attributes(self,`
`*args)`
	This subcommand returns or sets platform-specific attributes. The first form returns a list of the platform specific flags and their values. The second form returns the value for the specific option. The third form sets one or more of the values. The values are as follows:
	
	On Windows, -disabled gets or sets whether the window is in a disabled state. -toolwindow gets or sets the style of the window
	
	totoolwindow (as defined in the MSDN). -topmost gets or sets whether this is a topmost window (displays above all other windows).
	
	On Macintosh, XXXXX
	
	On Unix, there are currently no special attribute values.

`client = wm_client` `(self, name=None)`	Store name in `WM_CLIENT_MACHINE` property of this widget. Return current value.

`colormapwindows`
`= wm_colormapwindows`
`(self, *wlist)`
	Store list of window names (wlist) into `WM_COLORMAPWINDOWS` property of this widget. This list contains windows whose `colormaps` differ from their parents. Return current list of widgets if wlist is empty.

`command = wm_`
`command(self,`
`value=None)`
	Store `value` in `WM_COMMAND` property. It is the command which shall be used to invoke the application. Return current command if `value` is None.

`deiconify = wm_` `deiconify(self)`	`deiconify` this widget. If it was never mapped, it will not be mapped. On Windows, it will raise this widget and give it the focus.

`focusmodel = wm_`
`focusmodel(self,`
`model=None)`
	Set focus model to `model`, "active" means that this widget will claim the focus itself, "passive" means that the window manager shall give the focus. Return current focus model if `model` is None.

`frame = wm_frame` `(self)`	Return identifier for decorative frame of this widget if present.

`geometry = wm_`
`geometry(self,`
`newGeometry=None)`
	Set `geometry` to `newgeometry` of the form `=widthxheight+x+y`. Return current value if None is given.

`grid = wm_grid(self,`
`baseWidth=None,`
`baseHeight=None,`
`widthInc=None,`
`heightInc=None)`
	Instruct the window manager that this widget shall only be resized on grid boundaries. `widthInc` and `heightInc` are the width and height of a grid unit in pixels. `baseWidth` and `baseHeight` are the number of grid units requested in `Tk_GeometryRequest`.

`group = wm_group(self,` `pathName=None)`	Set the group leader widgets for related widgets to `pathName`. Return the group leader of this widget if None is given.

`iconbitmap = wm_`
`iconbitmap(self,`
`bitmap=None,`
`default=None)`
	Set bitmap for the iconified widget to BITMAP. Return the bitmap if None is given. Under Windows, the DEFAULT parameter can be used to set the icon for the widget and any descendants that don't have an icon set explicitly. DEFAULT can be the relative path to a `.ico` file (example: `root.iconbitmap(default='myicon.ico')`). See Tkdocumentation for more information.

`iconify = wm_` `iconify(self)`	Display widget as icon.

`iconmask = wm_`
`iconmask(self,`
`bitmap=None)`
	Set mask for the icon bitmap of this widget. Return the mask if None is given.

`iconname = wm_`
`iconname(self,`
`newName=None)`
	Set the name of the icon for this widget. Return the name if None is given.

`iconposition = wm_`
`iconposition(self,`
`x=None, y=None)`
	Set the position of the icon of this widget to X and Y. Return a tuple of the current values of X and Y if None is given.

`iconwindow = wm_`
`iconwindow(self,`
`pathName=None)`
	Set widget `pathName` to be displayed instead of icon. Return the current value if None is given.

`maxsize = wm_`
`maxsize(self,`
`width=None,`
`height=None)`
	Set max `width` and `height` for this widget. If the window is gridded, the values are given in grid units. Return the current values if None is given.

`minsize = wm_`
`minsize(self,`
`width=None,`
`height=None)`
	Set min `width` and `height` for this widget. If the window is gridded, the values are given in grid units. Return the current values if None is given.

`overrideredirect`
`= wm_overrideredirect`
`(self, boolean=None)`
	Instruct the window manager to ignore this widget if Boolean is given with 1. Return the current value if None is given.

`positionfrom = wm_`
`positionfrom(self,`
`who=None)`
	Instruct the window manager that the position of this widget shall be defined by the user if `who` is "user", and by its own policy if `who` is "program".

`protocol = wm_`
`protocol(self,`
`name=None, func=None)`
	Bind function `func` to command `name` for this widget. Return the function bound to `name` if None is given. `name` could be for example, `WM_SAVE_YOURSELF` or `WM_DELETE_WINDOW`.

`resizable = wm_`
`resizable(self,`
`width=None,`
`height=None)`
	Instruct the window manager whether this width can be resized in `width` or `height`. Both values are Boolean values.

`sizefrom = wm_sizefrom(self, who=None)`	Instruct the window manager that the size of this widget shall be defined by the user if who is "user", and by its own policy if who is "program".
`state = wm_state(self, newstate=None)`	Query or set the state of this widget as one of normal, icon, iconic (see `wm_iconwindow`), withdrawn, or zoomed (Windows only).
`title = wm_title(self, string=None)`	Set the title of this widget.
`transient = wm_transient(self, master=None)`	Instruct the window manager that this widget is transient with regard to widget `master`.
`withdraw = wm_withdraw(self)`	Withdraw this widget from the screen such that it is unmapped and forgotten by the window manager. Redraw it with `wm_deiconify`.
`wm_aspect(self, minNumer=None, minDenom=None, maxNumer=None, maxDenom=None)`	Instruct the window manager to set the aspect ratio (width/height) of this widget to be between `minNumer`/`minDenom` and `maxNumer`/`maxDenom`. Return a tuple of the actual values if no argument is given.
`wm_attributes(self, *args)`	This subcommand returns or sets platform-specific attributes. The first form returns a list of the platform specific flags and their values. The second form returns the value for the specific option. The third form sets one or more of the values. The values are as follows:
	On Windows, `-disabled` gets or sets whether the window is in a disabled state. `-toolwindow` gets or sets the style of the window
	totoolwindow (as defined in the MSDN). `-topmost` gets or sets whether this is a topmost window (displays above all other windows).
	On Macintosh, XXXXX
	On Unix, there are currently no special attribute values.
`wm_client(self, name=None)`	Store `name` in `WM_CLIENT_MACHINE` property of this widget. Return current value.
`wm_colormapwindows(self, *wlist)`	Store list of window names (wlist) into `WM_COLORMAPWINDOWS` property of this widget. This list contains windows whose `colormaps` differ from their parents. Return current list of widgets if wlist is empty.
`wm_command(self, value=None)`	Store `value` in `WM_COMMAND` property. It is the command which shall be used to invoke the application. Return current command if `value` is None.

`wm_deiconify(self)`	Deiconify this widget. If it was never mapped, it will not be mapped. On Windows, it will raise this widget and give it the focus.
`wm_focusmodel(self, model=None)`	Set focus model to model. "active" means that this widget will claim the focus itself, "passive" means that the window manager shall give the focus. Return current focus model if `model` is None.
`wm_frame(self)`	Return identifier for decorative frame of this widget if present.
`wm_geometry(self, newGeometry=None)`	Set `geometry` to `newgeometry` of the form `=widthxheight+x+y`. Return current value if None is given.
`wm_grid(self, baseWidth=None, baseHeight=None, widthInc=None, heightInc=None)`	Instruct the window manager that this widget shall only be resized on grid boundaries. `widthInc` and `heightInc` are the width and height of a grid unit in pixels. `baseWidth` and `baseHeight` are the number of grid units requested in `Tk_GeometryRequest`.
`wm_group(self, pathName=None)`	Set the group leader widgets for related widgets to `pathname`. Return the group leader of this widget if None is given.
`wm_iconbitmap(self, bitmap=None, default=None)`	Set bitmap for the iconified widget to `bitmap`. Return the bitmap if None is given. Under Windows, the `default` parameter can be used to set the icon for the widget and any descendants that don't have an icon set explicitly. DEFAULT can be the relative path to a `.ico` file (example: `root.iconbitmap(default='myicon.ico')`). See Tkdocumentation for more information.
`wm_iconify(self)`	Display widget as icon.
`wm_iconmask(self, bitmap=None)`	Set mask for the icon bitmap of this widget. Return the mask if None is given.
`wm_iconname(self, newName=None)`	Set the name of the icon for this widget. Return the name if None is given.
`wm_iconposition(self, x=None, y=None)`	Set the position of the icon of this widget to X and Y. Return a tuple of the current values of X and X if None is given.
`wm_iconwindow(self, pathName=None)`	Set widget `pathname` to be displayed instead of icon. Return the current value if None is given.
`wm_maxsize(self, width=None, height=None)`	Set max `width` and `height` for this widget. If the window is gridded, the values are given in grid units. Return the current values if None is given.

`wm_minsize(self, width=None, height=None)`	Set min `width` and `height` for this widget. If the window is gridded the values are given in grid units. Return the current values if None is given.
`wm_overrideredirect(self, boolean=None)`	Instruct the window manager to ignore this widget if Boolean is given with 1. Return the current value if None is given.
`wm_positionfrom(self, who=None)`	Instruct the window manager that the position of this widget shall be defined by the user if `who` is "user", and by its own policy if `who` is "program".
`wm_protocol(self, name=None, func=None)`	Bind function `func` to command `name` for this widget. Return the function bound to name if None is given. Name could be for example, `WM_SAVE_YOURSELF` or `WM_DELETE_WINDOW`.
`wm_resizable(self, width=None, height=None)`	Instruct the window manager whether this width can be resized in `width` or `height`. Both values are Boolean values.
`wm_sizefrom(self, who=None)`	Instruct the window manager that the size of this widget shall be defined by the user if `who` is "user", and by its own policy if `who` is "program".
`wm_state(self, newstate=None)`	Query or set the state of this widget as one of `normal`, `icon`, `iconic` (see `wm_iconwindow`), `withdrawn`, or `zoomed` (Windows only).
`wm_title(self, string=None)`	Set the title of this widget.
`wm_transient(self, master=None)`	Instruct the window manager that this widget is transient with regard to widget `master`.
`wm_withdraw(self)`	Withdraw this widget from the screen such that it is unmapped and forgotten by the window manager. Redraw it with `wm_deiconify`.

Index

D

Deactivate, event types 305
deiconify = wm_deiconify(self) method 326
denial of service (DOS) 245
deserialization 102
Destroy, event types 305
dialogs
  askdirectory(**options) 60
  askopenfile(mode='r', **options) 60
  askopenfilename(**options) 60
  asksaveasfile(mode='w', **options) 60
  asksaveasfilename(**options) 60
  working with 59-64
disabledforeground 299
display_final method 244
display_frame() method 241
do not repeat yourself (DRY) 38
Double, event modifiers 306
drag_items method 217
drawing application
  checklist 190
  developing 189
  features 190
  features, adding 214-218
  hotshot challenge 221
  objectives 190
drawing board. *See* root window
drawing program
  structuring 196-201
draw_pieces() method 132
drum samples
  loading 88-91

E

ElementTree 106
encoding 275
Enter, event types 305
Entry command 300, 323
event_add(self, virtual, *sequences) method
    313
event binding 29, 30
event details
  about 32, 306
  Alt_L 306
  Alt_R 306
  BackSpace 306

Cancel 306
Caps_Lock 306
Control_L 306
Control_R 306
Delete 306
Down 306
End 307
Escape 307
Execute 307
F1 - F11 307
F12 307
Home 307
Insert 307
keysym 306
KP_0 307
KP_1 307
KP_2 307
KP_3 307
KP_4 307
KP_5 307
KP_6 307
KP_7 307
KP_8 307
KP_9 307
KP_Add 307
KP_Begin 307
KP_Decimal 307
KP_Delete 307
KP_Divide 307
KP_Down 307
KP_End 307
KP_Enter 307
KP_Home 307
KP_Insert 308
KP_Left 308
KP_Multiply 308
KP_Next 308
KP_Prior 308
KP_Right 308
KP_Subtract 308
KP_Up 308
Left 307
Linefeed 307
Next 308
Num_Lock 308
Pause 308
Print 308

T

About Packt Publishing

Packt, pronounced 'packed', published its first book "*Mastering phpMyAdmin for Effective MySQL Management*" in April 2004 and subsequently continued to specialize in publishing highly focused books on specific technologies and solutions.

Our books and publications share the experiences of your fellow IT professionals in adapting and customizing today's systems, applications, and frameworks. Our solution based books give you the knowledge and power to customize the software and technologies you're using to get the job done. Packt books are more specific and less general than the IT books you have seen in the past. Our unique business model allows us to bring you more focused information, giving you more of what you need to know, and less of what you don't.

Packt is a modern, yet unique publishing company, which focuses on producing quality, cutting-edge books for communities of developers, administrators, and newbies alike. For more information, please visit our website: www.packtpub.com.

Writing for Packt

We welcome all inquiries from people who are interested in authoring. Book proposals should be sent to author@packtpub.com. If your book idea is still at an early stage and you would like to discuss it first before writing a formal book proposal, contact us; one of our commissioning editors will get in touch with you.

We're not just looking for published authors; if you have strong technical skills but no writing experience, our experienced editors can help you develop a writing career, or simply get some additional reward for your expertise.

Building Machine Learning Systems with Python

ISBN: 978-1-782161-40-0   Paperback: 290 pages

Master the art of machine learning with Python and build effective machine learning systems with this intensive hands-on guide

1. Master Machine Learning using a broad set of Python libraries and start building your own Python-based ML systems

2. Covers classification, regression, feature engineering, and much more guided by practical examples

3. A scenario-based tutorial to get into the right mind-set of a machine learner (data exploration) and successfully implement this in your new or existing projects

CoffeeScript Application Development

ISBN: 978-1-782162-66-7   Paperback: 258 pages

Write code that is easy to read, effortless to maintain, and even more powerful than JavaScript

1. Learn the ins and outs of the CoffeeScript language, and understand how the transformation happens behind the scenes

2. Use practical examples to put your new skills to work towards building a functional web application, written entirely in CoffeeScript

3. Understand the language concepts from short, easy-to-understand examples which can be practised by applying them to your ongoing project

Please check **www.PacktPub.com** for information on our titles

Python Geospatial Development Second Edition

ISBN: 978-1-782161-52-3   Paperback: 508 pages

Learn to build sophisticated mapping applications from scratch using Python tools for geospatial development

1. Build your own complete and sophisticated mapping applications in Python.

2. Walks you through the process of building your own online system for viewing and editing geospatial data

3. Practical, hands-on tutorial that teaches you all about geospatial development in Python

Python Data Visualization Cookbook

ISBN: 978-1-782163-36-7   Paperback: 254 pages

Over 60 recipes that will enable you to learn how to create attractive visualizationss using Python's most popular libraries

1. Learn how to set up an optimal Python environment for data visualization

2. Understand the topics such as importing data for visualization and formatting data for visualization

3. Understand the underlying data and how to use the right visualizations

Please check **www.PacktPub.com** for information on our titles

Made in the USA
Lexington, KY
29 December 2017